Native Americans Today

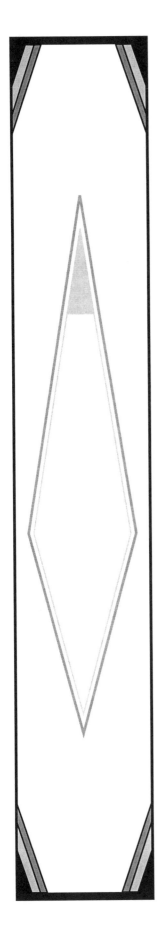

Native Americans Today

Resources and Activities for Educators, Grades 4–8

Arlene Hirschfelder

Yvonne Beamer

2000
Teacher Ideas Press
A Division of
Libraries Unlimited, Inc.
Englewood, Colorado

TEACHER IDEAS PRESS
A Division of
Libraries Unlimited, Inc.
P.O. Box 6633
Englewood, CO 80155-6633
1-800-237-6124
www.lu.com/tip

Library of Congress Cataloging-in-Publication Data

Hirschfelder, Arlene B.
    Native Americans today : resources and activities for educators,
  grades 4–8 / Arlene Hirschfelder, Yvonne Beamer.
        p.   cm.
    Includes bibliographical references and index.
    ISBN 1-56308-694-8 (pbk.)
    1. Indians of North America--Study and teaching (Elementary)
  2. Indians of North America--Study and teaching (Middle school)
  I. Beamer, Yvonne. II. Title.
  E76.6.H5   1999
  970.004'97'00712--dc21   99-16299
                                                          CIP

To my family and friends who were loving, supportive, and patient: Jiman (who didn't complain too much about washing the dishes every day), Clement, Fredlina, Yvonne, Pedro, Irma, Christina, Gelvin, Eric, Arlene, Dr. Zina, Sam, and Audrey.

— *Yvonne Beamer*

To Dennis, Brooke, and Adam, who once again tolerated another deadline with humor and unqualified support.

—*Arlene Hirschfelder*

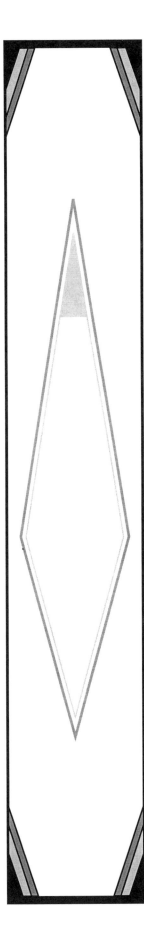

Contents

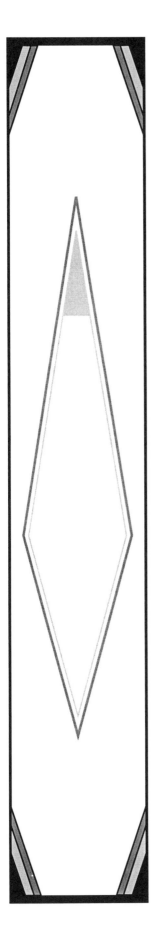

Acknowledgments

Yvonne is grateful to all of the following: Jeff Kalin, Joseph Bruchac, Jim Murphy, Karen Taylor, Carmen Katcher, Wanda Locklear at LRDC, Cindy Kane, Mrs. Bill Rieske, Kathryn Oneita, and all those who let me interview them for the biographies. Gel Stevenson shares my philosophy and style and did justice to the chapters that he cranked out for us; Christina Bryant lovingly shared her favorite teaching activities; and Ray Evans Harrell sleuthed down web sites (I hardly understand the process) of Native artists in the lessons on performers. Seven million thanks, Wado to each of you!

—Yvonne Beamer

Arlene Hirschfelder would like to give special thanks to the following people:

> Gary Heiman, nephew, friend, and computer whiz extraordinaire, who has tried to teach me everything from file management to VCR-plus. (And thanks to Jill and Carli for their patience!!)

> Lisa Charmont, gracious artist, designer, and educator who makes magic out of found objects.

> John Goodwin, our dear friend whose photographs grace my books, and who never never fails to respond to my eleventh-hour calls for images.

> Mary Emma Ahenakew, whose line drawings of powwow dress convey extraordinary beauty, grace, and dignity.

> Karen Warth, who brings back photographs from her trips west and lets me have my pick. Again, thank you for your generosity.

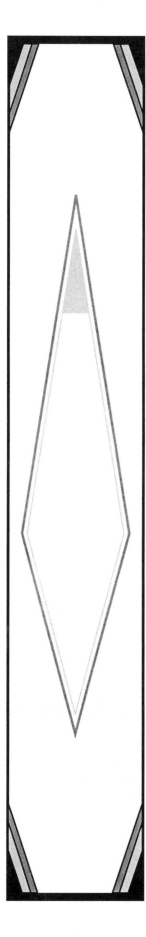

Introduction

November. Our phones never stop ringing. We are very popular people in November, because that is the one month that most of America wants a crash course in Indian culture. It is part of the American image—Thanksgiving, Pilgrims, turkeys, and . . . Indians. Not just any Indians, but only Indians who can show up in the school auditorium, heads adorned with paper headbands and feathers, faces painted with grease paint or lipstick, and hands dragging along a couple of paper turkeys. These honored Thanksgiving Indians are to share a feast of fish-fertilized maize, entertain "squaws" and "braves" on the "tom-tom," and deliver powerful oratories in pidgin English. (They must be careful not to awaken the sleeping "papooses!") Of course, these Thanksgiving Indians are also required to step lively to a rain dance song and then must stand with their stoic arms crossed over their stoic chests, while keeping a stoic expression on their faces.

After surviving over 50 combined years of Novembers training teachers and creating curricula, we decided to share some of our ideas with a broader audience. It is time to teach about Native peoples from September to June in every subject, from science to physical education. The Thanksgiving Indian, that nostalgic, romanticized, weary relic of the past, longs to join DDT, the Edsel, pet rocks, Jim Crow, lead paint, and indentured servants as a thing of the past.

Although this guide may seem like a time warp for some, skipping from seventeenth-century Thanksgiving Indians to film-making, motorcycle shop–owning, traffic-engineering Indians of the 1990s, we have not rushed anything. We are just introducing contemporary American Indians and focusing on Native issues of the twentieth century. If it feels like a few centuries of Native America have been omitted, argue with your librarians, textbook manufacturers, Hollywood, and the museums. In this book, we have tried to provide a realistic account of how things are today.

We have a lot of respect for teachers who try to integrate a true multicultural perspective into their curriculum. We know it is not easy. Usually the resources available to schools are outdated, biased, and just plain racist. In this guide, we have included materials that are affordable, if you have to purchase your own. In our years as educators, we have often had to do our own research, spend our own carfare gadding about trying to find good materials, and after we located them, buy them with our own money! Sometimes we have been forced to order through the school's distributors, only to find that the resources available were no improvement over existing materials in the school library.

The Native published resources suggested in this book may be more difficult to obtain. Nevertheless, it behooves you to try, because it is imperative to teach about Native Americans from a Native point of view. American Indians have for the most part been shunned in the publishing business, it is just more familiar and comfortable to present a non-Native perspective—stereotypes and cultural inaccuracies about American Indians are endemic. In the catalog and resource section, you will find a supermarket of good materials. Mail order is always a convenient way to shop! Nothing is more frustrating than not being able to find recommended sources. We have made every effort to check addresses and the availability of written and audiovisual materials. Also, we have tried not to duplicate chapter resources in the bibliography. Check both places to get as many sources as possible.

Many of the chapter resources list articles in the Indian press. While these writings may be more difficult to locate, it is worth the time and effort to contact these newspapers and try to have the articles photocopied or faxed. Addresses of periodicals are listed in the Resources, too. This is a guidebook about contemporary Native peoples, and newspapers and periodicals will have the most up-to-date information. Teachers and students should become as familiar with *News from Indian Country* and *Indian Country Today* as they are with the *New York Times* and *Chicago Tribune*.

The appendices feature Global Information Sources. Many of the lessons transport students beyond the classroom materials to the library filled with global information sources. From the *Readers' Guide to Periodical Literature* to *School Library Journal* to *Census Data* and InfoTrac, students will become familiar with and able to research any subject. Not only that, many lessons urge students to make changes—either in changing offensive names of geographic features or changing offensive athletic team names, mascots, and logos. We want students to be able to think, question, and hopefully contribute to our global community in a fair and informed way.

In our lesson plans, we have tried to cover diverse areas. As stated previously, at the end of each chapter is a resource section that will guide you to further activities. Almost all of the lessons have been student and teacher tested. We recommend that you use the lessons as part of your overall curriculum. If you are teaching gymnastics, use the chapter on recreation. If you are teaching math or architecture, integrate the lesson on housing into your presentation. The food lesson works well in a math or science class, and "Where We Live" lessons can be adapted for geography or American history. This method demonstrates that Indians live in this century and do all kinds of things. Also, the student can interact with American Indian culture, rather than drive by like a tourist. The biographies featured in this book give form and life to real people; students should read all of them.

We have cross-referenced lessons and chapters so that you can have a whole language approach. The lessons on tribal names and visual arts can both be used with written arts, for instance. We have included a glossary of selected vocabulary used in the lessons. Teachers can best determine which words need defining.

Each lesson is formatted in the following order: Grade Level, Materials, Time, Objectives, Activities, Enrichment/Extensions, Readings (if any), and Resources. We have targeted certain grade levels for most of the lessons, but *you* know your students. Please feel free to adapt the lessons up or down a few grades. Some of the materials are contained in the lesson, or we have provided information for ordering them. Feel free to augment the suggested materials. The time recommended for completing the lesson is a projection; your group may work slower or faster. Several of the chapters feature reading(s) that you can either share with your students or use for your own preparation. However, some readings should be given to students—either photocopied or read aloud as indicated in the Activities section.

This book has a limited amount of space, and we included as many activities as possible. Feel free to add your own or integrate ours with other lessons. You and your students can come up with some great ideas!

Our hope is that all peoples will be included in your curriculum and that your students will reflect the diversity of cultures in this country. It would be great if both Indian and non-Indian teachers were teaching this to Indian and non-Indian students! In teaching about Native Americans or any group, we find it advantageous to cite examples in other cultures. For instance, in the section on adolescents, all cultures recognize teenagers, but some have rituals and others do not.

We chose our subjects based on our experiences with educators. These lesson plans reflect the information we feel is necessary to give a realistic and diverse view of American Indians. It is by no means complete! We are not experts on American Indians and do not presume to speak for all Indian people. There is no one American Indian viewpoint, just as there is no one way of thinking shared by all Americans whether of Arab, Irish, Pakistani, Russian, African, English, Japanese, or Puerto Rican descent!

However, a few of the lesson plans were developed by experts in a particular field. New York City Arts in Education teacher Christina Bryant, Cherokee and Shinnecock, lent some of her very successful curriculum to the visual arts. Maestro Ray Evans Harrell, Oklahoma Cherokee, an artistic director and conductor, gave a Native artistic point of view to the lesson plan for performing arts. Lisa Charmont, an educator, artist, and designer, made her hogan lesson so realistic that we wanted to move in. Dr. Gelvin Stevenson, Oklahoma Cherokee, is an investment counselor for Indian Nations and a past editor for *Business Week*. He very skillfully designed the lessons on Indian-owned companies, casinos and gaming, and sovereignty so we could all understand it!

It would be effective to teach the lessons in a traditional Indian way, experientially. Use a talking stick (see Lesson 4.7, page 84) to create a climate of respect in the classroom. No one is allowed to speak except the person who holds the stick; everyone must wait for a turn. Try to position students in a circle rather than rows. Respect for differences of opinion should be fostered. Allow the group to make decisions together and talk out different points of view—encourage students to convince each other to agree, instead of letting the majority vote rule. Wherever possible, we have tried to interject these methods into the activities. To help you not make glaring errors, we have provided a list of NO-NOs.

NO-NO 1!! No using masks. Do not make them, wear them, or display them. Masking, a feature of many Native religious traditions throughout North America, is used in a large number of contemporary ceremonies. If masks are mishandled, it is believed that disaster can result. They are sacred; many are seen as living and must be fed. Look them up in the library if you don't believe us, but do not ask students to make or wear them. Indian children never wear sacred masks. You can foster respect for these and other sacred objects by making them off-limits in the classroom. Indian masks, whether they are donned by Apache Crown Dancers or part of the healing rituals of the Iroquois False Face Society, are not Halloween costumes!

NO-NO 2!! No making or playing drums! Drums are sacred objects, regarded as alive and representing the heartbeat of an Indian Nation, the earth, and the universe. Used in ceremonies, each drum is a distinct individual with a name and a voice. Asking students to make drums often perpetuates the old "tom-tom" stereotype. Introduce students to Indian songs using available recordings of social Indian music (make sure you do not use sacred music) or take them to a concert or powwow. We've listed plenty of resources in the audiovisual section.

NO-NO 3!! No headdresses! Students will learn that Indian people do not walk around in feathered headdresses. And Native children rarely ever wear headdresses. In the past, they were worn during war dances, battles, and ceremonies. Have students learn about the gus-toweh of the Six Nations (Iroquois). Feathers and beads do not define Indian identity.

NO-NO 4!! No kachinas, sandpaintings, or pipes! These are also part of religious ceremonials, sacred objects meant to be used by special people in an honored way. Yes, we do know that some kachinas are sold as dolls, but we prefer that you not even attempt to address any sacred subjects. Sandpaintings are not permanent works of art like oil paintings; they are used only for healing and then destroyed. Pipes should not even be displayed—there are simply too many rules to follow to respect the customs.

NO-NO 5!! No Thanksgiving pageants! Please do not create a pageant that not only distorts the past, but, as we have already stated, makes Indians into unreal characters whose sole purpose for living was to help the downtrodden Pilgrims. In our experience, November is the only month that America feels compelled to even mention Indians, and then it is only in the context of being helpful to whites. Don't do it! Write to the Wampanoag people and ask them about Thanksgiving.

NO-NO 6!! No giving Indian names! Some youth organizations or "new agers" give Indian names or so-called English translations of Indian names. Most Indian people have English, Spanish, or French surnames, and it is insulting to see non-Indians sporting names like Wind In The Grass or Princess Bear Claw. Oftentimes, Indian people are asked, "What kind of name is David Smith for an Indian?" With 500 years of oppression and all matter of things being forced on Native peoples, it is not a surprise that Native people have Italian, Spanish, Irish, or English names. For a spoof on "Indian names," view the video *Harold of Orange* by Gerald Vizenor.

NO-NO 7!! No assuming that you do not have Indian students in your class! Not everyone is identifiably Indian. Sometimes Indian children do not want to be singled out as being different and may not disclose their ethnicity. If you do have Native American students, remember that they are just children like your other pupils and may not be experts on their heritage. Do not ask them their opinions or interpretations or anything else that may embarrass them. Let them take the initiative and talk to their parents. If you are a Native American teacher, we know you'll understand what we mean!

NO-NO 8!! No using terms like "them" and "us," our culture, their ways. In a multicultural society, who are the "them" and who are the "us?" Do not start lessons with the European or American white standard every time. In a lesson on music, for instance, begin with instrument and scales developed by the Chinese. Begin a science lesson with African-inspired architecture or a government lesson with the Iroquois Confederacy. It is inappropriate and tragic to stunt the thinking of our youth by constantly making one group better, smarter, wiser, etc. As we have seen in our country, segregation does not work. And integration has not been successful because respect for different cultures, history, and standards of beauty have *not* been integrated. Language is powerful, so drop the "them" and "us."

It was really hard to write this book. Rather, it was difficult to narrow down what we had room to include. Several times, we laughingly put an idea for a lesson aside and said, *This is for Native Americans Today: Resources and Activities for Educators, Grades 4–8, Volumes Two Through Ten!* We would like to hear from you. What worked? How did you improve the lesson? Is there anything else you are just dying to teach? Now that the Thanksgiving Indian has retired, there is more room for truth, justice, and the "American Indian Way!"

U.S. Indian Lands and Communities (Partial Listing)

Lower Elwha
Makah
Ozette
Quileute
Hoh
Port Gamble
Quinault
Port Madison
Skokomish
Squaxin Island
Shoalwater
Chehalis
Grande Ronde
Siletz
Fort Bidwell
Karok
Hoopa Valley
Round Valley
Yerington
Carson
Dresslerville
Washoe
Numerous small rancherias
Morongo
Soboba
Ramona
Cahuilla
Pachanga
Pala
Pauma
Rincon
San Pasqual
Mesa Grande
Viejas
Jamul
Sycuan
La Posta
Campo
Manzanita
Palm Springs
Cabazon
Augustine
Santa Rosa
Torres-Martinez
Los Coyotes
La Jolla
Santa Ysabel
Inaha-Cosmit
Capitan Grande
Cuyapaipe
San Manuel
Death Valley
Timbi-sha
Shoshone Band
Colorado River
Gila Bend
Papago

Lummi
Jamestown
Klallam
Nooksack
Tulalip
Kalispel
Muckleshoot
Puyallup
Colville
Spokane
Coeur d'Alene
Nisqually
Yakima
Umatilla
Warm Springs
Cow Creek Band of Umpqua
Burns Paiute
Klamath
Fort McDermitt
Summit Lake
Pyramid Lake
Reno Sparks
Lovelock
Fallon
Yomba
Walker River
Fort Independence
Tule River
Lone Pine
Santa Ynez
Fort Mohave
Hualapal
Chemehuevi
Yavapai
Camp Verde
Gila River
Cocopah
Quechin
Gila Bend
Maricopa
Papago

Swinomish
Upper Skagit
Stillaguamish
Sauk Suiattle
Kootenai
Blackfeet
Spokane
Duck Valley
Elko
Ely
Duckwater
Moapa
Las Vegas
Havasupai
Kaibab
Goshute
Winnemucca
Te-Moak
Skull Valley
NW Shoshone
Payson
Salt River

Rocky Boys
Fort Peck
Flathead
Fort Belknap
Northern Cheyenne
Crow
Nez Perce
Wind River
Uintah & Ouray
Navajo
Ute Mountain
Southern Ute
Hopi
Paiute
Turtle Mountain
Fort Berthod
Standing Rock
Cheyenne River
Lower Brute
Pine Ridge
Rosebud
Jicarilla Apache
Picurls
Taos
Santa Clara
San Juan
San Ildefonso
Pojoaque
Nambe
Tesuque
Cochiti
Santo Domingo
San Felipe
Santa Ana
Isleta
Mescalero
Tigua
Pawnee
Cheyenne
Arapaho
Wichita
Caddo
Kiowa
Jemez
Zia
Acoma
Sandia
Zuni
Ramah Navajo
Laguna
Alamo Navajo
Canoncito
Fort Apache
San Carlos
Fort McDowell
San Xavier
Pascua Yaqui
Kickapoo

Inuit
Athapascan
Yupik
Tlingit
Haida
Aleut
Annette Island
(Alaska not to scale)

Legend

- ▨ Federal Indian Reservations
- • Federal Indian Reservations
- ▲ State Indian Reservations
- + Other Indian Communities

Bois Forte
Deer Creek Vermillion Lake
Red Lake Red Cliff
Devils Lake
Bad River Grand Portage
White Earth L'Anse Lac Vieux Desert
Sisseton Leech Lake Hannahville
Sandy Lake Bay Mills
Mille Lacs Fond du Lac Sault Ste Marie
St. Croix Ontonagon Grand Traverse
Crow Creek Lac du Flambeau Grand Traverse
Upper Sioux Lac Courte-Oreilles Sokaogan Chippewa
Flandreau Shakopee Prairie Island Potawatomi
Lower Sioux Menominee Oneida
Yankton Ottawa +
Winnebago Stockbridge-Munsee Isabella
Santee Sioux Sac and Fox Potawatomi
Omaha Winnebago
Sac and Fox
Iowa
Kickapoo
Potawatomi + Cherokee
Peoria Quapaw
Tonkawa Shawnee Ottawa
Ponca Kaw Wyandot
Otoe Osage Seneca Cayuga
Miami E. Shawnee
Modoc
Iowa Cherokee
Chickasaw Creek
Shawnee Seminole
Potawatomi Choctaw
Sac and Fox
Kickapoo + Ouachita
Coushatta
Mississippi Choctaw
+ Choctaw
Tunica-Biloxi + Creek
Alabama-Coushatta
Chitimacha + Houma

Micmac
Houlton Maliseet Indian Town
Pennocook Pleasant Point
Ganienkeh Penobscot
St. Regis + Abenaki
Abnaki Nipmuk-Hassanamisko
Oneida
Tonawanda Onondaga
Tuscarora Shagticoke
Paugusett Wampanoag
Oil Springs Narragansett
Allegheny Mashantucket Pequot
Cattaraugus Mohegan
Paucatuck Pequot
+ Miami Shinnecock
+ Alegheny Poosepatuck
+ Nanticoke
+ Miami + Piscataway-Conoy

Mattaponi
Pamunkey

+ Cherokee

+ Meherrin
+ Haliwa-Saponi
+ Coree
+ Coharie
Cherokee + Hattadare
+ Kaweah
+ Cherokee + Lumbee
Catawba + Waccamaw
+Tuscarora

+ Cherokee
+ Creek

Poarch Creek + Cherokee

Brighton Seminole
Big Cypress Seminole Dania
Miccosukee

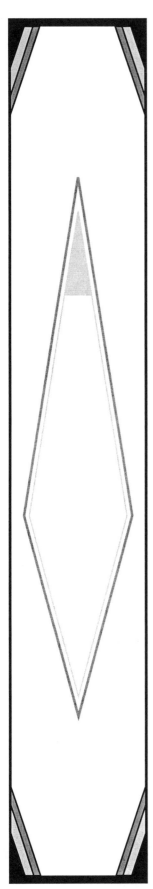

Basic Ground Rules

As Julie Andrews so lyrically stated in "The Sound of Music," "Let's start at the very beginning, that's a very good place to start." A good beginning for your students is to learn what is offensive to American Indians (or is it Native Americans?), and how they can help their communities be more respectful of Indian people. The seven lessons in this chapter focus on correct and accurate terminology, anachronisms, and sovereignty. Students become familiar with the special relationships that Indian Nations have with federal and state governments that are different from ethnic groups like African Americans, Asian Americans, or European Americans.

After completing the lessons in this chapter, your students will read and think more critically. Students will practice questioning their educational resources and will probably challenge the stereotypes and inaccuracies they encounter in the media, school, homes, and extracurricular activities. Our experience has been that once students question the truth, they are usually eager to spread the word.

Lesson

1.1

Terminology: American Indians or Native Americans?

Grade Level
4–8

Materials
Student Reading: "What's Correct: American Indian nor Native American?"

Time
One class period

Objectives
- Students learn that neither "American Indian" nor "Native American" is the correct/right term. Both are acceptable and interchangeable.

- Students learn that both are collective terms for hundreds of different cultures that prefer to be called by their own tribal names.

Activities
After students read "What's Correct: American Indian or Native American?" they can survey what students think is the correct term. After obtaining the results, they can teach classmates that both terms are correct.

Enrichment/Extensions
Research. Students can research what Native and non-Native writers have to say about the terms "Native American" and "American Indian." See Resources.

📖 Reading

What's Correct: American Indian or Native American?

Have you noticed that some books and newspapers use the term "American Indian" and others use "Native American"? Which is correct? The answer may surprise you. Both are. Although "Native American" is popular with some Indian people and non-Indians, it is not the only correct term to use. Tim Giago, former publisher of the Rapid City, South Dakota–based *Indian Country Today*, an important Indian newspaper, wrote on December 4, 1991, "We use 'American Indian,' 'Indian,' or 'Native American,' but we prefer to use the individual tribal affiliation when possible."

After Giago wrote this column, *Indian Country Today* received many calls and letters pointing out that all those born in the Americas can refer to themselves as Native American. The term "Native American" is used most commonly in the United States, especially in bookstores and by publishers. Keep in mind that both collective terms, Native Americans and American Indians, refer to hundreds of different cultures who prefer to be called by their tribal names.

Resources

Students and Teachers

Harjo, Suzan Shown. "Foreword," in *North American Indian Landmarks* by George Cantor. Detroit: Visible Ink, 1993.

Harjo argues that all the collective terms are "awkward" and more emphasis should be placed on tribal names, especially traditional tribal names.

Lesson

Terminology: Eskimo or Inuit?

Grade Level

4–8

Materials

Student Reading: "Eskimo Versus Inuit"

Time

One class period

Objectives

- Students learn that the word "Eskimo" has been dropped from use throughout much of Canada and replaced by "Inuit." It means "the people" in dialects across northern Canada and northwest Alaska.

- Students learn that in Alaska the word "Eskimo" rubs some Alaska Natives the wrong way, but the word "Inuit" does not solve the terminology problem.

Activities

Students read "Eskimo Versus Inuit" and discuss why Canadian Inuits wanted change. Discuss why the word "Inuit" may not be a suitable term for Eskimos in Alaska.

📖 Reading

Eskimo Versus Inuit

Have you noticed that some books and newspapers use the term "Eskimo" and others use "Inuit"? Which is correct? In Canada, the word "Eskimo" has practically disappeared because people prefer to call themselves Inuit, meaning "the people" in the Inuit language.

Many people in Canada saw the term "Eskimo" as derogatory. Most dictionaries and many reference books describe the word "Eskimo" as an Algonquian word that means "eaters of raw meat." Some linguists argue that the word originated with the Montagnais and actually means "snowshoe netter." Nevertheless, in the 1600s, French-speaking explorers picked up the term "Eskimo" and so too the rest of the world.

By the 1970s, Native political activists in Canada pressing for Native rights rejected the term and demanded to be called "Inuit." The Canadian government agreed to the demand. Today, government agencies, the media, and academic scholars rarely use the word "Eskimo."

In Alaska, the word "Eskimo" is also beginning to bother some Alaska Natives, mainly because it is not the name they call themselves in their own language. The word "Inuit," however, may not be the solution. The problem is that in Alaska, there are two language and culture groups—the Inupiaq and Yup'ik. Both words mean "a real person." (The plurals are Inupiat and Yupiit—the real people.) Although both Inuit and Inupiaq mean the same thing, the word "Inuit" does not exist in Yup'ik, the most widely spoken Eskimo language in Alaska. Inuit is as foreign a term in Bethel, Alaska, as Eskimo. So the best solution seems to be to use the words preferred by both cultural and language groups in Alaska—Yup'ik and Inupiaq.

Resources

Teachers

Fienup-Riordan, Ann. *Eskimo Essays: Yup'ik Lives and How We See Them*. New Brunswick, NJ: Rutgers University Press, 1990.
On pages 5 and 6, there is an excellent discussion of terminology.

Lesson

Terminology: S-word

Grade Level
6–8

Materials
Student Reading: "You Can Change That Name"

Time
One class period

Objectives
- Students learn that the "s-word" or "squaw," an Algonquian word, has evolved into a derogatory term for Native women that offends them.

- Students learn that across the nation some tribes and Native people have changed or are trying to eliminate the names of geographic features named "squaw," because the word offends Native women.

- Students learn there is a procedure for changing the names of geographic features.

Activities

After reading "You Can Change That Name," students comb the map of their state to see if there is a geographic feature or city using the word "squaw" or any other derogatory term. If so, students debate whether the name should be changed. If so, students can send for information from the U.S. Board on Geographic Names.

📖 Reading

You Can Change That Name

If you want to change the name of a lake, stream, hill, or other geographic feature, there's a way to do it. The U.S. Board on Geographic Names, a federal body created in 1890, has set up procedures for changing local names that are derogatory to a particular person, race, or region. (There are also procedures for proposing names for unnamed domestic geographic features.) Any person or organization, public or private, may request the Board to render a formal decision on proposed name changes. Write for a "Domestic Geographic Name Report" from the Executive Secretary, U.S. Board on Geographic Names, 523 National Center, Reston, VA 22092.

Native Americans consider the word "squaw" offensive. There is disagreement on the origin of the term. Regardless of its origins, the term "squaw" has evolved into a derogatory term that offends American Indian women. Some dictionaries, such as the standard edition of *The American Heritage Dictionary*, cite the word as offensive.

The term "squaw" has extensive use in North America. Besides countless place names, including California's popular ski resort "Squaw Valley," it has been perpetuated in printed matter and public discourse since the colonial period.

Across the nation, some tribes and Native people have changed or are trying to eliminate the names of lakes, creeks, buttes, hills, and other geographic features named "squaw" because the word offends Native women.

Because of the efforts of Anishinaabe (Chippewa or Ojibway) high school students, the state of Minnesota enacted a law mandating the elimination of the term "squaw," or the "s-word," as the students and their supporters began calling it, from place names in the state. The Minnesota law, Chapter 53–S.F. No. 574, states:

> On or before July 31, 1996, the commissioner of natural resources shall change each name of a geographic feature in the state that contains the word "squaw" to another name that does not contain this word. The commissioner shall select the new names in cooperation with the county boards of the counties in which the feature is located and with their approval.

Two students, Dawn Litzau and Angelene Losh from Minnesota's Cass Lake-Bena High School, began a campaign in 1994 to change Leech Lake Reservation place names, Squaw Point and Squaw Lake. In letters to congressional representatives, tribal officials, and newspaper editors, they explained why the "s-word" is offensive to Native American women. They also sought support from other students by circulating petitions. After receiving positive responses, a Name Change Committee was formed at their school.

Following the success of affecting a name change from "Squaw Point" to "Oak Point" locally, the Name Change Committee began extending its efforts statewide. Researching locations using the "s-word" in place names, committee members identified sites via Minnesota's Department of Natural Resources. Dawn, Angelene, and their advisor, Muriel Litzau, testified before both state Senate and House committees concerning the legislation. Their efforts paid off when the bill received overwhelming support in Minnesota's full Senate and House of Representatives. It was signed into law by Governor Arne H. Carlson on April 18, 1995. As of September 1, 1996, 16 of 19 place names in the state of Minnesota had been changed, with two counties failing to comply with the law.

In their original letter objecting to the use of the word "squaw" for place names, Dawn Litzau and Angelene Losh likewise state, "We suggest that the word 'squaw' be replaced with *'ikwe'* which means woman in Ojibway, or *'nimaamaa'* meaning mother." Tribal languages representing differing cultures include rich, beautiful terminology related to gender and its associated status. In some tribal languages, for example, the word for mother or grandmother is the same as that for earth. There are also age-appropriate terms, such as those for baby girl, baby daughter, or baby sister, all the way to old age.

The Name Change Committee continues to work for change on this issue, using its experience in Minnesota as a model. Today, similar efforts are under way in several other states. In Oregon, the Burns Paiute Tribe requested in 1993 that the name of Squaw Butte, a peak east of Burns, Oregon, be changed to Paiute Butte. The Oregon Geographic Names board agreed to support the name change.

In Montana, the Northern Cheyenne Tribal Council got rid of the name Squaw Hill also in 1993. The hill was renamed Head Chief and Young Mule Memorial Site after two heroic warriors who died there at the hands of the U.S. Cavalry.

Resources
Students and Teachers

Bowker, Ardy. "The 'Princess' or the 'Squaw,' " in "Racism and Stereotyping in Native America." *Sisters in the Blood—The Education of Women in Native America*. Bozeman, MT: Montana State University, 1993, 33–36.

"Northern Cheyenne Choose Dignity over 'Squaw Hill' Designation." *Indian Country Today*. May 5, 1993.

"Ojibwe E-Quay: A Testimonial." *The Circle*. July 1996.
   Squaw Lake name change.

"Oregon to Rename Squaw Butte." *Indian Country Today*. September 29, 1993.

"Squaw: A Name That Hurts" and "Twisting a Word Toward Racism." *Indian Country Today*. April 7, 1993.

"Squaw: A Word That Offends." Reprinted from *Minneapolis Star Tribune*. *Indian Country Today*. June 22, 1994.

Lesson

1.4

Stereotypes in General

Grade Level
6–8

Materials
Student Reading: "Ten Terrific Tips for Spotting Stereotypes"; greeting cards, toys, cartoons, comic books, magazines, food packages, T-shirts, music cassettes and CD covers, advertisements, business logos, and so on; photo of stereotypes (Figure 1.1)

Time
Two class periods

Objectives
- Students learn the meaning and function of stereotyping—a fixed and often mistaken notion of how a whole group of people thinks, behaves, and dresses.

- Students begin to learn how to identify stereotypes of Indian people.

- Students learn sources for contemporary, realistic images of Native American people.

Activities
1. Students discuss the meaning of stereotyping and give examples.
2. Students read "Ten Terrific Tips for Spotting Stereotypes," look at the photograph, and identify five reasons why the objects are stereotypes.
3. Students discuss the impact of Indian stereotypes on themselves and on Indian children.
4. Students brainstorm possible sources for contemporary and realistic images of Indians including magazines like *Faces*, *Native Peoples*, *National Geographic*, *Arizona Highways*, and *New Mexico Magazine*; calendars; historical societies; museums; good books like those listed in the bibliography of this teaching guide; Indian-published newspapers and magazines (see Resources at back of book, page 227); and Indian-published curriculum (see Resources at back of book, page 223).
5. Students collaborate on a class exhibition that displays both stereotypic and accurate images of contemporary Indians. Students can photocopy or bring in examples of Indian stereotypes found on clothing, food packages, toys, ads, cartoons, comics, greeting cards, magazines, and children's books. Students can invite other classes to their exhibition.

Enrichment/Extensions
Research. Students in seventh and eighth grades can do a content analysis of the presence or absence of Indian stereotypes in periodicals like *Seventeen*, *Teen*, *Mad Magazine*, *Family Circle*, and *Newsweek* depending on back issues available in the school or town library. Students should choose a magazine(s) and survey every single issue in a given time period, keeping track of stereotypes in advertisements, cartoons, and collectors' art (dolls, plates). Make an illustrated

report for the class showing the number of and kinds of stereotypes. It is also a stereotype if Native people are not represented at all.

Creative Writing. Students can write a letter to greeting card companies, clothing or toy manufacturers, or others explaining why stereotyped images of Indians offend them. The assignment also involves finding the addresses of these companies in directories located in reference rooms of most libraries.

📖 Reading

Ten Terrific Tips for Spotting Stereotypes

1. Watch for little Indian boys and girls from unidentified tribes running around in feathers, fringed buckskin clothing, and moccasins in an unidentified past and unidentified place.

2. Watch for Indian children and adults who are denied the courtesy of a name: "Little Indian" or "mama Indian," for example.

3. Watch out for "I-for-Indian" (as in illustrated alphabets) that turns human beings into objects.

4. Watch out for Indian anachronisms, past-tensed Indians in contemporary settings.

5. Watch out for animals dressed up as Indians. This makes the Indian less than human.

6. Watch out for Indians that are treated like toys.

7. Watch out for non-Indian children and animals "playing Indian" or disguising themselves as Indians. To suggest that non-Indian children or adults can become Indian by putting on a feather insults a Native person's identity. Being Indian is not a profession or a costume, but a condition of being human.

8. Watch out for Indians equipped with tomahawks, bows and arrows, spears, and guns. These weapons make Indians look violent and threatening.

9. Watch out for words like "squaw," "brave," and "papoose." These words do not evoke the same images as do the words "woman," "man," and "baby."

10. Watch out for books that mistreat Indian spiritual practices. Masks, pipes, drums, and rattles are sacred objects, not classroom decorations or props.

Figure 1.1. Examples of stereotypes. Photograph by John Goodwin.

Resources

Students

Video. "Images of Indians: A Series."
    A five-part series examines Hollywood movie stereotypes and their effects on the Indians' self-image. Each segment is about 28 minutes. Order from Native American Public Telecommunications, PO Box 83111, Lincoln, NE 68501.

Teachers

Doxtator, Deborah. *Fluffs and Feathers: An Exhibition of the Symbols of Indianness. A Resource Guide.* Brantford, ON: Woodland Cultural Center, 1988.
    Articles in this exhibition catalog discuss the range of Indian images in historical and contemporary Canadian society (same for U.S. society). Film, books, ads, and toys are examined. This profusely illustrated book includes a good bibliography.

Hirschfelder, Arlene, Paulette Molin, and Yvonne Wakim, eds. *American Indian Stereotypes in the World of Children.* 2nd ed. Lanham, MD: Scarecrow Press, 1999.
    Numerous articles spell out stereotypes in children's books, toys, textbooks, sports teams, and Y-Indian Guide programs. Lengthy bibliography.

Jojola, Theodore S. "Public Image," in *Native America in the Twentieth Century: An Encyclopedia,* Mary B. Davis, ed. New York: Garland, 1994, 483–86.
    From Columbus to Chief Illiniwek (University of Illinois mascot), this Isleta Pueblo scholar sums up Indian images and the need for Natives to revise their own images.

Slapin, Beverly, and Doris Seale. *Through Indian Eyes: The Native Experience in Books for Children.* Philadelphia: New Society Publishers, 1992.
    Collection of essays, poetry, critical reviews of 100 children's books by and about Indian peoples; a checklist for evaluating children's books for anti-Indian bias; recommended bibliography and Native publishers.

Stedman, Raymond William. *Shadows of the Indian: Stereotypes in American Culture.* Norman, OK: University of Oklahoma Press, 1982.
    Study draws on literature, art, and popular culture to describe the counterfeit images attached to Indians. Illustrations and a lengthy bibliography.

Lesson

Past-Tense Stereotyping

Grade Level
4–8

Materials
Student Reading: "Indians in the Past Tense"; children's books about Indians in libraries or homes

Time
One class period

Objectives
- Students learn that most publishing houses print books that dwell on the past histories of Native American life. They learn there are relatively few books about Native people today.

- Students learn that reading only books about Indians in the past reinforces the stereotype that Indians have vanished or are past-tensed, not contemporary.

- Students use *School Library Journal* and other journals that review children's books to understand the process by which librarians buy books for their collections.

Activities
1. Students, either in groups or singly, count books (fiction and nonfiction) in the school or town library or home that deal with the past (before 1900). Students then count books that deal with Indians in the twentieth century. Discuss the results in class.
2. Students discuss the effects of reading only about Indians in the past.
3. Students read "Indians in the Past Tense" and discuss why it is important to read more books about Indian life in the twentieth century.
4. Students write a class letter to the school or town librarians asking them to order books about American Indians in the twentieth century. Enclose a wish list of titles. Students can find titles and reviews of books about twentieth-century Indians in back issues of *School Library Journal, Publishers Weekly, VOYA,* or *Horn Book.* Many children's librarians use these journal reviews to guide them in buying books for their collections.

📖 Reading

Indians in the Past Tense

Most people in the United States know little about Native American people in the twentieth century. How many people know that Simon Ortiz, Acoma Pueblo, and N. Scott Momaday, Kiowa, both famous award-winning writers, pen books for children? How many have seen Hattie Kauffman, Nez Percé, an Emmy award–winning reporter on *CBS This Morning*? How many know that a painting by Jaune Quick-to-See Smith, Salish/Shoshone/Cree, landed on a poster celebrating the 1993 inauguration of President Bill Clinton? How many know there are Indian rock musicians, folk singers, and dozens of Native people producing and directing movies? How many know there are over two dozen tribal colleges and Indian newspapers?

One reason why you probably don't know about all these people is that you are bombarded daily with time-frozen unrealistic Indian images. Faces of past-tensed Indians with headdresses decorate some of your clothing. Some of you have played with cowboy-and-Indian sets or other toys that picture past-tensed Indians. You may watch Indians kill white settlers, army soldiers, or other "good guys" on television, in the movies, or in animated cartoons. Your school textbooks tell you about bloody conflicts between Indians and Europeans and the U.S. Army during the seventeenth, eighteenth, and nineteenth centuries and then stop there. Happy Birthday cards picture past-tensed feathered Indians talking in broken English or bad grammar. Many of you across America cheer for school sports teams with mascots that parade around in buckskin, beads, and feathers. At Halloween, some of you trick-or-treat in fake nineteenth-century Indian costumes. At Thanksgiving, some of you take part in school pageants wearing plastic headdresses and fake buckskin clothing.

Anachronisms, people or things chronologically out of place, also confuse students. Indian anachronisms make students think that the only way a person can be identified as "Indian" today is by wearing feathers, buckskin, and living in a tipi. Anachronisms don't show Indians living in houses and dressing in jeans, T-shirts, and sneakers listening to rock just like everyone else.

Why make a fuss about past-tensed pictures and anachronisms? Because only seeing these kinds of images makes people, young and old, confused about who American Indians are. Only reading about Indians in the past might make you think Indians have vanished or you might think Indians still lead a past-tensed life. Neither idea is true.

Lesson

1.6

Anachronisms

Grade Level
5–8

Materials
Student Reading: "Indians and Anachronisms"; A-B-C, counting, and picture books

Time
Two class periods

Objectives
- Students learn to define, identify, and give an example of an anachronism.

- Students learn that anachronisms of Indian people lead to believing that the only way a person can be identified as Indian today is by wearing feathers, buckskin, and living in a tipi.

- Students learn anachronisms tend to turn Indian people into objects, no longer human.

Activities
1. First explain to students that an anachronism is a person or thing that is chronologically out of place and give some examples—a jet plane flying over an Indian village in 1609; a train in the dinosaur age; an Indian dressed in buckskin clothing and wearing a headdress going to work in a law firm.
2. Ask each student to create an anachronism to confirm understanding of what the concept means.
3. After reading "Indians and Anachronisms" ask students to look for anachronisms of Indian people under "I-is-for-Indian" (and other letters as well) in A-B-C, counting, and picture books. Ask students to look at the images used to illustrate other letters (objects, animals, and so on) and compare them with the Indian images. If an illustration shows an Indian head minus the body, point out to students that the "Indian head" has been turned into a symbolic object and no longer represents a human being.
4. If students find an anachronism of an Indian in a book with a recent publication date (the book is probably still in print), have students compose a letter to the publisher explaining why they think the image should be changed.
5. Small groups of students create a Top Ten List poster with reasons why anachronisms hurt Indian people today. Have each group share its Top Ten List.

Enrichment/Extensions
Research. Have students look in their hometowns for anachronisms of Native people. Suggest students begin by looking at town seals (Hackensack, New Jersey, uses Chief Oratamin who lived in the mid-1600s on its seal), billboards, store windows, and signs with business logos, for example, Mohawk Carpets, Mutual of Omaha Companies, Lawn Chief grass mower, Pontiac car, banks, restaurants, inns, and so on. Students can photograph/draw the image and

make an illustrated report of their findings. Have them discuss the end result of seeing these anachronisms on a daily basis.

Have students write a poem expressing feelings about seeing anachronisms of Indians all around them.

📖 Reading

Indians and Anachronisms

There are too many alphabet and counting books for children with past-tensed Indians showing up alongside contemporary objects, animals, or fantasy people. This juxtaposition creates an anachronism, a confusion of past and present, a person chronologically out of place. Many children conclude that Indians look past-tensed today and that the only way a person can be identified as "Indian" is by wearing feathers, buckskin, and living in a tipi. Too many tourists visiting Indian reservations ask "Where's the tipi?" As one teenage Chippewa girl once said in *Parade* magazine, "Some people just don't get it, that we live in houses now." Furthermore, Indian teens wear jeans, T-shirts, and sneakers and listen to rock and rap just like everyone else.

Anachronistic images don't portray how Indians live and dress today or in the past. That's because the I-for-Indian and count-an-Indian images are stereotypes to begin with. No other ethnic group is so constantly treated as an anachronism employed to illustrate letters of the alphabet, phonics, counting activities, and other language arts activities.

Resources

See Resources, page 9, Stereotypes in General.

Lesson 1.7

Sovereignty

Grade Level

6–8

Materials

Student Readings: Two readings about sovereignty in Indian country; map of world and U.S. map with Indian nations; materials for a collage

Time

One class period

Objectives

- Students will think about the characteristics that define a sovereign nation.

- Students will learn the meaning of sovereignty as it applies to Indian Nations.

Activities

1. Students make a list of a dozen nations and identity them on a map.
2. Students discuss what makes each of those countries a sovereign nation. List the characteristics on the board. (Hints: national boundaries, a political structure, common language, customs, identity as a people or a nation.)
3. Students discuss two readings about sovereignty in Indian country. Identify 12 Indian Nations on the U.S. map.
4. Students discuss whether the sovereignty of Indian Nations is the same or different from other nations in the world.
5. Discuss whether a nation or a government can be partly sovereign. Can a nation be sovereign in some respects but not in others?

Enrichment/Extensions

Art. Students make a collage of pictures that represent characteristics of sovereign nations.

Political Science. Discuss the relationships of states to the federal government. How is that relationship similar and different from the relationship of Native American nations to the federal government?

 **Reading**

Sovereignty

From Robert J. Lyttle (Cheyenne/Arapaho),
Attorney, Norman, Oklahoma, 1999.

Sovereignty in its simplest form means governmental power over people and land. Governments possess sovereignty. The United States has sovereignty, each state has sovereignty, and Indian tribes have sovereignty. The sovereignty of the United States comes from each state. The original 13 colonies each had their own sovereignty over their land and people after the American Revolution. When the 13 colonies decided to form the United States, they gave a portion of their sovereignty to the central government of the United States, therefore, the source of U.S. sovereignty is each state.

The United States is a limited sovereign. It's power is limited because the powers that states did not give to the federal government remain with the states. Similarly, Indian tribes are the source of their sovereignty. For thousands of years Indian tribes had the absolute power to govern their territory and the people within their territory. The United States did not "give" Indian tribes any governmental powers or sovereignty. Indian tribes existed for thousands of years before the United States was formed. For example, when the U.S. government encountered Indian tribes, they negotiated treaties as one sovereign government to another sovereign government. At the treaty negotiations, both the tribe and the United States would bring their sovereign rights to the table. In this way, each side made promises to the other to forge the agreement. Any powers that the tribe did not relinquish remain with the tribe to this day. Over the years, however, the U.S. government has unilaterally taken pieces of tribes' sovereignty away. Nevertheless, tribes still retain broad governmental powers over their territories and the people within their territories. As sovereign governments, tribes have power to pass laws addressing such matters as land use, criminal conduct, civil conduct, and business regulation.

Since the formation of the U.S. government, there has been tension between the powers of the states versus the powers of the federal government. Some people argue for a strong central government while others argue for "states rights" or more power to the states. Similarly, the distribution of powers between Indian tribes and the federal government is also constantly in dispute. Tribes, like states, argue that they are the source of their sovereign powers, that is, they have inherent sovereignty, and that the federal government only has limited powers over them. Overall, the extent to which the U.S. government will respect the sovereign rights of Indian tribes remains to be seen.

📖 Reading

Sovereignty in Indian Country

> From Charles F. Wilkinson. "The Idea of Sovereignty: Native Peoples, Their Lands, and Their Dreams." *Native American Rights Fund (NARF) Legal Review*, vol. 13, no. 4 (Fall 1988): 1–11.

. . . The fact is that we regularly use the word "sovereignty" today and we use it in a way markedly different from the classical definition. Of course, Native governments do not possess absolute power. Neither does the city of Honolulu or the city of New York, the state of Hawaii or the state of New York, the nation of Luxembourg or the Republic of Mexico, or, for that matter, the United States of America or the Union of Soviet Socialist Republics. None of them possesses complete power—world politics and internal national politics are far too complicated for that—yet we refer to all of them as sovereigns. . . . Today, we intuitively understand that sovereignty simply refers to an entity that possesses governmental powers. The working dictionary definition of sovereign is "an independent government."

A sovereign is a national, state, city, county, or Native government that can make laws and enforce them. Some sovereigns—such as Russia—have enormous power. They have nearly all of the possible aspects of sovereignty. Other sovereigns—such as the city of Lahaina or a rural county in Iowa—possess relatively few of the total sticks in the bundle that a sovereign could possess. Others—one might give examples the city of Honolulu or the Navajo Nation—are somewhere in between. But all of them share important things in common. They are not merely corporations or some kind of voluntary organization, such as a social club. They can make laws and enforce them.

Sovereignty, therefore, is easy to define in the real world. When one parses sovereignty out in this manner, there is nothing mystical or extraordinary about it. The reason is that sovereignty means power and when a people bands together to exercise its sovereignty that people is empowered. . . .

Far and away the greatest achievement, however, has been the attainment of political power. The overriding point of constitutional law and political science made by the U.S. Supreme Court in modern times is that there are three—not two, as we all were taught from grade school on—there are three sovereigns in our federal constitution system: the federal government, the states, and Native governments. American Indian tribes not only own their reservations, they rule them. Tribal laws govern land use, hunting, fishing, religious exercise, environmental protection, economic development, marriage, divorce, and adoption and custody of children. Indian tribes can tax in order to raise revenue. They have administrative agencies to regulate natural resource use, zoning, and numerous other activities. They have police and courts to enforce the laws. . . . In Indian country, the dominant laws are tribal laws, not state laws, and they are enforced by tribal officials, not by state officials.

Resources
Students

Cohen, Fay G., and Jeanne Heuving, eds. *Tribal Sovereignty: Indian Tribes in U.S. History.* Seattle, WA: United Indians of All Tribes Foundation, Daybreak Star Press, 1981.
Short introduction to Indian history, covering Indian governments and U.S. Indian policy.

Deloria, Vine, Jr., and Clifford Lytle. *The Nations Within: The Past and Future of Indian Sovereignty.* New York: Pantheon, 1984.
Of all the issues affecting Native people, sovereignty is critical. This book presents an Indian perspective that is clear and easy to understand.

Teachers

Clinton, Robert N. "Sovereignty and Jurisdiction," in *Native America in the Twentieth Century: An Encyclopedia.* New York: Garland, 1994, 605–11.
Scholarly article surveys sovereignty from first contact with Europeans to the present.

NARF Legal Review. Native American Rights Fund, 1506 Broadway, Boulder, CO 80302.
This quarterly publication chronicles some of the current legal battles being fought on behalf of Indian tribes by this highly regarded legal rights organization.

Pevar, Stephen L. *The Rights of Indians and Tribes: The Basic ACLU Guide to Indian and Tribal Rights.* Carbondale, IL: University of Illinois Press, 1992.
Readable legal handbook covering Native sovereignty and relationship to the federal government.

Prucha, Francis Paul. *Documents of United States Indian Policy.* Lincoln, NE: University of Nebraska Press, 1990.
This book contains legal documents that spell out U.S. government Indian policies. Any of Prucha's books are essential to understanding U.S. Indian policy.

———. *United States Indian Policy: A Critical Bibliography.* Bloomington, IN: Indiana University Press, 1977.
Lists books that deal with powerful intervention of the U.S. government into Indian self-government.

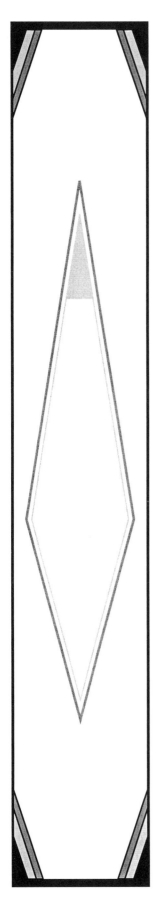

 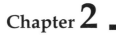

Chapter 2

Where We Live

Indians do not live in "cupboards" like a popular children's book and movie portray or in museums, but by now your students may be well aware of this. Where are Indian people? Non-Indian people are often surprised to learn that Native Americans may live in the same communities as they do and that the largest percentage of Indians do not live on reservations. Indians, like other Americans, move away from home to attend college, seek employment, or marry someone from a different area. Unlike most other Americans, Indians have also been forcibly relocated away from ancestral homelands by the U.S. government. The lessons in this chapter will help students understand that Indians live in every state and all kinds of communities; this can be quite enlightening even for Indian students!

A map exercise in Lesson 2.1 can be combined with Lesson 7.1, Indians in Careers/Employment. Lessons 2.2 and 2.3 will help students become aware of the states that have Indian names and why some tribes have changed their names. Lesson 2.2 may be used with Lesson 1.7, Sovereignty.

Lesson

2.1

Where We Live

Grade Level
4–8

Materials
U.S. map; map of contemporary Indian communities (pages xviii–xix); Indian census demographics for your individual state and Nation (included in this lesson); Student Readings: "U.S. American Indian Policies and Acts," "1990 Census Count," and "The Top Ten Cities with Native American Residents"; blank map of your state; compass; markers; construction paper; maps from the Web site: <www.gdsc.bia.gov/maps.htm epa1> (go to Indian Lands in the United States; then go to State and Regional Shaded Relief Maps). Contact Big Moon Traders, (801) 359-0306 for an accurate historical map.

Time
Three to four class periods

Objectives
- Students will be able to recognize their state, locate their state capital, and identify neighboring states.

- Students will become familiar with both historical and contemporary Indian communities within their state and understand why those communities have been altered.

- Students will learn specific U.S. government policies regarding Native Americans in the twentieth century and how those policies affected changes in Indian population.

- Students will learn to read a compass.

- Students will learn to construct a time line.

- Students will become familiar with reading and interpreting census data.

- Students will begin to acquire skills to make oral and visual presentations.

Activities

<u>First Class</u>

1. Give the class a brief lecture on U.S. Indian policy over the last 200 years. Show maps of the United States with historical and contemporary Indian communities. Initiate discussion on why Indian communities are so different today, for example, size, locations.
2. Divide the class into two groups. Group A: Give handout of Reading: "U.S. American Indian Policies and Acts," ruler, construction paper, tape or glue, markers. Have students discuss policies. Explain why and how time lines are used. Have students construct a time line of U.S. American Indian policies. Before next class, students will research policies in other sources. They should investigate different views than those presented here. See if they can locate any firsthand accounts of those affected by the policies. They will prepare to share their work with the entire class.
3. Group B: Give them a blank map of your state, historical map of Indian communities, markers. They will map all tribes that were once located in their state. For next class, they will research those Nations (each student can take one or two tribes).

<u>Second Class</u>

1. Group B: Group will display their maps and give names and numbers of Nations that were located in their state (before and after statehood).
2. Group will share a little information about each Nation. After the presentation, ask the following:

    Was the information presented in a nonstereotypical way?

    Do you think it was accurate?

    What sources did you use?

    Do you think Native authors wrote the books you used for your research? Explain your answer.

3. Group A: Group A will post their time line and lead a discussion about the different policies by asking the class the following questions:

    How did those policies change the lives of Indian people?

    Give some reasons why the enforcement of these policies would change the geographical locations of Indian peoples and/or communities.

    Do you think the acts were beneficial to the United States?

    Do you think any of the acts were beneficial to Native Americans?

Third Class

1. Show students a compass. Ask for volunteers to read the compass.
2. Have students stand and face cardinal directions according to the compass. Ask them to visualize what landmarks, roads, buildings, etc. are in each direction. See if they can locate the direction of their homes. Show them a map of the United States and locate their state. What direction is their state in relationship to the country, hemisphere, Arctic Circle, oceans, Mississippi River, Rocky Mountains, Mexico, Canada, etc.
3. Pass out a blank map of the state (with space enough to write on the outside of the map). Students will add cardinal directions on maps, state capital, and their own community. Add contemporary Indian communities (reservations, rancherias, etc.) to maps.
4. Give population for each tribe/Nation from state census information. Have students add demographics to the side of their maps. Example follows on page 21, Figure 2.1.
5. Now compare communities and members of all tribes residing in the state to the historical map. Are there differences? If so, why? Are students surprised that Native Americans live in their state?
6. Do not assume that there are no American Indians in your classroom.
7. Also, be careful not to use " them" and "us." Have students research the state census to find towns or cities where Indians reside. Add those towns to their maps. If you have Native American students in your class, please do not make them feel either special or different. Let them take the initiative. Now compare all of the maps. Stress differences in eras.

Enrichment/Extensions

Field Trips. Visit Indian communities.

Geography. Research Indian place names in your state and add them to the maps. Research methods for mapmaking. Have the class create a three-dimensional map of your state. Research Native American methods of mapmaking, traveling directions, and the importance of the four directions.

Literature. Research stories on directions, migration, geography.

Social Studies. Do an ethnic census of school/neighborhood. Make a population map of school with lines drawn to countries/tribes of students/teachers. Locate Indian organizations, community centers, etc. in your area.

Writing. Correspond with tribes in your state for information/pen pals.

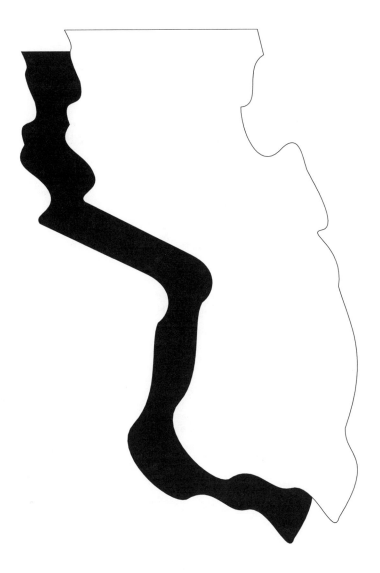

NEW JERSEY

Ramapo 326

Haida 3

Haliwa 26

Hidatsa 2

Cayuga 6

Mohawk 366

(etc.)

Figure 2.1. Blank map of New Jersey.

📖 Reading

U.S. American Indian Policies and Acts

National Indian policy has changed numerous times in the last 200 years. At times, tribes have been seen as nations who merited a geographical territory. Other times, the opinion has been that Indian tribes/Nations should be abolished or terminated and Indians assimilated into non-Indian society. These two conflicting positions seem to dominate. American Indian policy is still in a state of flux.

Native Americans share some of the same characteristics of other oppressed groups—poverty, alienation, poor health and health care, substandard education, discrimination, inadequate housing and employment. However, the overriding difference is that American Indians have a special legal relationship with the U.S. government. Legally, American Indians are domestic, dependent, sovereign nations. Below are a few official policies that have affected American Indians.

The Indian Removal Act of 1830 empowered the president to remove Indians from their ancestral lands and locate them west of the Mississippi River. Although this act required the consent of the Indians before ceding the land, Indian people were tortured and forced to sign treaties.

The Trade and Intercourse Act of 1834 made it illegal for individuals to buy land from Indian Nations.

From the 1850s on, whites were living all over North America and few areas were inhabited exclusively by American Indians. The Reservation Period sought to contain Indians in areas away from most white communities. In exchange, Native peoples were to be given protection, food, and clothing. Many starved or froze to death because provisions never came.

The Treaty of 1868, often called the Treaty of Fort Laramie, between the United States and various Lakota groups, recognized the Black Hills as belonging to the Sioux. White settlers and the U.S. military were supposed to stay out of the Black Hills forever. However, gold was discovered in 1873 and the treaty was not upheld by the United States because of the gold rush.

The General Allotment Act or Dawes Severalty Act of 1887 completely ignored traditional Indian society. Indian land that was held tribally or communally was divided into separate tracts for each family. All excess lands were then sold or given to white settlers. Furthermore, if Indians did not farm the land, it was also given away. Often, the Indian families did not have the money to buy tools and materials for farming. The end result was that by the early 1930s Indian lands were reduced from 138 million acres to 48 million acres.

The Curtis Act of 1898 dissolved all tribal courts, forced allotments, and put control of tribal monies under the secretary of the Interior.

In 1924, President Calvin Coolidge signed an act making American Indians official citizens of the United States. However, many Indians were already citizens. This act said that Indians could be citizens of the United States without having to give up citizenship of their Indian Nation.

In 1928, a government study called the Meriam Report was conducted to determine the quality of life on reservations. It stated that conditions were wretched; changes must be made.

The Indian Reorganization Act of 1934 or Wheeler-Howard Act reversed the Allotment Act and allowed tribes to organize governments. Some tribes were encouraged to manage their own resources, but the U.S. government through the Bureau of Indian Affairs still had to approve any decisions. Not all Nations agreed because this Act stated that the Indian government could not be traditional, but patterned after Anglo-American law.

Created in 1946 by Congress, the Indian Claims Commission was to settle land claims of tribes against the United States. Over $800 million was paid to tribes for lands stolen.

In 1948, the Hoover Commission recommended that the Bureau of Indian Affairs be transferred to the Federal Security Agency and stated that assimilation must be the dominant goal of public policy for Indians. Thus, the climate was set for some of the policies that followed.

The relocation policy officially began in 1948 when placement offices were opened in Denver, Salt Lake City, and Los Angeles. People were often forced from their homes on reservations to big cities in search of job opportunities. The Bureau of Indian Affairs offered on-the-job training, but oftentimes after the federal training money was spent, employers would not hire Indians on their own payroll. People were far from home, living in squalid urban conditions. Like before, assimilation was not working.

The termination policy became official in 1953 in the form of House Resolution 108. Congress intended to sever direct and historical federal relations with Indian tribes. The law was overturned in 1960 when state and Indian opposition blocked plans to terminate more tribes. Some of the Nations terminated were: Alabama-Couchatta of Texas; California rancherias and reservations; Catawba of South Carolina; Klamath tribe of Oregon; Menominee tribe of Wisconsin; Ottawa tribe of Oklahoma; Paiute Indians of Utah; Peoria tribe of Oklahoma; Ponca tribe of Nebraska; Uintah and Ouray Utes of Utah; 60 bands of western Oregon Indians; and Wyandot tribe of Oklahoma. Most of these tribes lost their lands, which passed into non-Indian hands.

The American Indian Civil Liberties Act of 1968 protected reservation Indians under the Bill of Rights. States would not be allowed to assume law and order jurisdiction on reservations without tribal consent.

The American Indian Policy Review Commission created in 1975 studied the effects of federal policies on Indians. The final report stated that forced assimilation should not be continued, and Indians should have the right to self-determination. The Indian Self-Determination and Education Assistance Act was passed in 1975.

The Indian Child Welfare Act, passed in 1978, gave authority to tribes for Indian child custody proceedings. This protected the Indian child from being adopted by non-Indian families, a common practice that was another form of assimilation or *cultural genocide*, which is destruction of the language, customs, and traditions of a people. Instead of killing people with guns and bullets, this kind of genocide destroys people's identity, spirit, and purpose for living with laws and government policies.

Indian peoples fought long and hard for the freedom to practice their own religions. Although the American Indian Religious Freedom Act of 1978 was finally passed, many Natives are still not allowed to worship in traditional ways. Forcing Indians to become Christians was another form of cultural genocide.

In 1988, the Indian Gaming Regulatory Act was passed to establish an Indian gaming commission to oversee the gaming industry and protect the tribes' interests.

The National American Indian Museum Act, passed in 1989, stated that Native human remains were to be returned to tribes, if requested.

In 1990, Congress enacted the Native American Grave Protection and Repatriation Act, which ordered all museums to inventory their collections of human remains and funerary objects and inform tribes of their whereabouts. If tribes desired it, they were to be returned.

📖 Reading

1990 Census Count

At present there are 515 tribes recognized by states or the federal government. There are an additional 100 or so who have filed for recognition. The following chart shows the number of American Indians in each state in 1990.

Oklahoma	252,420	Virginia	15,282
California	242,164	New Jersey	14,970
Arizona	203,527	Pennsylvania	14,733
New Mexico	134,355	Idaho	13,780
Alaska	85,698	Georgia	13,348
Washington	81,483	Maryland	12,972
North Carolina	80,155	Arkansas	12,773
Texas	65,877	Indiana	12,720
New York	62,651	Nebraska	12,410
Michigan	55,638	Massachusetts	12,241
South Dakota	50,575	Tennessee	10,039
Minnesota	49,909	Wyoming	9,479
Montana	47,679	Mississippi	8,525
Wisconsin	39,387	South Carolina	8,246
Oregon	38,496	Iowa	7,349
Florida	36,335	Connecticut	6,654
Colorado	27,776	Maine	5,998
North Dakota	25,917	Kentucky	5,769
Utah	24,283	Hawaii	5,099
Kansas	21,965	Rhode Island	4,071
Illinois	21,836	West Virginia	2,458
Ohio	20,358	New Hampshire	2,134
Missouri	19,835	Delaware	2,019
Nevada	19,637	Vermont	1,696
Louisiana	18,541	District of Columbia	1,466
Alabama	16,506		

📖 Reading

The Top Ten Cities with Native American Residents

Los Angeles, CA and suburbs	87,487
Tulsa, OK	48,196
New York, NY and suburbs	46,191
Oklahoma City, OK	45,720
San Francisco, CA and suburbs	40,847
Phoenix, AZ	38,017
Seattle-Tacoma, WA	32,071
Minneapolis-St. Paul, MN	23,956
Tucson, AZ	20,330
San Diego, CA	20,066

Resources

Please see Resources at the back of this book for information on contemporary people, census, maps, etc.

Students

Canby, William. *American Indian Law in a Nutshell*. St. Paul, MN: West, 1981.
    This is not specifically a student resource, but with help, it is understandable.

Teachers

American Indian Report. The Falmouth Institute, Inc. Publications Order Department, 3918 Prosperity Avenue, Suite 302, Fairfax, VA 22031.
    This monthly report lists Indian issues.

Francis, Lee. *Native Time: An Historical Timetable of Native Americans from 200,000 B.C. to 1994 A.D.* New York: St. Martin's Press, 1995.

Hirschfelder, Arlene, and Martha Kriepe de Montaño. *Native American Almanac: A Portrait of Native America Today*. New York: Prentice-Hall, 1993.
    This reference book has a lot of contemporary information on everything from education and maps to policies.

We the First Americans. U.S. Department of Commerce, Bureau of the Census, Population Division, Racial Statistics Branch, Washington, DC 20233.

Lesson

2.2

Tribal Names

Grade Level
   4–6

Materials
   Student Readings: "Why Some Tribes Have Changed Their Names" and "Name Changes in African Nation-States"

Time
   One class period

Objectives
   • Students learn that during the twentieth century, some tribes have cast off names given to them by Americans, English, French, Spanish, and others.

   • Students learn that during the twentieth century, some tribal peoples have expressed a preference or have formally changed their names to traditional names in their own language.

   • Students learn it is an exercise of sovereignty for a people to determine the name by which they want to be called.

Activities
   Student Reading: "Why Some Tribes Have Changed Their Names" and discuss why these Nations have changed their names. Discuss the concept of sovereignty.

Enrichment/Extensions
   Research. Students research nations in Africa that changed back to traditional names since the 1960s.

📖 Reading

Why Some Tribes Have Changed Their Names

   As the tribal sovereignty movement has grown in the United States, many tribes have fought for more local control in Native communities. Some tribes have even fought for control over their names. Many tribes have names that are very seldom their own names for themselves. Even when a Native name has always existed, non-Indian people persist in using alien terms. Take, for example, the tribal name "Delaware." On August 27, 1610, Sir Samuel Argall, captain of the sailing vessel *Discovery*, sailed into the bay, which was subsequently named De La Warre Bay in honor of Sir

Thomas West, third Lord De La Warre and governor of the Virginia colony. The numerous Indian bands living along the shore of this bay and the river that fed into it were viewed by the English as the Indians on the De La Warre River, later simplified into the Delaware River Indians or Delaware. But the Indians' original name for themselves was and is Lenni Lenape. Another example: The tribal name Nez Percé came from the French word for pierced nose. This tribe supposedly practiced the custom of piercing the nose for insertion of a piece of dentalium. The tribe's name for itself is Nimipu. And finally, the tribal name Fox was also derived from a French word. When the French first met with a clan of the Mesquakies (the traditional name for the tribe) in the early 1600s, they saw a sign of a fox that these people were carrying. The French recognized the animal as a fox and from then on, the Mesquakies became known as the Fox—through the translation of the French word "renard" into fox.

Indians themselves have gradually been forced to live with or even accept these alien names because of the pressure stemming from non-Indian custom. But this is all changing. Some tribes are reclaiming their own traditional names and making it official.

One of the first Indian Nations to take back its name was the Tohono O'odham, who in 1984 were sick and tired of being called "Papago," a derogatory Spanish corruption of the Indian word "bav" for "bean eaters." Members of the tribe then, as well as now, refer to themselves as the Tohono O'odham or The Desert People. Only outsiders called them Papagos. But no longer. The Tribal Council approved a change in the new tribal constitution, and tribal members on three southern Arizona reservations approved it.

In 1993, the Sisseton-Wahpeton Sioux dropped "Sioux" from its name, no longer wanting to be known by a French misinterpretation of an enemy's word. The Tribal Council officially rejected the name "Sioux" and adopted the word their ancestors called themselves, Dakota, a word meaning "allies." As of October 29, 1993, the tribe's letterhead and every other document from the tribe read Sisseton-Wahpeton Dakota Nation. "Sioux" is believed to be a mispronunciation of the last syllable of the word *nadowessiwag*, used by the Ojibway to describe the people who were then their enemies.

In 1994, the Winnebago Tribe of Wisconsin renamed itself the Ho-Chunk Nation, a name that traditionally referred to this people. The name means "big voice" or "mother voice."

In 1996, the Devil's Lake Sioux Tribe of North Dakota changed the name of its reservation to the Spirit Lake Nation. The tribe used to refer to themselves as *Mniwakan oyate*, which means Spirit Lake Nation. The name Devil's Lake came from white settlers in the late nineteenth century.

📖 Reading

Name Changes in African Nation-States

In the last two decades of the nineteenth century, almost the whole of the African continent was taken under European control. Beginning in the late 1950s, the indigenous peoples in African nation-states broke colonial ties and won their political independence from European nations. This led to a number of these nations changing their names:

1957	The Gold Coast	Ghana
1960	Dahomey	Benin
1964	Nyasaland	Malawi
	Northern Rhodesia	Zambia
	Southwest Africa	Namibia
1966	Bechuanaland	Botswana
1968	le de France	Mauritius
1974	Portuguese Guinea	Gambia
1977	Somaliland	Djibouti
1980	Rhodesia	Zimbabwe

Resources
Students and Teachers

Chart of traditional Indian nation names (before and after contact) in Vine Deloria Jr. *God Is Red.* New York: Dell Publishing, 1973, 365.

Hodge, Frederick Webb. *Handbook of American Indians North of Mexico.* 2 volumes. Smithsonian Institution Bureau of American Ethnology Bulletin 30, 1907–1910.
   Several reprints available. Look up hundreds of tribal names in these volumes located in most library reference sections.

Lesson

2.3

Place Names

Grade Level
4–5

Materials
Student Reading: "States with Indian Names"

Time
One class period

Objectives
- Students learn that 27 states have Indian names.

- Students learn there still are ancient Indian place names attached to some cities, villages, counties, mountains, hills, rivers, lakes, bays, and other geographic features in every state in the nation. Some of the names are in the original Indian language and some are translated into English.

- Students learn that Indian place names (1) tell history; (2) show respect for people or animals associated with them; (3) name activities that are important to people; and (4) describe features of the land like a visual map.

Activities
1. Pass out the list of 27 states with Indian names. Students fill in these names on a blank map of the United States. Students discuss the function of each state place name.
2. Teachers prepare a list of some of the Indian place names within the state (or a group of students can do the research and prepare the list for the class).
3. Students plot the Indian place names on a blank map of the state, or using an actual map of the state, highlight each name, or find another technique to show the Indian place names.

Enrichment/Extensions
Creative Writing. Students "rename" their town or city based on its geographic features or other visual characteristics.

Field Trip. Students search their neighborhoods for street names named after Indian tribes, individuals, or in Indian languages. Bring a list to class with the names and their meanings.

Research. Students search the state map for cities, towns, rivers, or other geographic features with French, Spanish, or German names and get these names translated. Categorize the names by language.

📖 Reading

States with Indian Names

Alabama. The word comes from an Indian tribe originally called the Alabamas or Alibamons, who in turn gave the name to a river from which the state is named.

Alaska. The word is either from the Eskimo word *alakshak*, meaning "peninsula," or the Aleut word *Alaxsxaq*, designating "their land"; also said to mean "great lands."

Arizona. Many authorities attribute the meaning to a word that means arid zone or desert. Others claim the name is Aztec, from *arizuma*, meaning "silver bearing." Still another version attributes the origin to the Tohono O'odham (Papago) tribe of Arizona, who named it from the locality in which they lived called Arizonac, meaning "site of the small springs." This place was near the present town of Nogales, and in the early 1700s silver was discovered near there, which gives some credence to the Aztec word *arizuma*.

Arkansas. Origin is uncertain. According to some, the word is from the Algonquian language. Others say that Arkansas is a French version of *Kansas*, a Sioux Indian name for "south wind people."

Connecticut. The word appears to be derived from the Indian word *Quonoktacut*, interpreted by some to mean either "river whose water is driven in waves by tides or winds" or "long river," or "the long (without end) river."

Idaho. The origin of the word is uncertain. Some claim it derives from an Indian word of unknown meaning, while others claim it means "gem of the mountains." Some claim the word to be a Shoshone translation of *edah hoe,* meaning "light on the mountain."

Illinois. The word comes from the Illini Indian word meaning "men" or "warriors," supplemented by the French adjective ending *ois.*

Indiana. The word presumably comes from the fact that the land lying along the Ohio River was purchased from the Indians. Others claim it was named for the Indian tribes who settled in western Pennsylvania.

Iowa. The word comes from an Indian tribe called Ah-hee-oo-ba, meaning "sleepy ones" or "drowsy ones." They lived in the valley of the state's principal river, which they named for the tribe, and, in turn, the name was applied to the state.

Kansas. The state was named for the Kansas or Kanza tribe of the Siouan language family whose name translates as "south wind people" or "wind people."

Kentucky. The origin and meaning are controversial. Some claim it comes from the Indian word *Kentake*, meaning "meadow land." Some claim it comes from the Shawnee word meaning "at the head of a river," inasmuch as they used the Kentucky River in traveling around the area.

Massachusetts. The word comes from the Algonquian language and means "great-hill-small-place," possibly for the hills around Boston as seen from the bay.

Michigan. The word comes from the Algonquian word *Mishagamaw*, meaning "big lake" or "great water"; it is also said to be from *Michi*, meaning "great" and *gama*, meaning "water."

Minnesota. The word comes from the Sioux word meaning "cloudy water" or "sky-tinted water"; it derived its name from the river of the same name.

Mississippi. The word means "great river" or "gathering in of all the water," sometimes referred to as the "father of waters," indicating the Indians were aware of the immensity of the river.

Missouri. The word is from a tribal name denoting "muddy water" and named for the large river.

Nebraska. The Sioux word describes the river from which the state gets it name, meaning "shallow water" or "broad water." Also said to be an Oto Indian word meaning "flat river," referring to the Platte River.

New Mexico. The word was used by the Mexicans to refer to the territory north and west of the Rio Grande in the sixteenth century. It may have been derived from the name of the Aztec war god Mixitli.

North Dakota. The word comes from the Sioux name meaning "allies." Allies was used to signify the common name of the confederated Sioux tribes.

Ohio. The Iroquois Indian word means "beautiful river," taken from the river of the same name.

Oklahoma. Believed to have been coined about 1866 by a Choctaw-speaking missionary; the Choctaw Indian word means "red people."

South Dakota. The word comes from the Sioux Indian name for "allies." Allies was used to signify the common name of the confederated Sioux tribes.

Tennessee. The word is of Cherokee origin from a tribe located at a village site called Tanasee. The state is named for its principal river, which has been interpreted by some as meaning "bend in the river."

Texas. The word is generally accepted as an Indian word meaning "tejas" or "friends" or "allies."

Utah. The name is taken from the Ute Indians who inhabited the region, but the origin of the word is unknown.

Wisconsin. The word is believed to be an Indian word, but the meaning is uncertain. The state was named after its principal river, which is said to mean "wild rushing channel" or "holes in the banks of the stream in which birds nest."

Wyoming. Authorities interpret this name as either "extensive plains" or "mountains, with valleys alternating."

Resources
<u>Students and Teachers</u>

Hodge, Frederick Webb. *Handbook of American Indians North of Mexico.* 2 volumes. Smithsonian Institution Bureau of American Ethnology Bulletin 30, 1907–1910.
  Several reprints available. Look up hundreds of place names and geographic features in these volumes located in most library reference sections.

Lambert, Eloise, and Mario Pei. *The Book of Place Names.* New York: Lothrop, Lee and Shepherd, 1959.

Rasky, Susan F. "What's in a Name? For Indians, Cultural Survival." *New York Times.* August 4, 1988.
  Discusses project to restore the ancient place names on maps of the White Mountain Apache tribe in Apache, Arizona. The vast majority of the names describe features of the landscape.

Stewart, George R. *American Place Names: A Concise and Selected Dictionary for the Continental U.S.A.* New York: Oxford University Press, 1970.

Weatherford, Jack. "The Naming of North America," in *Native Roots: How the Indians Enriched America.* New York: Ballantine, 1991, 214–33.
  Lively discussion about the way Indian people named their environment, about American settlers who toyed with Indian names, and about French and Spanish names that are direct translations of older Indian names.

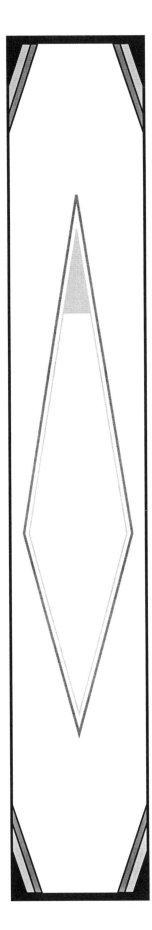

Chapter 3

Growing Up, Growing Old: A Few Events Along the Way

The few times there is an Indian theme or role on film or television, it often centers on mysticism, alcoholism, or deprivation of some sort. This chapter focuses on the four stages of life—child, adolescent, adult, elder—and cites an example or event in each, presenting a more realistic view of some of the ceremonies and customs than the media portrays. Also, students will learn that Native Americans have had great difficulties in maintaining traditional religions, although these spiritual ways are still practiced today. The last lesson helps students understand that many Indian elders have an extremely hard life and how some young Indian people place more importance on youth than the aged, a concept foreign to Indian tradition.

The lesson on adults is about a math teacher, and like all the biographical readings in this book features a "real" Indian person. Feel free to use the reading in the lesson on "Indians in Careers/Employment."

Lesson

3.1

Personal Naming Traditions

Grade Level
4–5

Materials
Student Reading: "Native American Naming Practices"

Time
One class period

Objectives
- Students learn that tribes have different name-giving traditions and ceremonies that are important to cultural identity.

- Students learn the meaning of their own names: given, surname, and nickname.

- Students learn members of every culture have naming practices, but details vary from culture to culture.

Activities
1. Students read "Native American Naming Practices" and compare tribal naming traditions with their own.
2. Students ask parents/guardians who named them where their given and last names came from (given names from relatives, the Bible, Greek mythology, or another language; surnames from occupations, place of residence, given name of father, or a descriptive nickname).
3. Students ask whether they had a naming ceremony (perhaps some of them remember). If so, write a description of it and share it in class.
4. Students discuss in class whether they have nicknames. If so, where do they come from (physical features, reputation, abbreviation)?

Enrichment/Extensions
Research. Students research the history of first and last names and do an oral report. Students research the naming practices of other cultures and do an oral or written report.

📖 Reading

Native American Naming Practices

Depending on the tribe, Indians acquired their names at different points during their life. Some people, like the Tewa of New Mexico, gave babies their everyday names several days after birth, selecting them from natural phenomenon appropriate to the season. The Lenape (Delaware) Indians named a child at three or four years of age when the parents were sure the Creator intended the child to remain in their care. The Hopi people of Arizona initiated boys and girls between the ages of 6 and 10 into religious organizations and gave them ceremonial names to indicate their change in ritual status. Among the North Pacific Coast peoples, middle-aged persons between the ages of 45 and 60 received names that made them bona fide members of lineages. Until then, they were considered only relatives of lineage members.

Traditionally, in many Native cultures, a person could acquire many names throughout life. The Navajos first provide a kinship name that identifies a person's relationship to other family members. Such names translated into terms such as one's maternal nephew who is the middle son of one's youngest sister. Navajos also nickname their children and provide a Euroamerican name used in school or non-Navajo situations. They also give people "holy" or "war" names that are part of one's personal power. Navajos consider it impolite to use these names in a person's presence because names with power wear out from overuse. In many Native cultures, some names are kept secret. In others, the name, while secret, is rarely used because people use nicknames.

Traditionally, the Dakota/Lakota (Sioux) receive three or four names over a lifetime. The birth name shows the order of birth into a family, such as first-born daughter or last-born son. Children also receive nicknames, and, later, a medicine person gives an honor name to the child referring to great deeds of the child's ancestor.

Many tribes name children after distinguished tribal relatives, elders, or ancestors in hopes the child later will live up to the attributes of the name. In the past, some men acquired a dozen or more names in a lifetime by performing a succession of distinctive deeds. In many tribes, after the death of such a warrior at a prescribed time, relatives gathered and chose a young man to bear the name.

In recent years, more Native people have been giving their children Indian names and ceremonies, even if the children have English names. It's a way of keeping Native cultures alive.

Resources
Students

Old Coyote, Henry. "The Power of the Word," in *Respect for Life: The Traditional Upbringing of American Indian Children*, Sylvester M. Morey and Olivia L. Gilliam, eds. New York: The Myrin Institute, 1974, 35–38.
Crow naming practices are described by a Crow elder in conversational style.

Poster. "Why Our Children Should Have Indian Names." North American Indian Traveling College. R.R. 3, Cornwall Island, ON, Canada K6H 5R7.

Stewart, George R. *American Given Names: Their Origin and History in the Context of the English Language*. New York: Oxford University Press, 1979.
   A dictionary of names from historic to present times. Especially good introduction about naming practices in America.

Video. "I Am Different from My Brother: Dakota Name-Giving." 1981. 20 minutes. Real-life docu-drama depicts the Name-Giving Ceremony of three young Flandreau Dakota Sioux children who receive their traditional Indian names from their grandparents. Available from Native American Public Telecommunications. (See Audiovisual Resources, page 225.)

Wiles, Sara. "Arapaho Names: Treasured Gifts." *Tribal College Journal*. Vol. 7, no. 3 (Winter 1996): 29–31.
   Description of how giving of names is still a "vital and important tradition" among the Northern Arapaho of the Wind River Reservation of Wyoming. Six names are discussed.

Teachers

Hinton, Leanne. "Names." *News from Native California*. Vol. 9, no. 4 (Summer 1996): 7–9.
   Describes different California Indian past-day naming practices and tells how many Native Californians are bringing back traditional names and naming ceremonies. Contemporary Wukchumne naming ceremonies are described.

Weslager, C. A. "Delaware Indian Name Giving and Modern Practice," in *A Delaware Indian Symposium*, Herbert C. Kraft, ed. Harrisburg, PA: Pennsylvania Historical and Museum Commission, 1974, 135–45.
   After summarizing information about Euroamerican surnames (especially objectional ones like Hitler), writer describes bygone traditional Delaware naming practices. He then describes a name-giving ceremony in 1972 in which he was given a Delaware name.

Lesson

3.2

Adolescents

Grade Level
   4–8

Materials
   Student Readings: "The Apaches," "The Story of Changing Woman," and "Our Life Today as White Mountain Apaches"; poster board or newsprint for chart; pens and paper for letter writing

Time
   One class period

Objectives
   • Students learn that all societies have rites of passage when moving from one stage of life to another.

- Students become familiar with an Apache Celebration, Nah-ih-es (Sunrise).

- Students develop a sense of Apache geography, culture, and values.

- Students will explore their own values.

Activities

1. Ask students to name some events that signify changes in age, for example, obtaining a driver's license, starting kindergarten, school graduation, later curfew, going out without parents or adults, selecting classes, getting married, etc. Are any of these changes celebrated with a special party or religious ceremony?
2. Share with the class that most cultures around the world have or had ceremonies or celebrations to mark the passage from one stage of life to another. Ask them for some examples: Sabaa (celebrated among some Muslims), birthday parties, Communion (Catholic), Bar/Bat Mitzvah (Jewish), Kinaalda (Navajo), etc.
3. Explain that the class will be learning about the Sunrise Dance or Nah-ih-es, the Apache womanhood ceremony for young girls. Locate the Apache communities on the map. Share a little about the Apache from the readings in this section. Read (or have a student read) to the class the story of Changing Woman.
4. Divide the class into two groups; select a recorder and reader.
5. Give each group the Reading: "Our Life Today as White Mountain Apaches" and discussion questions. Have each group read and address questions.

    The entire community shares in Telly's ceremony. Do you think that is important? If so, why?

    Certain objects are symbols in the Sunrise Dance, for instance, the cane and eagle feather mean long life. Find other objects in the story and describe what they symbolize. (There are quite a few.)

    What is an important number for Apaches? Why?

    At birthday parties and other celebrations, presents are given to the honored guest. How and why is the Sunrise Ceremony different?

    Do you think Telly feels special and honored by her Nah-ih-es?

    Do you think that other people have the same respect for girls as the Apaches do? Give some examples.

Enrichment/Extensions

Community Resources. A spiritual/religious leader can visit class and discuss ceremonies marking passage from childhood to adulthood. Students can research American Indian organizations for young people and write them for information. Some possibilities are Native American Education Programs or reservation schools.

Community Service. Give a celebration for younger children being promoted to a higher grade. Help them cross the bridge and give them an idea of what is expected of them in their new grade.

📖 Reading

The Apaches

The Apaches at one time lived in a very large area from central Texas to central Arizona and from southern Colorado to the Mexican states of Chihuahua and Sonora. The region is diverse—high mountains, deserts, and plains. Today, there are nine Apache reservations, and Apaches live in many areas of the United States. Most reservation dwellers speak the traditional language.

There has been a resurgence of the traditional religion in many Apache communities. Many young girls are able to have a Nah-ih-es, a ceremony that was denied their mothers because American Indian religious practices were prohibited by the government. During the ceremony, the following story about Changing Woman is acted out and retold.

📖 Reading

The Story of Changing Woman

A long time ago, there was a terrible flood. Water covered everything—all creatures and every bit of land. Every living creature perished except one person, Changing Woman. She managed to survive by sealing herself inside an abalone shell. Eventually the waters receded, and she climbed out of the shell. Changing Woman roamed the earth, creating beautiful places wherever she went—mountains, valleys, and wonders such as Monument Valley and the San Francisco Peaks. Changing Woman settled in Oak Creek Canyon, a lovely tranquil place, but she was very lonely because she was the only living creature. No animals, birds, butterflies, or people were left. She felt very sad.

One day Changing Woman was surprised to hear someone speaking to her. A voice instructed her to go to a certain place and kneel down when the sun comes up. She did this for three days, but nothing happened. She was about to give up, when the voice spoke to her again and told her to do it a fourth time. After she knelt to the sun for the fourth time, she became pregnant by the sun and gave birth to a boy.

The voice spoke to her again and told Changing Woman to kneel by the dripping water four times. She did it three times and was about to give up. After kneeling to the water the fourth time, she became pregnant by the water and gave birth to another son.

These three people, Changing Woman and her two sons, were the first people on Earth and the ancestors of all people.

The Apache people honor Changing Woman as the first mother of the people. She is the perfect woman, an example for all to admire. In Apache culture, as in many Indian cultures, women are very important. The children become part of their mother's clans, not their father's; the mother is the earth; the father is the sun.

The Changing Woman Ceremony honors a girl's change from childhood to womanhood, a symbol of life going on.

📖 Reading

Our Life Today as White Mountain Apaches

By Kathryn Oneita

My name is Telly. I am Apache and I'm 12 years old. I'm from the White Mountain Reservation in Arizona. I live in the town of Whiteriver. . . . Phoenix is about five hours away by car. The roads are steep and kind of dangerous where they wind through the mountains.

There's lots to see on the trip to Whiteriver. The steep hills and deep canyons on either side of the road are very colorful. They have layers of deep red rust, gray, white, brown, and green. It looks as though Ussenk, the Giver of Life, took a huge brush and painted the face of the desert. . . . My dad bought a really neat Jeep Cherokee because it's able to climb over the rough hills and plow through the muddy ruts in the winter.

It's late summer now. School is about to start. There won't be any more carnivals or climbing down the cliffs to swim. My brother and I won't be able to chase the wild ponies that roam in the hills. Sometimes we're lucky or fast enough to catch one. If we do, we usually get a few bruises. It's fun to ride into the hills. I like to imagine what it must have been like for our ancestors. They rode their mustangs in these same hills. I pretend I am one of them as I ride the mountain trails.

I'll be in Junior High this year. I'm looking forward to the dances and football games. I may even try out for cheerleader. My school will be putting on a Christmas play. I want to try out for a part.

My favorite school subject is computer science because my dad sells computers. He showed me how to use them. My dad's also a contractor. He builds things. He helped to build the hospital and elementary school here in Whiteriver. He even built the house we live in.

My mom is a firefighter. She had to train a long time to learn how to fight forest fires. It's hard work and it can be very dangerous. You have to be strong. When there is a fire, she has to work very long hours. She gets dirty and hot. She puts her life in danger in order to save others and save the forests. Mom is proud of the kind of work she does. . . .

Something very, **V-E-R-Y** important is going to happen to me in two weeks. I'm having my Sunrise Dance. It lasts for four days. It's the biggest ceremony of the White Mountain Apache tribe. It's performed when an Apache girl passes from childhood into womanhood. My mother never had a Sunrise Dance, so she is excited about mine. She explained how important it is. She told me, "Then you will live to an old age. You will be strong during your life."

My parents have spent a year getting ready for the ceremony. They asked our relatives to help them. A medicine man helped choose my sponsors. The sponsors have to be an older couple who are not related to us. I will call them my godparents. My mother and father will take an eagle feather to the home of my godmother. They will place it on her foot and ask her to prepare a dance for me. When she picks it up, she has answered "Yes."

Mother told me what will happen at my Sunrise Ceremony. The first night my godmother will pin an eagle feather on my head. This will help me live until my hair turns gray. She will fasten an abalone shell in my hair so that it lies on my forehead. This is the sign of Changing Woman, mother of all Apache people. During the whole ceremony, Godmother will massage my body. She is giving me all her knowledge through her hands. That night the crown dancer will dance around the fire. I will follow him because he represents spirits who protect us.

The second day is Saturday and it's going to be hard. It's like an endurance test. The men begin to chant at dawn. The chant is really a prayer. I have to kneel on a buckskin pad and move my body like I'm dancing. I face the sun, who is the Creator. After I have done this, I must run around a sacred cane and prove my strength. My godmother and other women in my family will run behind me. My dress will be made of buckskin and it will be heavy. Mother says I won't even notice. My spirit will carry the burden.

On Sunday, the third day, my godfather will direct my dancing. He will take an eagle feather in each hand. My father will stand next to him holding my sacred cane. When I am a very old woman, I will use this cane to help me walk. The handle of the cane is decorated with the feathers of the oriole. The oriole is a sweet-tempered bird. It will help me to be sweet-tempered, too.

On both Saturday and Sunday, I am showered with bright yellow powder. This is the pollen of the cattail. It is holy to my people. We use it as a blessing. Perhaps as many as a hundred people will walk by me. Each one will take a handful of pollen and shake it over my head. Each person will say a silent prayer for me. In return, I will pray to the sun, asking for blessings on all those people who are sharing this special time with me.

Next, my father pours candies and kernels of corn over me. This will protect me from hunger in my life. Then my whole family passes out gifts to the guests. This means we hope that the people will *always* have plenty to eat.

The number Four is the most important number to Apache people. There are four seasons and four directions. It is a sacred number. On Sunday, Godfather paints me with a mixture made from pollen, cornmeal, and ground-up stones of four colors. He paints me from the top of my head to the bottom of my buckskin boots. This means I am protected from all four sides. Later on, the paint will dry and brush off my outfit. I will be able to wear the outfit at any Apache dance. I am proud of my outfit because many people helped to make it. My Aunt Linda sewed the buckskin top. Another aunt cut and rolled about 200 small pieces of tin into little cones. When they are sewn on the dress, they will jingle. It will make me sound like wind in the trees when I walk. . . .

Mother says that for four days, I won't be able to take a bath, touch my skin, or drink from a glass. Godmother has made a string that will attach to the neck of my dress. A cloth and a tube will be tied to the string. The cloth will be used to wipe my face. I will drink from the tube. It is made from reeds.

The men from the tribe will build a tipi frame. I must dance through it several times on Sunday so that the spirits will always make sure I have a home. Late in the day my mother will follow me through the tipi for the last time. When darkness comes, the dancing will be done.

On Monday morning many people will come to visit me and offer their blessings. Aunt Zoe will be proud if I don't cry. In the Apache tribe, the people in the mother's clan are very important. Aunt Zoe is my mother's sister, and I will listen carefully to what she tells me. I want to make her proud. By the end of the fourth day, I will be a young woman instead of a little girl.

When we say thank you to Godmother, we'll do it in a big way. We will have a feast. All our relatives have made dozens of dresses, quilts, and blankets. These will be given away to our guest. It takes a lot of hard work and a long time to pay back all the people who have come to my Sunrise Dance.

I'm really glad my family is able to have a Sunrise Dance for me. Not all Apache families can afford it or still believe it's important. But it's part of our tradition. My parents care for me. They want me to grow up in the right way. The Sunrise Dance *is* the right way for Apache girls.

Resources

<u>Students</u>

(See Lesson 3.3, page 42.)

Barlow, Kathleen. "Coming of Age Ceremonies." *Faces*. Vol. 4, no. 5 (February 1988): 4–8.
This article talks about different ceremonies around the world, including the Kinaalda.

Bruchac, Joseph. *Flying with the Eagle, Racing with the Great Bear*. New York: Bridgewater Books, 1994.
A collection of strong stories of passage from boyhood to manhood. Several different Indian Nations are covered.

Ingpen, Robert, and Philip Wilkinson. *A Celebration of Customs and Rituals of the World*. New York: Facts on File, 1994.

Rites of Passage in America: Traditions of the Life Cycle. Philadelphia: The Balch Institute for Ethnic Studies, 1992.
Exhibition catalog with great text and photographs from many different cultures.

Roessel, Monty. *Kinaalda: A Navajo Girl Grows Up*. Minneapolis, MN: Lerner Publications, 1993.
Full-color photographs by Roessel of his sister's rite of passage.

Ross, Gayle, and Joseph Bruchac. *The Girl Who Married the Moon: Tales from Native North America*. New York: Bridgewater Books, 1995.
This exciting book tells stories of transitions from girlhood to womanhood from many different tribes.

Seymour, Tryntje Van Ness. *The Gift of Changing Woman*. New York: Henry Holt, 1993.
This book gives a clear description of the Apache womanhood ceremony.

<u>Teachers</u>

Heth, Charlotte. *Native American Dance: Ceremonies and Traditions*. Golden, CO: Fulcrum, 1992.
Beautiful book has great text and photographs of many traditions, including the Sunrise Ceremony.

Lesson

3.3

Adolescents, Different and Alike: Teen Problems Today

Grade Level
7–8

Materials
Books with Native American teen writings

Time
One class period

Objectives
- Students learn that adolescents from different cultures have some similar problems.

- Students will write a poem about "Alike" and "Different."

Activities
1. Either in small groups or the whole class, students read at least two books with writings by young Native Americans. (See Resources.)
2. After each group shares what it has learned about the problems facing Native American adolescents, discuss the common problems. Students discover problems that are similar and some that differ. Have students make and display a chart of positive and negative things associated with being a teen.
3. Students write a poem "Different but Alike," in which one verse deals with "Different" and the other deals with "Alike."

Enrichment/Extensions
Art. Students can make a collage of events, feelings, symbols of being a teen.

Discussion. Students discuss belief held by many people that teens today have more problems than teens did a long time ago. Some think it may be because teens do not know what is expected of them and that their changes in life are not recognized by celebrations and ceremonies.

Literary Arts. The class can create an anthology of writings and visual art about teen issues.

Resources
Students

Ashabranner, Brent. *To Live in Two Worlds: American Indian Youth Today.* New York: Dodd, Mead, 1984.
Indian students discuss the problems they face living with Indian values in a white world.

Citykids. *Citykids Speak on Prejudice.* New York: Random House, 1994.
The voices of kids from Citykids, a New York–based, not-for-profit multicultural foundation dedicated to the survival of today's youth.

Gravelle, Karen. *Soaring Spirits: Conversations with Native American Teens.* Danbury, CT: Franklin Watts, 1995.

Seventeen teens from different regions and backgrounds talk about their lives, hopes, and anger over being stereotyped, and the problems they face.

Hanging Loose Press. 231 Wyckoff Street, Brooklyn, NY 11217.

This publisher of the literary magazine of the same name has published two anthologies of fiction and poetry with the writings of high school students: *Smart Like Me: High School–Age Writing from the Sixties to Now* (1990), and *Bullseye: Stories and Poems by Outstanding High School Writers* (1995).

Hirschfelder, Arlene, and Beverly R. Singer, eds. *Rising Voices: Writings of Young Native Americans.* New York: Ivy Books, 1992.

In six chapters of poems and essays, young people celebrate their families and rituals and protest oppression and prejudice.

Just Talking About Ourselves: Voices of Our Youth. 2 volumes. Penticton, BC: Theytus Books, 1994.

Stories, poetry, and visual art reflect the harsh realities of Native youth in British Columbia.

Merlyn's Pen, Inc.

Publishes anthologies of writings by American adolescent writers.

Lesson 3.4

Adults

Grade Level
4–8

Materials
Student Readings: "Jim Murphy" and "indian math and the wolf from texas"; paper; pencil; blackboard

Time
Two class periods

Objectives
- Students will learn that Indian people still practice their religion.

- Students will learn that people can have many roles in life.

- Students will learn about values and the role adults play in the survival of culture.

- Students will show appreciation for adults in their lives.

- Students will write a story or poem.

Activities

First Class

1. Read students background information. Initiate discussion based on the following.

    How many different roles does Jim Murphy have?

    Why do you think Native people were not allowed to openly practice their religion?

    Why do you think people have respect for Jim Murphy?

    Look at the routine of some adults in your community or family. How do their routines differ from children's? List them on the board.

    In the story about Mr. Murphy, he wants his children to be part of the Cherokee community with an extended family around. Do you think that it is important to children to be part of a community? Why?

    What did adults do to help you today? List them on the board. (For example, they made breakfast, drove me to school, made sure that our homes and schools had electricity, drove the garbage truck, prepared school lunch, answered school phones, paved roads, etc.)

    What do you think it is important for adults to teach children?

    Who are the people in your community who teach you values—how to live, how to behave?

    Make a wish list of how you would like your community to be (for example, no drugs, safe streets, free food, enough jobs, etc.).

Second Class

1. Read the poem, "indian math and the wolf from texas," to the class. One of Mr. Murphy's students wrote the poem about him.
2. Pose the following questions to students:

    How does Alex describe Mr. Murphy?

    What things did Mr. Murphy teach Alex?

    In most Indian cultures, calling someone "uncle" is a term of respect and endearment. Do you think Alex has respect for Mr. Murphy?

    Who is Will Rogers and what do you think Alex meant when he compared him to Mr. Murphy?

    Did Alex stay in touch with Mr. Murphy after he finished high school?

3. Students spend some quiet time thinking about adults and choosing one they feel has helped them in their lives. For the next class (or in class, time permitting) they will write a song, poem, story, or advertisement expressing gratitude and admiration.

Enrichment/Extensions

Art. Students can make a "giveaway" to honor their adult on appreciation day. (See Lesson 4.9, page 98.)

Community Service. Students can have an appreciation day for people that they wrote about in class. Serve Native American foods. See Lesson 4.6, page 77, for further information.

Literature. Students can read a biography or autobiography about someone they admire. Instead of writing a book report, have students write an award presentation for that person. Their selections should be people who have really helped people, the environment, animals, etc.

📖 Reading

Jim Murphy

Inoli stood up from his task to stretch his legs. He looked around the sun-drenched meadow, acknowledging friends and relatives gathered for the New Moon Ceremony, a monthly ritual of the Cherokee. The families and their guests were talking quietly, catching up on news, adjusting their traditional clothing, and waiting for the ceremony to begin. Inoli bent down to finish his job of lighting the sacred fire, the symbol of completing the circle and the continuance of the people.

Inoli, whose English name is Jim Murphy, is the Firekeeper for the Nuyagi Keetoowahs, a fellowship of Cherokee who practice the original religion. He assists the Medicine Priest, lays the fire, and often doubles as Raven, or speaker for the Priest. Although he did not ask for this job, the community thrust it upon him. They trusted Inoli with the Firekeeper's task because he is steady, responsible, and understands the importance of keeping the old ways.

At one time, the Keetoowahs were a secret society, hiding from the Christian missionaries and the U.S. government. Until the American Indian Religious Freedom Act was passed in 1978, it was illegal for Indian people to practice their traditional religions. Since Indian people do not separate spirituality and culture, several traditions and lifestyles were in danger of being destroyed. But the Cherokee, like so many other Native peoples in North and South America, organized a secret society to keep the faith and culture strong.

Today, the Keetoowahs observe many ceremonies, but still keep some secrecy, just for protection, and Inoli keeps the fire for all. The Cherokee have also been influenced by other tribes and non-Indians, and have developed a few ceremonies they did not have before, like weddings and namings. It is a lot of work to prepare for a Keetoowah ceremony, and Inoli is kept quite busy.

The Priest calls the people to the circle, and the New Moon Ceremony begins. It is time to focus on the community and show gratitude for the many blessings—time to give thanks for each other, the plants, the animals, elements, stars, land, and all of creation. Inoli listens to the prayers and makes sure that the fire continues to burn even though several hours may pass.

The Priest ends the prayers and there are some discussions and announcements. Inoli still keeps his post by the fire. The feasting and dancing begin! Dancing is a big part of every ceremony; some dances are just for fun and others have deeply spiritual significance. And, of course . . . food is as important as the dancing!

The families have all brought food to share and dishes to pass. Special plates are prepared for the Priest and Firekeeper, elders, and sick so they will not have to serve themselves. Christina takes a plate to Inoli, who can finally sit down and relax a little bit. This is the weekend, but on Monday, Inoli goes back to work, away from this beautiful ceremonial place in this quiet meadow to his job as Jim Murphy, New York City math teacher.

Jim has been an educator for 29 years—a principal for 4, a private school teacher for 2, and a public school teacher for 23. His Indian customs have oftentimes caused conflict with the administration, because he believes that it is improper to tell anyone how to think or believe, including his students. Imposing his views on others is not something that Jim likes to do.

Many years ago, Jim realized that students were afraid of math and science, and since these are Jim's areas of instruction, he set out to do something about it. He began to study string figures. At first, he researched many different Indian tribes and their traditions around string figures. Then he researched peoples all over the world to find out how they used the art. Finally, Jim began to invent all kinds of complex mathematical figures and a system of notation, which allowed him to keep order in his investigation. He had devised an innovative method for teaching math based on the wisdom of preliterate people around the globe! All of Jim's students readily learned to form the figures and used his system to learn practical applications of math principles. In his 16 years of teaching mathematical string figures, Jim has never had a student fail to master math!

Affectionately called Mr. Strings, Jim always has strings around his wrists and entertains and teaches wherever he goes. "He is like the Pied Piper," said an elder at one ceremonial, "always able to engage the kids and teach them something, too."

Jim has taught other teachers how to use string figures to teach math and is always on hand to help students in his classes as well as Indian students from many different schools who need tutoring. He is a member of the American Association for the Advancement of Science and the International String Figure Association. Besides string figures, Jim plays guitar, sings in a band, and enjoys sports.

A father, Jim thinks that it is very important for his three children to be a part of the Cherokee community. One of the main reasons that he wanted to commit to being a Keetoowah was that his children would have an extended family of cousins, aunts, uncles, and grandparents. In the traditional Indian way, the tribe and clans are all related—separate individuals, but all one people. Jim is active in his children's schools and volunteers for class activities. He feels responsibility for all children, not just his own, and youngsters often end up at Jim's house when they are in trouble. He always takes time to listen and counsel; he is fair, and young people respect his opinion.

Back to Jim, the Firekeeper. The ceremony is over, dancing and feasting ended, and it is time to pack away all of the ceremonial objects. Inoli is glad for this connection to his roots here in New York, so far away from his family in Texas. He left Texas for Harvard University many years ago, one of only 15 men of color in a class of 1,250 students. It was difficult, and he was very lonely. Today, at the ceremony, there was a special dance for two young people leaving for college, and Inoli was grateful that these traditions and ceremonials would help keep them strong. As he said his last good-bye and got into his car to head for the city, Inoli knew that the Cherokee Sacred Fire would always burn, and that someday he would be honored to pass the position of Firekeeper to a younger member of the Keetoowahs.

📖 Reading

indian math and the wolf from texas

there is laughing wolf
uptown in
the wilds of New York,
transplanted from Texas.
a "bad" man, Texas Cherokee,
known for his rough nature and
savage demeanor, so tough

as to write poetry in volumes
opening slowly like
yellow roses in
a warm room.

all that and
the only teacher who could
get through to our
thick, adolescent, inner-
city-school brains; and just
by using loops of strings.

teaching complex
mathematical paradigms,
exploring permutations
within the memories of
your own
dancing fingers making
"cats-cradle" webs, learning
pre-literate "indian math."

in high school, he was
the "String-Man"
also called Murphy, and
on the occasional weekend
left his den to tend
the sacred Keetoowah fire
as Black Fox.

when i first asked
my uncle Murphy about
anything indian, it
was to find some silver or
turquoise jewelry, and

in the same way
that Will Rogers never
read the newspapers, Murphy
didn't know anything about that
just knew about
a Cherokee holiday i might
want to attend, where
it was, and who to

ask for in order to
get myself there.

seven years later
i find myself standing
next to my uncle every
month or so, tending the
ancient fire and making
silent conversation
with strings.

Alex SherKer, Abenaki
Art Student, University of Massachusetts

Resources

Students

New Mexico People & Energy Collective. *Red Ribbons for Emma.* Stanford, CA: New Seed Press, n.d. PO Box 3016, Stanford, CA 94305.

Emma is an elder and a hero! She has been fighting the power companies on her reservation to stop polluting. Great photos!

Video. "Haudenosaunee: Way of the Longhouse." Icarus, 1982. Icarus Films, 153 Waverly Place, New York, NY 10012 (212) 727-1711.

This highlights the traditional life of the Iroquois or Six Nations, their contemporary issues, and the strength of their community that is built on their traditional knowledge.

Video. "I Know Who I Am." Hotevilla, AZ: IS Productions, 1979. Upstream Productions, 420 First Avenue West, Seattle, WA 93119.

Shot on the Makah, Puyallup, and Nisqually reservations, Indian identity is seen as grounded in the life of the family.

Teachers

Beck, Peggy, and Anna Lee Walters. *The Sacred Ways of Knowledge.* Tsaile, AZ: Navajo Community College Press, 1977.

Blackman, Margaret, ed. *During My Time: Florence Edenshaw Davidson, A Haida.* New York: Douglas and Mcintyre, 1982.

This autobiography has historical information about the Haida as well as Davidson's story.

Brand, Joanna. *The Life and Death of Anna Mae Aquash.* New York: James Lorimer, 1978.

Aquash, a Micmac from Nova Scotia, was an activist who was murdered on the Pine Ridge Reservation.

Lesson  3.5

Elders

Grade Level
4–5

Materials
Student Reading: "Honor the Elders"

Time
One classroom period

Objectives
- Students learn that in Indian families, grandparents/elders have been important teachers of traditions.
- Students learn that the lives of Indian elders are difficult today.

- Students learn that elders in all communities have important stories and lessons to teach younger generations.

Activities

1. After reading "Honor the Elders," students list various roles grandparents/elders play in Indian families.
2. Students discuss 10 problems facing Indian elders today that interfere with their traditional roles.
3. Students discuss the roles and problems of their own grandparents/elders and compare these with the roles and problems of Indian grandparents.
4. Students interview a grandparent/elder in the community to learn about their traditions, herbal remedies, stories, and other information they wish to share with young people. Have students share these in class. (See Appendix A, page 209.)

Enrichment/Extensions

Research. Students read one of the books listed in the Resources section and do an oral report about five things they have learned from Indian elders that they did not know before they read their words.

Community Service. Plan a social event, a giveaway, to honor grandparents or elders in the community. (See Lesson 4.9, page 98.) Since some children may not have a grandparent, please be sure children know they can bring an aunt, uncle, elder from the community, or elder from a local nursing home.

📖 Reading

Honor the Elders

Indian elders traditionally had a great deal of authority in their households and communities. They accumulated great experience in caring for children, understanding human nature, and governing people. They were honored and entitled to certain privileges that other tribal members did not have.

Elders had the right to give advice, lecture, and counsel younger people. They told children stories that taught them the laws of their people as well as moral lessons. The experience and wisdom of elders entitled them to be part of tribal governments. They served as judges, lawyers, doctors, teachers, clergy, and politicians in their communities.

Today, many Indian people still regard elders as valuable storehouses of the cultures, histories, and languages of Indian groups. Some elders know how to conduct ceremonies properly, how to prepare healing remedies, how to speak the language. They know how to make objects of great beauty without patterns or blueprints.

All over the United States, many elders are mindful that tribal information might go to the grave with them. They are recording traditional stories, ceremonies, languages, and other information to preserve their tribes' cultures for future generations. Elders visit classrooms at Indian preschools, elementary and high schools, and community colleges, teaching classes and telling traditional stories. They attend elder-and-youth conferences and share their knowledge.

Elders still play an important role in their communities. Many help raise their grandchildren. Others serve as foster grandparents to children without parents. Some elders work with younger tribal members who have health problems like alcoholism and drug abuse.

The 1990 census reported about 8 percent of all Indian and Alaska Native elders were 60 years old and older. Many elders face serious problems. The have small incomes, in many cases only welfare payments, that do not permit them to live in good health and in dignity. Elders who live to be 62 receive small Social Security payments from the government, as do all Americans at this stage of life. Their homes do not have enough heat, or clean water, or decent plumbing. Often they do not have enough money for food, so they never eat properly. Some live alone and cannot prepare their own meals, take medicine, or bathe and dress themselves. The census revealed that 38 percent of the nation's Native elders 65 and older living in rural areas lived below the poverty line.

Many Indian elders also have serious health problems. They suffer from arthritis, diabetes, cancer, and liver disease. Many cannot see or hear and cannot afford dentures, hearing aids, eyeglasses, or counseling. Because many elders do not have cars, they can't get the medical care they need. Nor do they get the legal assistance they need to help them write wills or fill out difficult government forms.

A new kind of problem for elders is the lack of concern younger tribal members sometimes have for them. As a result, some elders are lonely, isolated, and neglected.

Tribes are trying to tackle the problems of their elders in a variety of ways. Some have winter assistance programs providing blankets, hauling water, and bringing firewood to elders who need these life-sustaining things. Some Nations transport elders to and from sites where meals are served or deliver "meals on wheels" to house-bound elders. Some tribal members shop for groceries, do the laundry, make beds, bathe and dress elders, take blood pressure, and supervise medicine. Some Nations run nursing homes, a new experience for Indians. Traditionally, elders stayed in their own homes, cared for by families. But today, the traditional practice of generations of families living together has broken down. Single families now live in urban communities far from their grandparents.

Resources
Students

Audiocassette. "Messages from the Grandparents," in *Spirits of the Present*. Tape 1, side A. 30 minutes. Produced by Radio Smithsonian and Native American Public Telecommunications (NAPT), 1992. Available from NAPT.
Listen to the voices and wisdom of elders.

Audiocassette: "Wisdomkeepers: Meetings with Native American Spiritual Elders." (See Wall and Arden, 1992.) Available from Audio Literature, PO Box 7123, Berkeley, CA 94707-1502.
Set of two tapes with almost three hours of elders talking based on the book below.

Johnson, Sandy. *The Book of Elders: The Life Stories and Wisdom of Great American Indians.* San Francisco: HarperCollins, 1994.
Photographs and words of 31 traditional elders (men and women) belonging to 20 tribes.

McFadden, Steve. *Profiles in Wisdom: Native Elders Speak About the Earth.* Santa Fe, NM: Bear and Co., 1991.
Interviews with 17 elders.

Video. "Nokomis." 54 minutes. Produced by Sarah Penman, 1984.
Three Ojibway women talk about childhood, schooling, treaty issues, repatriation of sacred objects from museums, and the need to pass along knowledge to their grandchildren. Distributed by Cinnamon Productions, 19 Wild Rose, Wesport, CT 06880. (203) 221-0613.

Wall, Steve. *Wisdom's Daughters: Conversations with Women Elders of Native America.* New York: HarperCollins, 1993.
Text and interviews with 13 women elders from 10 Indian Nations.

Wall, Steve, and Harvey Arden. *Wisdomkeepers: Meetings with Native American Spiritual Elders.* Hillsboro, OR: Beyond Words Publishing, 1990.
Photos and words of 17 elders (men and women) from 13 Indian Nations.

Teachers

Baldridge, Dave. "Elders," in *Native America in the Twentieth Century: An Encyclopedia*, Mary B. Davis, ed. New York: Garland Publishing, 1994, 185–87.
Essay discusses elders in the past, present, and future.

National Indian Council on Aging (NICOA), 6400 Uptown Boulevard, NE, Suite 510W, Albuquerque, NM 87110.
This 20-year-old organization publishes books about Indian elders, most recently: *The NICOA Report: Health and Long-Term Care for Indian Elders,* 1996. NICOA defines an Indian elder as 55 years and older.

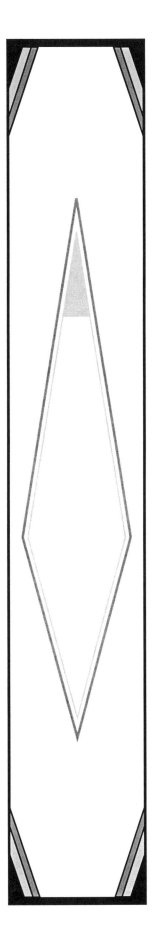

Chapter 4

A Day in the Life . . .

Native Americans, like any other people, live in apartment buildings, eat pizza, bowl, shop at the mall, dance at clubs, go on picnics, get their hair styled, play video games, skateboard, serve on the PTA, and listen to rap music. However, there are things that many (not all) Native Americans do that are different from other Americans and unique to Indian cultures, like attending powwows and dressing in traditional Indian outfits. The lessons in this chapter provide awareness of a few unique aspects of Indian lifestyles.

The lesson about Navajo hogans created by Lisa Charmont introduces students to round architecture and how to make a model to scale, while learning about Navajo traditions.

The food lesson can be a science fair project idea. Both the food and games activities can be learned and shared on your school's international or field day. The games lesson can be integrated into a physical education program as well.

Lesson

4.1

Hogans: Navajo Dwellings

Grade Level
6–8

Materials
Student Reading: "The Development of the Hogan and Its Meaning"; one section of corrugated cardboard measuring 12 inches by 12 inches; one section of corrugated cardboard measuring 7 inches by 21 inches with ribs running lengthwise; pointed scissors; ruler; pencil; masking tape or white glue; photocopies of template; photos of corrugated cardboard (or cardboard sample) and completed model; photos of hogans on-site

Time
Two class periods

Objectives
- Students dramatize the sense of roundness in a structure.

- Students construct a scale model of a female stacked-log hogan.

Activities
1. After clearing a space, students form one or two circles, either next to one another or a smaller circle within a larger one. While the students spin in circular formation, the following poem from *Little Herder in Autumn* may be recited by one or more students in the center.

> The Hogan
>
> My mother's hogan is round
> and earth-color.
> Its floor is smooth and hard.
> It has a friendly fire
> and an open door.
> It is my home.
> I live happily
> in my mother's hogan.
>
> From *Little Herder in Autumn*, by Ann Nolan Clark.
> Ancient City Press, Santa Fe, New Mexico. Used
> with permission.

2. Teacher should make the model first and bring the sample to class so students can visualize and examine what they are going to make.
3. After completing the motivational activity, students discuss feelings about the movement and read "The Development of the Hogan and Its Meaning."

4. If available, show students photographs of actual hogans. (See Resources, page 60.) Follow this by showing students the photograph of the pieces of corrugated cardboard (Figure 4.1) and the hogan model (Figure 4.2).

Figure 4.1. Pieces of corrugated cardboard. Photograph by John Goodwin.

Figure 4.2. Photograph of corrugated cardboard hogan.
Photograph by John Goodwin.

5. Show students a copy of the hogan template to be used. (See Figure 4.3, page 56.) Explain to students that this is to be used to trace panels for constructing a hexagonal (six-sided) hogan. (Ask students what the name of an eight-sided hogan would be—octagonal.) Tell students that today some hogans are constructed for gatherings with as many as 12 sides.

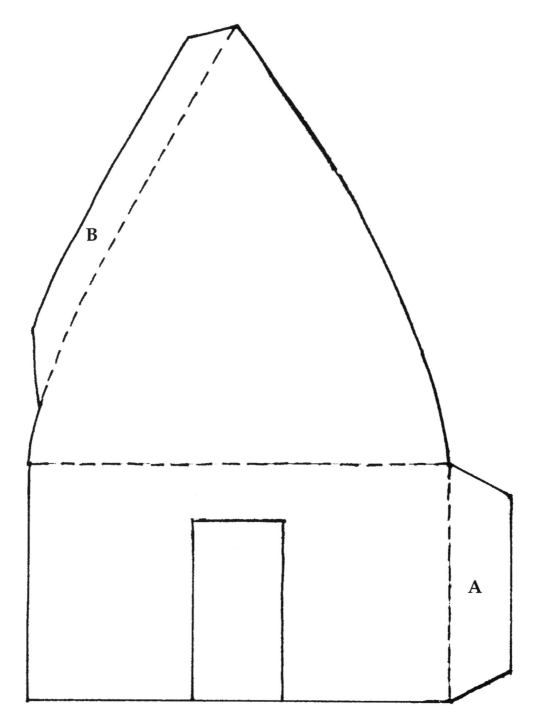

Figure 4.3. Hogan template. Line work © Lisa Charmont.

6. Explain to students that the 12-inch-by-12-inch piece is to be used for the site. Tell them to mark one side of the board "East" with the pencil to designate the side the door must face.

7. Tell students that models are built to scale. Scales simply replace a large measurement (1 foot) with a smaller measurement (¼ inch). The hogan model is built on the scale of ¼ inch = 1 foot. This means that each foot of a real hogan equals ¼ inch of the model. Draw this on a piece of paper or chalkboard to illustrate. Every inch of the model represents 4 feet of a real hogan. Therefore, the model 7 inches in diameter represents a hogan measuring 28 feet in diameter (7-inch diameter of model times 4 feet of a real hogan = 28 feet). If possible, measure 28 feet in the classroom to suggest the actual size of a real hogan.

8. Duplicate "Simplified Directions for Making a Model of a Hogan" for each student.

> Tell students they must first cut out the hogan template along the edges and carefully cut around and preserve tab "A" and tab "B." Cut out the door opening.

> After cutting out the template, it must be traced a total of six times (with tab "B" flattened out onto the side of the 7-inch-by-21-inch corrugated piece of cardboard. Fold in all the tab "As," "Bs" and trace the outline of the actual template on top of the first tracing. Tell students that the corrugated ribs must be in a horizontal position as they trace the template onto the cardboard.

> Cut out the panels from the cardboard, preserving the tabs.

> Next comes scoring, which enables panels to bend cleanly at a slight angle. With a ruler and pencil, draw a line straight across from corner to corner to separate the sides of the hogan from the roof panels. (See Figure 4.4.) Scoring can be done with the pointed edge of a scissor. Carefully go over the correct lines as indicated. Score just enough to break the paper layer, then bend gently inward. Continue to bend gently to the top, making the roof panels curve inward.

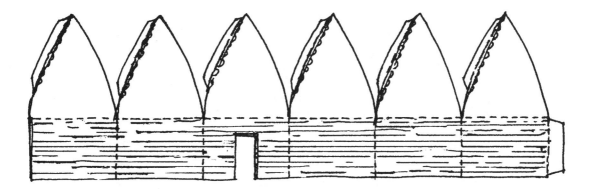

Figure 4.4. Draw a line from corner to corner to separate the sides of the hogan from the roof panels. Line work © Lisa Charmont.

Peel off the outer paper covering of the cardboard below the score line, exposing the corrugated core on the side panel section only, not the roof area. Tabs "A" and "B" must be peeled to leave a single layer of paper covering the bottom/inside of the tab.

Score between each panel on the lines indicated on Figure 4.5, then bend at the score; the panels are now pliable and may be joined at tab "A" with white glue. Hold to dry in place.

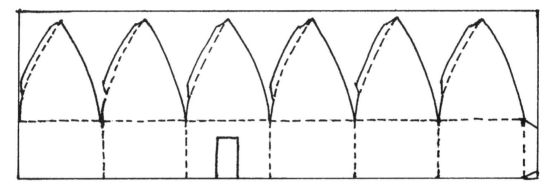

Figure 4.5. Score the panels. Line work © Lisa Charmont.

Gently bend each roof panel inward to form a dome. Join the roof panels with white glue (using a small amount dries faster) and with masking tape on the inside, using small pieces. No adjustments are needed if the alignment of panels is in a straight line. Join the side panel and tab "A" to complete.

Using the scissor point, make a small hole and begin cutting a rectangular hole at the top of the roof in the center. Make a smoke hole cover from scraps to fit the opening. Use small pieces of tape, attached from the inside to make hinges.

Use a piece of scrap cardboard to make a door measuring 3 feet wide by 6 feet high (times 1½).

Place the model hogan on the site with the door facing east.

Enrichment/Extensions

Art. Students may make collages of circular structures (residential, commercial, secular) from around the world using copies or drawings of library materials along with student-made drawings and photographs made on-site of local architecture.

Design. Design a circular home using multilevel or intersecting circles.

Mathematics. Other commonly used scales are ⅛ inch = 1 inch and ½ inch = 1 inch. Ask students if the scale of the hogan model was ½ inch = 1 inch, what would a 7-inch hogan model represent in an actual hogan diameter? (14 feet in diameter). If the scale of the hogan model was ⅛ inch = 1 inch, what would a 7-inch hogan model represent in a real hogan? (56 feet in diameter). Change the diameter of the hogan model and have students calculate dimensions of a real hogan.

Research. Students research house blessings of other cultures.

📖 Reading

The Development of the Hogan and Its Meaning

The Navajo creation story reveals the origins of the first hogan, the first home built by the holy people in the Underworld. Its use and design are described as a holy place having a square roof and a supporting post at each of the four corners. The roof was covered with earth and bark. This type of hogan is still in use today in parts of Arizona and New Mexico and is called a temporal in Mexico.

When First Man and First Woman entered the Fourth World (the world as we know it) from the Underworld, they had to find a suitable site to build a new hogan. When people build hogans today, great care is given to making a good selection for a building site.

The present-day hogans consist of several designs. The two most often used by Navajos are the forked stick or male hogan and the stacked log or female hogan. The forked stick hogan has two legs and is named for its canelike shape with three poles jutting from the pointed top. The front entrance is lower than the top and often extends several feet from the main structure, causing the hogan to appear to be kneeling with arms extended forward. The stacked log hogan design was developed 150 years ago by Draw-an-Arrow-All-the-Time, a warrior living near the eastern face of Navajo Mountain. Seeking to protect himself from the enemies nearby, he built this fortlike structure by setting logs in a circular formation on the ground. The walls rose straight up and to complete the roof, the logs became smaller as they neared the top, continuing the circular formation, forming a dome shape. Spaces between the logs were filled with smaller sticks and finished with cedar bark and mud. At the top, a smoke hole allowed smoke from the centrally located fire to escape. The door faced east and there were no windows. The hogan's design reflects many symbolic concepts. When other Navajos saw the new home, they soon built others similar to it.

The typical hogan dwelling has six to eight sides and is about 16–25 feet in diameter. With the introduction of better axes and saws about 100 years ago, bigger medicine hogans could be constructed with 6 to 12 sides and perhaps 50 feet in diameter.

Before a hogan is lived in, a Blessingway rite is performed by a medicine man or the male head of the household. The female head of the household cooks a small portion of food in the cooking area and the ceremony, consisting of at least three prayers and 4 to 12 songs, is performed. The medicine man spreads corn pollen or white cornmeal at the main posts moving in a clockwise direction. This ritual makes the hogan strong and good. A blessed hogan protects those who live within it and fosters happiness and prosperity. More than a home, a hogan is a place of spiritual centering.

Today, some hogans are constructed of modern building materials and use efficient sources of power, such as solar energy. Navajos prefer to live in modern versions of hogans, preserving their culture and concepts of life and living.

Simplified Directions for Making a Model of a Hogan

1. Cut out the template, including tabs.

2. Trace the template (including the tabs) six times and then trace over each area with the tabs "A" and "B" folded in six times.

3. Cut out the panels, preserving the tabs.

4. Score and bend where sides and roof sections meet and between each side panel.

5. Peel outside layer of paper on side panels.

6. Join tab "A" to first panel; line up carefully to keep them even. Connect all six templates using tab "A."

7. Bend roof panels in gently, then glue tabs "B" to form roof. Work slowly and carefully. Use a small amount of glue. Tape will hold it together while drying.

8. Cut a rectangular hole at center of roof.

9. Cut a smoke hole cover and a door from scraps.

10. Place on-site with door facing east.

Resources
Students

Bradley, Hassell G. "Solar Hogans: Houses of the Future?" *Natives Peoples* (Spring 1990): 44–50.
  About the Colorado Solar Hogan Project on the University of Colorado campus.

Calloway, Sydney M., Gary Witherspoon, et al. *Grandfather Stories of the Navahos.* Phoenix, AZ: Navajo Curriculum Center Press, 1974.

Grimes, Joel. *Navajo: Portrait of a Nation.* Englewood, CO: Westcliffe, 1992.
  Photos of hogans.

Karavasil, Josephine. *Houses and Homes Around the World.* Minneapolis, MN: Dillon Press, 1986.
  Full-color photos include round structures.

Knevitt, Charles. *Shelter: Human Habitats from Around the World.* San Francisco: Pomegranate Art Books, 1994.
  Shows examples of circular shelters.

Muskett, Evaleen. "The Hogan." *Native Monthly Reader.* Vol. 3, no. 8 (1991–1992): 91–92.

Roessel, Monty. *Songs from the Loom: A Navajo Girl Learns to Weave.* Minneapolis, MN: Lerner Publications, 1995.

Time-Life Editors. "Architecture Based on Tradition," in *Winds of Renewal*. Alexandria, VA: Time-Life Books, 1996, 108–15.
    Full-color photos of six modern building styles that reflect traditional Native structures. Gorgeous photo of the Ned Hatathli Cultural Center at the Navajo Community College in Tsaile, Arizona, a six-sided glass hogan!

Yue, Charlotte, and David Yue. *The Igloo*. Boston: Houghton Mifflin, 1988; *The Pueblo*. Boston: Houghton Mifflin, 1986; *The Tipi: A Center of Native American Life*. New York: Knopf, 1984.

Teachers

Krinsky, Carol. *Contemporary Native American Architecture: Cultural Regeneration and Creativity*. New York: Oxford University Press, 1996.
    Photos of contemporary hogans and dozens of other modern-day examples of Native architecture based on tradition.

Nabokov, Peter, and Robert Easton. "Hogan, Ki and Ramada," in *Native American Architecture*. New York: Oxford University Press, 1989, 322–47.

Lesson

Clothing

Grade Level
4–5

Materials
Student Readings: "What Native American Clothing Reveals" and "Academic Dress"; books with photographs of contemporary Indian people

Time
Two class periods

Objectives
- Students learn that what we wear tells something about ourselves.

- Students learn that everyday Native American people wear the same kinds of clothes as everyone else: jeans, T-shirts, sweaters, and sneakers, but wear traditional clothes for ceremonies, powwows, and other special occasions.

- Students learn that designs on Native clothing relate to nature.

- Students learn that some clothing helps identify who or what you are.

- Students learn that influence on clothing styles is a two-way street. American Indians and Inuits have influenced the way other Americans dress. Euro-Americans have influenced the way Native people dress.

• Students learn that Indian identity does not depend on the clothes (or feathers) people wear.

Activities

1. Have students discuss what clothing tells us about people. Allow at least 20 minutes for discussion. Clothing tells what kind of climate people live in; tells what communities people come from, for example, Guatemalan village weaving designs, Amish; tells whether people are in mourning or joyous; tells rank/combat duty/honors in military; uniforms tell what people do for a living, for example, police, firefighters, nurses; tells clan membership; tells whether people are athletes; school uniforms tell whether a student goes to private or parochial school; tells position/status, for example, academic regalia; tells where people come from, for example, Scotland—tartans, Palestine—kaffiyeh; tells personality and lifestyle, for example, punk rockers, preppy; tells religious beliefs, for example, yarmulke; tells about people's modesty, for example, Muslim women—chador.

2. After reading "What Native American Clothing Reveals," have students go to the school or town library and take out at least six to eight books with photographs of contemporary Native American people. Students can also bring in magazines like *National Geographic* and *Native Peoples* that carry articles about contemporary Indian peoples. Divide class into small groups and give each group two or more books or magazines depending on the total number available. Each group should choose a reporter who keeps notes. Ask the groups to look at the clothing Indian people wear today and discuss what the garments tell about them. Allow at least 15 minutes. Allow each group to decide how to report its findings. (See Bibliography for books with photos of contemporary Native people.)

3. Ask students what clothes, shoes, or jewelry they wear has been copied or influenced by Native styles and designs (moccasin-styled shoes, parkas, fringed and beaded clothes). Have the class survey students and teachers in other classrooms to see if they wear anything inspired by Indian dress. Students can make a bulletin board or classroom display of clothes, shoes, and jewelry inspired by Native Americans.

4. Ask students to pair up. Have each student in the pair look at the other and discover three things the partner's outfit tells about that person.

Enrichment/Extensions

Art. Students can make a drawing, painting, or collage of a favorite outfit.

Creative Writing. Students can write a poem or essay about a special outfit and what it tells about them.

Field Trip. Students can visit a local museum and study clothing worn in centuries past or by people from other countries, with an eye to what the clothing tells about men and women.

Research. Students can study and make a report about clothing from other cultures: Scotland, tartans (plaids); Ghana, kente cloth; Guatemala, Mayan *huipil* (loose blouse) village designs; Panama, Kuna *mola* designs.

Students research Seminole/Miccosukee patchwork clothing and make a piece of paper patchwork. Students experiment by changing colors and widths of paper. (See Figure 4.6, page 67.)

📖 Reading

What Native American Clothing Reveals

Like all peoples, American Indians wore clothes for a variety of reasons. The most important factor was the need to protect themselves from the climate, whether hot, cold, wet, or dry. The local environment largely determined the materials people used to make protective clothes. Eskimo people survived the harsh Arctic winter clothed in superbly tailored fur garments made from animals. The Eskimo parka, with its loose-fitting design, allows an insulating layer of air between the Arctic cold and the body. On the other hand, men along the Northwest coast went naked most of the time. When rains came, they put on capes and hats of shredded cedar bark or other fibers that acted like umbrellas.

Terrain also affected the clothing people wore. Desert people wore hard-soled moccasins to protect their feet from thorns, cactus spines, and rocks. The Indians living in the Southeast wore swamp moccasins as they sloshed through lowland marshes. People traveling in snow country used snowshoes. Some in the Pacific Northwest went barefoot because they spent so much time in canoes or on sandy beaches. Indians near forests wore garments with short fringes that would not catch in the underbrush, but Indians living on the plains adored their long, fluttering fringes.

There were other functions of clothing. They communicated tribal identity. People in the same tribe wore the same type of moccasins decorated with a similar style of beadwork and wore a certain cut of garment. Within the tribe, a person's clothing and accessories communicated such things as membership in certain societies, military exploits, and socioeconomic status. In certain tribes, the many ceremonials permitted participants to display their status. Each cylinder on a Tlingit chief's hat represented a potlatch or feast he gave to substantiate his claims to prestige.

Clothing communicated stages of life. During some tribal puberty ceremonies for adolescents, youngsters wore special clothing. Some garments showed the wearer was ready for marriage and adulthood. Some showed a person was in mourning for a loved one. Not only did people cut their hair (a widespread custom in North America), they put on specific items of dress, like the mourning belt of the Shasta of California, woven from the hair of the deceased.

Nowadays, Native people wear jeans, shirts, sweaters, and sneakers most of the time and save their traditional clothes (type of clothing worn for centuries by people who share the same nationality, religion, or customs) for dances, powwows, ceremonies, and other special occasions. There are several tribal groups, however, that wear distinctive "new" traditional clothing every day. Around the turn of the century, Seminole and Miccosukee women in southern Florida acquired hand-cranked sewing machines, cloth, and thread. With these tools, they developed patchwork clothing. They cut and sewed tiny pieces of different-colored cloth into long strips. Then they sewed these long strips of complicated geometric designs in continuous rows to make large pieces of material. Today, just about every Miccosukee woman, man, and child in Florida wears something decorated with rows of colorful geometric patchwork designs, either a vest, coat, jacket, dress, blouse, shirt, cape, or baseball cap. Miccosukee men especially like to wear their jackets over manufactured every-day clothing. These clothes have become an identifying mark of Florida Indians.

For more than 100 years, Navajo women have worn fitted velvet and velveteen blouses with full, long, cotton skirts. They saw this style of dress on non-Indian women in the late 1860s, liked what they saw, and created their own version, which is now considered "traditional" dress.

As you can see from this last example, the way people dress is influenced by what they see other people wearing. This is the way it has always been throughout history. When one group of people encounters another, they borrow things from one another. And clothing is usually the first thing exchanged. From the first contact with Europeans, Indians liked the new clothing and materials they saw, so they adopted some of them. The newcomers changed the Indian way of dressing, but Indian styles also influenced the way Europeans dressed. Clothes borrowing works both ways. That's why today, manufacturers produce moccasin-type shoes, parkas, headbands, and ponchos adapted from Indian styles. Look around and you will see plenty of examples of "Indian-style" beading, fringe, and other traditional designs added to contemporary fabrics and styles of dress.

📖 Reading

Academic Dress

In 1932, the American Council on Education approved a code for academic dress still in effect. In colleges and universities, gowns have the following characteristics. The gown for the bachelor's degree has long, pointed sleeves and is worn closed. The gown for the master's degree has an oblong sleeve and is open at the wrist. The gown may be worn open or closed. The gown for the doctoral degree has bell-shaped sleeves. It may also be worn open or closed. There are no trimmings for the bachelor's or master's degree, but the gown for the doctoral degree has black or colored velvet covering the front and three bars of velvet across each sleeve.

Different colors of velvet are associated with the different academic subjects:

Arts, Letters, Humanities	White
Nursing	Apricot
Commerce, Accounting, Business	Drab
Physical Education	Sage Green
Education	Light Blue
Public Health	Salmon Pink
Engineering	Orange
Science	Golden Yellow
Fine Arts, including Architecture	Brown
Social Work	Citron
Music	Pink

Resources
Students

Appelton, Leroy H. *American Indian Design and Decoration*. New York: Dover, 1971.
Over 700 black-and-white drawings of Native design from different regions of North and South America. Many of the designs appear on clothing.

Cobb, Vicki. *Super Suits*. Philadelphia: J. B. Lippincott, 1975.
Author describes super suits, special protective clothing for firefighters, deep-sea divers, mountain climbers, and astronauts.

Hendrix, Janey B. *Changing Fashions of the Five Tribes*. Park Hill, OK: Cross Cultural Education Center, 1982.
Author introduces children to traditional dress of the Five Tribes (Cherokee, Choctaw, Chickasaw, Creek, Seminole) before and after contact with Europeans. Book includes paper dolls and clothing (for coloring) from different historical periods, some of which are still worn at stomp dances, powwows, and ceremonials. Craft activities are also included.

MacLean, Charles. *The Clan Almanac: An Account of the Origins of the Principal Tribes of Scotland: Illustrated with the Examples of the Tartans Adopted by Each*. New York: Crescent Books, 1990.
Identifies tartans (plaid pattern), each belonging to a different Scottish clan.

Perl, Lila. *From Top Hats to Baseball Caps, from Bustles to Blue Jeans: Why We Dress the Way We Do*. New York: Clarion Books, 1990.
Survey of fashion from the late 1800s through the early 1900s. The author deals with the reasons people wear clothing. Line drawings and bibliography of other books and articles about clothing.

Sensier, Danielle. *Costumes: Traditions Around the World*. New York: Thomson Learning, 1994.
Book gives brief but careful descriptions of traditional clothes worn by people in Europe, North America, Central and South America, Africa, Asia, Australia, and New Zealand. Author emphasizes how clothes give clues about people's customs, climate where they live, and type of work they do.

Stribling, Mary Lou. *Crafts from North American Indian Arts: Techniques, Designs, and Contemporary Applications*. New York: Crown, 1975.

Whispering Wind: American Indian Past and Present. Bimonthly magazine published by Written Heritage, 8009 Wales Street, New Orleans, LA 70126-1952.
Hobbyist magazine with focus on past and present traditional clothing arts of Indian people. Many full-color and black-and-white photographs of authentic clothing.

Whitney, Alex. *American Indian Clothes and How to Make Them*. New York: David McKay, 1979.
Book includes instructions for making Navajo blouses, Seminole patchwork dress and shirts, Pueblo poncho shirt, and jewelry.

Wood, Margaret. *Native American Fashion: Modern Adaptations of Traditional Designs*. New York: Van Nostrand Reinhold, 1981.
Book has instructions for current designs of representative garments from Navajo, Apache, Pueblo, Seminole (five sample patchwork patterns and photos of patchwork clothing), Iroquois, Great Lakes area, Plains, and Northwest Coast women. The fashion history of each region is also included.

<u>Teachers</u>

Paterek, Josephine. *Encyclopedia of American Indian Costume*. New York: W. W. Norton, 1994.
    More than 150 photographs and illustrations show the variety of clothing, everyday and ceremonial, created by scores of tribes in 10 cultural regions. The author includes a "Transitional Dress" category that notes everyday and ceremonial garments worn today. Bibliography by regions.

Lesson  Seminole-Miccosukee Patchwork Clothing

Grade Level
    4–5

Materials
    Student Reading: "Seminole-Miccosukee Patchwork Clothing"; U.S. map with locations of Florida reservations; books, magazines, scissors, glue, multicolored construction paper

Time
    One class period

Objectives
- Students learn that Seminole and Miccosukee men and women are famous for their unique and vibrantly colored patchwork clothing—coats, jackets, "big shirts" (long shirts), skirts, blouses, capes, vests, and baseball caps.

- Students learn that patchwork clothing is an art form.

- Students learn that patchwork clothing became popular after the turn of the century when Seminole women adopted the use of sewing machines.

- Students learn that patchwork is a technique of cutting and sewing tiny pieces of different-colored cloth into long strips (bands) of fabric. The long strips of complicated geometric designs are sewn together in continuous rows to make large pieces of material.

- Students learn that patchwork clothing is a mark of identity for Florida Indians.

Activities
1. Introduce students to Seminole and Miccosukee Indians who live in southern Florida today. Students locate Seminole and Miccosukee reservations on a map of southern Florida.
2. Show students the photo of Seminole patchwork (Figure 4.6) and students read "Seminole-Miccosukee Patchwork Clothing" that explains how Seminole and Miccosukee women make this kind of clothing.

3. Divide the class into small groups. Give each group a magazine or book with patchwork clothing. Ask each group to study the clothing and make observations about what they see. Allow 10 minutes. Ask each group to report about their findings. (Students will doubtless notice the distinctive patchwork garments.)

4. Using background reading, share with the class information about patchwork clothing and tell students they are going to make a patchwork strip with paper instead of cloth.

5. Pass out construction paper of different colors, scissors, and glue.

6. Teachers should first make a piece of paper patchwork using instructions and show students an example of what they are going to make.

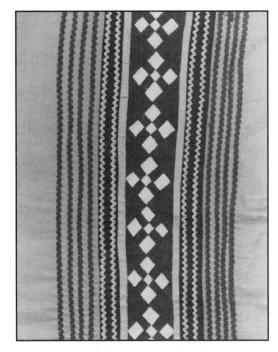

Figure 4.6. Photograph of Seminole patchwork.

Instructions for Paper Patchwork

1. Glue four strips of different color paper together.

2. Cut apart the stripe combination on the diagonal.

3. Reposition the pieces.

4. Glue the pieces back together in a new position.

5. Trim the strip so there is an even horizontal line at the top and bottom. Add a black border at the top and bottom.

6. Do the same thing with four different colors.

7. Experiment by showing different widths of color. Cut horizontally as well as diagonally and reposition the pieces for new effects. There is no limit to the patterns you can make.

📖 Reading

Seminole-Miccosukee Patchwork Clothing

The Seminoles and Miccosukees, like Native people everywhere, adopted what they wanted from non-Indians and used the new materials in a way that fit into their world. Around the beginning of the twentieth century, Seminole and Miccosukee women went to local trading posts and exchanged alligator hides, furs, and the plumes of exotic birds for hand-cranked sewing machines. Later they acquired treadle sewing machines. The women found the new machines could quickly sew pieces and strips of cloth together to make beautiful clothing for their families. Before long the women were creating a new art form as well as creating the mark of Florida Indian identity.

Patchwork involves cutting small pieces of different-colored cloth into geometric patterns and sewing them together into long strips or bands. Then the long rows of patchwork are sewn together to make larger pieces of materials that are turned into skirts, shirts, aprons, women's dresses, little girl's pinafores, men's jackets, vests, pot holders, and dolls. Patchwork designs have evolved from simple stripes into elaborate diamond, square, and zigzag shapes with accents of ricrac. And women created a multitude of designs by simply changing color combinations or geometric forms.

Patchwork designs come from the woman's imagination and sewing ability. Sometimes patchwork makers plan the patterns; other times they simply sews bands of patchwork without any grand scheme in mind. Either way, designs are not drawn or written down. There are no set patterns; the designs are created in the woman's head or remembered. Colors do not have special meanings and are not assigned to designs. Although certain women are known for creating certain patterns, these designs are not owned and can be used by anyone. Women exchange designs freely. Today, Seminole and Miccosukee women continue to come up with new ideas and designs.

Resources

Students

Capron, Louis. "Florida's Emerging Seminoles." *National Geographic* (November 1969): 716–33.
Full-color photos show patchwork clothing.

Downs, Dorothy. *Art of the Florida Seminole and Miccosukee Indians.* Gainesville, FL: University Press of Florida, 1995.
Plenty of examples of patchwork clothing.

Garbarino, Merwyn S. *The Seminole.* New York: Chelsea House, 1989.
A picture-essay "Patches of Color" shows examples of patchwork in full-color, close-up photos and offers an excellent summary of the development of patchwork clothing.

Hanisko, Dorothy. *Simply Seminole: The Excitement of Making Banded Patchwork.* Lincolnwood, IL: Quilt Digest Press, 1995.
Instructions for 35 designs in full color.

Lourie, Peter. *Everglades: Buffalo Tiger and the River of Grass*. Honesdale, PA: Boyds Mill Press, 1994.
    Some examples of patchwork clothing in this book about the ecology of the Everglades.

Teachers

Blackard, David M. *Patchwork & Palmettos: Seminole-Miccosukee Folk Art Since 1820*. Fort Lauderdale, FL: Fort Lauderdale Historical Society, 1990.
    Exhibition catalog covers basketry, finger weaving, beadwork, silver work, patchwork, and dolls dressed in patchwork clothes. The development of patchwork clothing is discussed decade by decade from 1920 to the present. Contains numerous black-and-white and full-color photos plus drawings of common patchwork designs.

Bradkin, Cheryl Greider. *The Seminole Patchwork Book*. Atlanta, GA: Yours Truly, 1980.
    Patterns for over 50 patchwork designs pictured along with instructions.

West, Patsy. "i. laponki: The Florida Seminoles in the 1930s." *Native Peoples* (Spring 1996): 26–32.
    Discussion on how the antigovernment i. laponki (Seminoles) benefited economically by posing for tourists; includes examples of patchwork clothing responsible for promoting strong tribal identity.

Wood, Margaret. *Native American Fashion: Modern Adaptations of Traditional Designs*. New York: Van Nostrand Reinhold, 1981, 49–57.
    The chapter "Seminole Clothing Styles" includes a history of patchwork clothing, five sample Seminole patchwork patterns, and photos of clothing with patchwork.

Lesson

4.4

Eagle Feathers

Grade Level
4–8

Materials
Student Readings: "Eagles," "The Eagle Symbol in U.S. Culture Today," "Eagle Feather on 1989 NASA Shuttle," and "Flags"; books about eagles and the American flag; photos of pow-wow dancers; books about Indian art

Time
Two class periods

Objectives
• Students learn that the eagle has been honored by all cultures.

• Students learn that eagle feathers are important to and honored by Indian people in much the same way the American flag is honored.

- Students learn how Indian people use eagle feathers and eagle designs in their religious ceremonies, powwow clothing, and artistic designs.

- Students learn that the symbol of the eagle is honored in U.S. culture today and its image is used on flags, seals, and in many other areas.

- Students learn appropriate and realistic information about the Native use of eagle and other feathers to counter stereotypes.

Activities

1. Ask students or small groups to research eagles and list five reasons why the bird is held in high regard by people from all cultures.
2. Share information about the ways Indian people honor the eagle and its feathers. (See Readings.) Especially share information about the rituals surrounding an eagle feather that is dropped. (See "When a Feather Drops," page 96.)
3. Ask students to research rituals performed when an American flag is dropped and make comparisons with rituals when an Indian dancer drops an eagle feather.
4. Ask students to look for examples of eagle feathers and/or symbols of eagles in photos of powwow clothing and headgear and Indian art.
5. Ask students to research the Great Seal of the United States; the seals of the U.S. Supreme Court; Departments of State, Justice, Postal Service, Defense, Air Force, Army, Navy, and Marine Corps; state seals (Alabama, Illinois); and businesses (American Airlines) that use eagle symbols.
6. Ask students to contrast Native use of eagle feathers with images of feathered Indians found on greeting cards, food packages, toys, children's books, and advertisements, and determine whether they are used in a realistic, appropriate, and respectful manner.

Enrichment/Extensions

Art. Students can make a drawing, painting, or collage using the eagle as the design element or design a postage stamp with an eagle design.

Creative Writing. Students can write a poem or essay about eagles that tells why cultures around the world honor them.

Field Trip. Students can canvas their hometown (or phone book) to see if any businesses, organizations, or town offices use the eagle as a logo or trademark. Students can visit a local museum and look for eagle designs in clothing worn by people from other countries and in other centuries.

Research. Students can study and make a report about the ways other cultures honor the eagle. Students can research postage stamps and coins with eagle designs issued by the United States and other nations. Students can study stories told by different Native cultures about eagles (also called thunderbirds) and eagle feathers. Students can contact their town government and find out what rituals local officials perform if the U.S. flag touches the ground, floor, or water.

Students can study and make an illustrated report about the headdresses of Native American tribes, including the eagle feather headdresses of the Plains Indian Nations (Sioux/Lakota, Cheyenne), *gustoweh* of the Haudenosaunee (Iroquois), the "Big Head" headdresses of the central California tribes, and stand-up bonnets of the Blackfeet.

Science. Students can research different types of eagles, eagle feathers, and their habitats. Students can find out how many eagles are living in their state and whether there are laws to protect them.

📖 Reading

Eagles

Of all the birds held in high regard by Native people of North America, the eagle (also called the thunderbird) was and is still honored because of its majesty, strength, power, wisdom, and solitary, mysterious nature. Some believe that eagles are messengers between people and the Creator.

Eagle feathers were, and are, of great importance. The striking headdresses of Plains tribes, made of eagle feathers, are worn during ceremonies and powwows. Eagle feathers and designs appear on sacred objects like pipes and rattles. Fans made of the eagle's primary feathers are still used in ceremonies. Clothing may contain eagle feathers or eagle designs. The bustle worn by a male dancer is usually made of eagle feathers if the dancer is a war veteran (or turkey or pheasant feathers if the person is not a veteran). Light, fluffy, and airy eagle down is attached to prayer sticks, sacred masks, headdresses, and dance garments.

Since eagle feathers are special, there are certain rules regarding use. Veterans, men or women, who have served their country or community in battle are symbolized by the eagle feather. If the veterans are dancers, they may wear eagle feathers on their roaches, turbans, or headdresses. People who have done good deeds can receive eagle feathers and use them on their garments. Eagle feathers may also be given as gifts to people during ceremonies.

If a dancer at a powwow accidentally drops an eagle feather or one falls off his clothing, a special ceremony must occur before any other activity can take place. A war veteran is the only person who can pick up the feather and return it to the owner. During this ceremony, drummers and singers sing special songs.

The eagle has given its name to many clans. It is probable that nearly every tribe in the United States had (and still has) an eagle clan at some period in its history. The Chippewa (Ojibway) tribe, however, does not have an eagle clan. Because the eagle holds such a high place of respect among the people, Chippewas feel no person can hold such a high place as the eagle and cannot be represented on the same level.

The Pueblo peoples of New Mexico honor eagles by performing in public an Eagle Dance in the spring. The Pueblo people associate the eagle with rain, thunder, lightning, and curing powers. Two young men dressed as eagles, one a male, the other a female, emulate the movements of these birds in flight. Eagle dance outfits differ from pueblo to pueblo, but generally the man's body is painted and he wears a headdress with a long, curved beak, great feathered wings over his shoulders and arms, and a feathered tail attached to his belt in back. Dance steps, gestures, and movement also vary from pueblo to pueblo. The eagle also holds an important place in Indian art. The bird has been depicted in all art forms created by Indians, including pottery, baskets, textiles, beadwork, quillwork, and paintings.

📖 Reading

The Eagle Symbol in U.S. Culture Today

The eagle is also important in American culture. Flags and seals sport eagle designs. The Great Seal of the United States; the Seal of the President of the United States; the seals of the U.S. Supreme Court, Department of Justice, Department of State, Department of Defense, Air Force, Navy, Army, and Marine Corps; states of Alabama and Illinois; and the Congressional Medal of Honor all show eagles.

📖 Reading

Eagle Feather on 1989 NASA Shuttle

Marsha Ivins, NASA payload specialist, carried a special eagle feather from her alma mater, the University of Colorado, when she rocketed into space on the space shuttle *Columbia* in December 1989. The CU-Boulder Advocacy Committee presented the eagle feather to the university because of its commitment to Indian and minority affairs. The feather has five colored beads on one side of the shaft representing the five races of people—red, white, black, brown, and yellow. Four beads on the other side represent the four sacred directions, the four seasons, and the four periods of life—birth, youth, adulthood, and death.

📖 Reading

Flags

In 1923, at a national conference on flag etiquette in Washington, D.C., patriotic organizations declared that the flag "represents a living country and is itself considered as a living thing." The participants put together a written U.S. Flag Code that explained how to care for and display the flag properly. In 1942, the U.S. Congress made these rules of etiquette the law of the land. Small changes were made to the code in 1954 and 1976. You can find the Flag Code in Public Law 344. Reference sections of most libraries house a set of U.S. public laws.

The Flag Code contains the following statement under "Respect for the Flag," "Our Flag should never touch anything beneath it, such as the ground, the floor, water, or merchandise." The Flag Code is silent about procedures to follow if a flag touches the ground, floor, or water. But the code does suggest that when a flag becomes weatherworn or damaged and no longer fit for display, it should be destroyed in a dignified manner, preferably by burning.

Resources
<u>Students</u>

Adams, John Winthrop, ed. *Stars and Stripes Forever: The History of Our Flag.* New York: Smith-mark Publishers, 1992.
This history begins with flags created in the 13 colonies and includes a complete guide to the use and display of the flag.

Appelton, Leroy H. *American Indian Design and Decoration.* New York: Dover, 1971.
Over 700 black-and-white drawings of Native designs.

Armbruster, Ann. *The American Flag.* New York: Franklin Watts, 1991.
Chapters cover flag makers, the flag in battle, the flag and the Constitution, plus an appendix with flag facts and etiquette.

Beans, Bruce E. *Eagle's Plume: The Struggle to Preserve the Life and Haunts of America's Bald Eagle.* New York: Charles Scribner's Sons, 1996.
Story about the eagle's significance in American culture.

Johnson, Linda Carlson. *Our Nation's Symbols.* Brookefield, CT: Millbrook Press, 1992.
One chapter deals with our national emblem, the bald eagle, plentiful in 1782 when it was chosen but nearly wiped out by DDT (an insect killer) in the twentieth century. Also covered is The Great Seal (bald eagle), which we all see every time we look at a dollar bill.

Krause, Chester L., and Clifford Mishler. *1999 Standard Catalogue of World Coins.* Iola, WI: Krause Publications, 1998.
This book has a complete listing by date since 1801 of over 52,000 actual-size coin photos, many with eagle designs.

Parry-Jones, Jemima. *Eyewitness Guides: Eagle.* New York: Dorling Kindersley, 1997.
Scores of full-color photos of birds of prey plus information.

Specialized Catalogue of U.S. Stamps. Sidney, OH: Scott Publishing, 1995.
Many examples of postage stamps with eagles.

<u>Teachers</u>

Tucker, Priscilla. *The Return of the Bald Eagle.* New York: Stackpole, 1994.
Read about eagles in cultures around the world, about four main groups of eagles that encompass 59 species, and eagles in popular culture. The writer follows the bird's decline in the nineteenth and early twentieth centuries to its resurgence. There is a survey of bald eagle hangouts in North America.

Lesson

4.5

Feathered Headdresses of the Plains Nations

Grade Level
4–8

Materials
Student Reading: "Plains Indians and War Honors"; U.S. map with locations of Plains Indian reservations; photographs of contemporary Indian people and powwow books; greeting cards, comic books, and other items with images of feathered "headdresses"

Time
One class period

Objectives
- Students learn the names of some of the Plains Nations and learn the locations of their reservations in the northern and southern plains states. These are the peoples who have worn (and still wear on ceremonial occasions) eagle feather headdresses, arguably the best-known headwear of any people in the world.

- Students learn accurate and realistic information about Plains Indian eagle feather headdresses.

- Students learn that the eagle feather headdress communicates the wearer's accomplishments in battle (U.S. military service in the twentieth century) and reputation/prestige within the community.

- Students learn that today the eagle feather headdress is worn on ceremonial occasions, not every day as portrayed in U.S. popular culture.

- Students learn that most nations recognize the achievements of their armed forces and understand that headdresses are somewhat like the war decorations worn today by people in the U.S. Army, Air Force, Marine Corps, and Navy.

- Students learn that the "headdresses" on greeting cards, toys, comic books, etc. are usually inaccurate and inappropriate.

Activities
1. Students first study the names and locations of Plains Indian reservations on the U.S. map. They learn these were and are the peoples who have worn (and still wear on ceremonial occasions) eagle feather headdresses (Arapaho, Arikara, Blackfeet, Cheyenne, Comanche, Crow, Hidatsa, Mandan, Omaha, and Sioux—Dakota and Lakota).

2. Students study photographs of Plains Indian headdresses in photo books about contemporary Indian people and powwows and list who wears them (adults, not children) and occasions during which they are worn (ceremonial, not every day). (See Resources, page 96, and Bibliography for list of "Photography Books.")
3. Students read "Plains Indians and War Honors" and discuss the way feathers identify military achievements of the wearer.
4. Students research the war decorations of the U.S. armed forces and learn how stars, ribbons, and medals identify their rank and military achievements .
5. Students compare authentic headdresses with images found on greeting cards, toys, comics, and children's books and determine whether they are used in a realistic, appropriate, and respectful manner.

Enrichment/Extensions

Art. Students can research and make illustrations of headdresses showing the different tribal styles as well as the meaning of notched, clipped, or dyed feathers.

Creative Writing. Students can research and write about the meaning of notched, clipped, and dyed feathers in headdresses.

Field Trip. If possible, arrange a class trip to a museum with headdresses in its collection. Compare and contrast Plains Indian headdresses with the headgear of Kuba kings, Ekonda leaders, Pende chiefs of Zaire, the headdresses of Mekeo men from Papua New Guinea, the headdresses of Karajá shamans of Brazil, or other cultures in Africa or South America.

Oral History. Interview a relative or friend about their service rank or war decorations in the Army, Air Force, Marine Corps, or Navy. If you are permitted to look at the uniform, draw a picture of the war medals/ribbons to go along with the interview. (See Appendix A, page 209, for Oral History Guidelines.)

Research. Students study and make an oral/illustrated report about the headdresses of Native American tribes including the *gustoweh* of the Haudenosaunee (Iroquois), the "Big Head" headdresses of the central California tribes, stand-up bonnets of the Blackfeet and adjacent tribes, otter-fur turbans of the Ioway and Osage, and others.

📖 Reading

Plains Indians and War Honors

In the past, war honors of Plains Indians were ranked in grade and differed from tribe to tribe. In general, the highest honor in all the tribes went to the warrior who struck an enemy with the hand, coup stick, bow, or lance and got away unharmed (known as "counting coup"). Every Plains tribe enabled its warriors to show off their exploits. One way was by wearing honorary insignia. The Lakotas used the tail feather of the male golden eagle as an insignia. The way it was notched or painted signified the wearer's war honor. A Lakota (Sioux) warrior who earned the highest honor (counting coup) wore erect in his hair a white-tipped feather from the tail of a golden eagle. A Lakota warrior who earned the second-highest honor could wear an eagle feather projecting from the side of the head. A Lakota warrior who attained more than one honor of the first three grades was entitled to wear an elaborate ornament in the back called a "crow," decorated with rows of eagle feathers. On the other hand, Crow warriors wore wolf tails at the heels of their moccasins to show they had counted coup. The Comanches showed that achievement with symbols on their war shields.

During the twentieth century, military service provided a substitute for traditional warfare and a means of gaining and earning respect—and an eagle feather. Armed forces found honor during World War I, World War II, the Korean War, and in Vietnam and Desert Storm. Nowadays, people can also earn a feather for their educational or professional achievements.

Resources
Students

"American Indian Headdresses" (1990), reproduced in *Specialized Catalogue of U.S. Stamps*. Sidney, OH: Scott Publishing, 1995.
    In 1990, the U.S. Postal Service issued five 25-cent stamps, each with a full-color tribal headdress: Assiniboine, Cheyenne, Comanche, Flathead, and Shoshone.

The Army Officer's Guide. Harrisburg, PA: Stackpole Books, 1988.
    In Part Four: Regulations at a Glance, there is a well-illustrated section on Decorations, Service Medals, and Badges.

Gabor, R. *Costume of the Iroquois*. Ohsweken, ON: Iroqrafts, 1980.
    Order from Tuscarora Road, Six Nations Reserve, R.R. 2. Ohsweken, ON, Canada NOA 1MO.

Gibbons, Cromwell. *Military Decorations and Campaign Service Bars of the United States*. New York: U.S. Insignia, 1943.

Kerrigan, Evans E. *American War Medals and Decorations*. New York: Viking, 1964.

Morgan, Lewis Henry. *League of the Iroquois*. Rochester, NY: Sage and Brothers, 1851; reprint ed. Secaucus, N.J.: The Citadel Press, 1975.
    The *gustoweh* is described and illustrated on page 265.

"Native Headdresses." Brantford, ON: Woodland Indian Cultural-Educational Centre, 1977.
    Well-illustrated drawings of the *gustoweh*, ceremonial headdresses of the Mohawk, Oneida, Onondaga, Cayuga, and Seneca, plus those of the Tuscarora and Delaware peoples and women's headwear. Order from 184 Mohawk Street, Box 1506, Brantford, ON, Canada N3T 5V6.

Paterek, Josephine. *Encyclopedia of American Indian Costume*. New York: W. W. Norton, 1994.
    Arranged by tribes within geographic regions; see Headgear.

Video. "Plains Indian War Bonnet: History and Construction." 50 minutes. Order from: Written Heritage, PO Box 1390, Folsom, LA 70437. $19.95 (800) 301-8009 or (504) 796-5433.

Teachers

Mishkin, Bernard. *Rank and Warfare Among the Plains Indians.* Lincoln, NE: University of Nebraska Press, 1992. (Originally published in 1940.)

In the section entitled "Kiowa Rank," Mishkin describes the formal rank hierarchy of the Kiowa and the Kiowa code of military achievement consisting of a series of deeds, some of which have higher value than others. Successful military performance was essential to achieving rank.

Phillips, Ruth B. "From *Gus-to'-weh* to Glengarry," in "Moccasins into Slippers: Woodlands Indian Hats, Bags and Shoes in Tradition and Transformation." *Northeast Indian Quarterly.* Vol. 7, no. 4 (Winter 1990): 26–36.

Illustrations and discussion about *gustoweh* and transformations it has undergone in media and form.

Reader's Digest. *America's Fascinating Indian Heritage.* Pleasantville, NY: Reader's Digest Association, 1978.

On pages 195–98, there is a discussion of counting coup and the way the Lakotas altered feathers to reflect specific kinds of exploits.

Lesson

4.6

Food

Grade Level
4–6

Materials
Student Readings: "Jeff Kalin," "Food Riddle Game" (one for each student), and "Recipes"; variety of art materials, cookbooks, food (see recipes), cooking and eating utensils

Time
Three to four class periods and one special time for feast, if feasible

Objectives
- Students will appreciate the role of Native Americans in world food production.

- Students will prepare Native-inspired dishes for a feast day.

- Students will hone math skills by enlarging recipes to accommodate the class.

Activities

First Class

1. Read students "Jeff Kalin," then open class dialogue.
2. Discussion Questions

    What are some foods that were first grown in this hemisphere?

    Name some Native American farming techniques.

    What is a primitive technologist?

    What dishes do you eat at home that have Native foods in them?

3. After discussion has ended, have students make a collage of Native foods or recipes using Native foods. If you intend to host a feast day and invite guests, students can make invitations with the same theme.

Second Class

1. Pass out "Food Riddle Game" sheets and have students complete them. Discuss answers. Divide class into teams and have them create additional food riddles that will stump the other team. This is a good library research project. Have students research traditional stories of food origins. Make sure that stories are tribally specific, that is, Lakota, Choctaw, Navajo, Mohawk, and so on. Riddles, stories, and food collages can be displayed at feast day.

Third Class (Feast Day)

1. Prepare for cooking activity. If circumstances allow, it would be a great field trip to let students share in the food shopping. There are many Native recipe books, or you can use the main dish and dessert included in this lesson.

Enrichment/Extensions

Art. Make cookbooks for gifts. Students can invent their own recipes or everyone in class can make a contribution.

Community Service. Prepare Indian recipes and share with a day care or nursing home. Try not to visit at holiday times when other groups visit.

Field Trip. Visit the supermarket and find as many indigenous foods as possible. Visit a farm.

Guest Speakers. Invite someone to class who works with food: nutritionist, chef, dietitian, farmer.

Literature. Research and learn stories about food.

Science. Research methods of Native farming. Make a matrix using different Nations, locations, foods, and farming techniques. Grow some food or herbs in the classroom. Compare nutritional values of foods. See what foods can be eaten together to make a balanced meal.

Writing. Have students write stories about their favorite foods, after researching their nutritional value.

📖 Reading

Jeff Kalin

"I look at my garden and I am thankful that I am able to have a good relationship with the earth. I guess you could say that I grow heritage foods, cultivated the way my ancestors did for thousands of years," said Jeff Kalin as he leaned on his broad blade hoe and surveyed his little farm.

"Native people grew thousands of different foods in this hemisphere before Europeans arrived," Jeff explained, "but I will just name a few. Peppers, chili peppers, tomatoes, onions, peas, beans, squash, tomatoes, guava, pineapples, potatoes, sweet potatoes, corn, popcorn, chocolate, vanilla, avocado, zucchini, quinoa, amaranth, wild rice, pumpkins, cranberries, peanuts, cashews, pecans, coffee, lima beans, sunflower seeds, tapioca, raspberries, walnuts, and cherries are just some of the foods developed in this hemisphere by Indian agronomists."

"Not only did our agronomists grow some of the world's most important food products," Jeff went on to say, "but we also had very innovative ways of farming. We were the first peoples to use terrace farming, dry farming, slash-and-burn agriculture, and were real experts at companion or symbiotic planting. Even our traditional stories, like the Iroquois story of *The Three Sisters,* tell us how to plant so that the soil will not be depleted, and the plants will nourish one another. Modern scientists are looking at Native farming techniques like the Chinampas Gardens in Mexico to learn how better to farm today. Botanists are trying to understand the Native science of growing plants together that help each other. For instance, Indian people hybridized corn so that it has many seeds firmly attached to the cob and many leave sheaths to protect it from birds, insects, and other predators. It cannot disperse its own seeds and is the only plant in the world entirely interdependent with humans."

Jeff Kalin, of Cherokee descent, grows many indigenous crops in his Connecticut garden and is a primitive technologist. He studies the way Native peoples lived hundreds and thousands of years ago and is able to replicate their farming methods, pottery, tools, jewelry, and other items. Sometimes Jeff plants a seed of ancient corn that has been preserved for centuries or determines how to reconstruct a water pot by looking at a pottery shard found in an archaeological dig.

Jeff, his wife, and children live on a small farm and try to follow a lifestyle that is natural and environmentally sound. They not only grow traditional Native foods, but they also preserve them in traditional ways as often as possible. They also hunt much of their food and prepare deer and rabbit meat in tasty recipes. At one time, their stream had a very low production of trout, so Jeff built trout condos, and the fish moved in!

Jeff acquired much of his knowledge from Native peoples in Central and South America where he farmed for many years. To get to his place, he had a two-day walk, including going over a 13,000 foot mountain and passing through several different types of environments, including tundra and rainforest. His closest neighbors were a two-hour walk away. In the little community of five families, they grew and shared crops of corn, beans, squash, yucca, many kinds of potatoes and sweet potatoes, melons, arrowroot, peanuts, platanos, papayas, onions, and lettuce. Slash-and-burn and companion planting were some of the techniques Jeff used, and his only tools were a broad-bladed hoe and machete. There was always enough to eat, and he needed very little money. He felt that people seemed more rational there; their relationship to the earth was different. And . . . that is how Jeff tries to live in Connecticut!

In workshops given by Jeff and his family, they teach people how to grow food without chemicals that pollute the earth. They also give instruction in most of the ancient arts, including flint napping, maple sugaring, cooking, and pottery. The entire family makes items to sell at powwows, and they are often called upon to design Indian motifs for movies and commercial buildings. The Kalins pride themselves on living close to the earth in a good way. Jeff said that most of the things they use are recycled, and once they are finished with it, it has been used up.

"I try to be an active participant with the natural world," Jeff said. "Our lives are interwoven with other living beings. Our ancestors developed over half of the food that is grown all over the world today. If it were not for American Indians, the Irish would not have the potato; the Italians would be missing tomatoes; Africans would never have tasted cassava; and the Chinese would not be adding peanuts to their stir fry!"

Food Riddle Game

(Don't forget to omit answers from student copies.)

1. I can be baked, fried, mashed, or stuffed and have famous sisters in Idaho and Maine.   *Potato*

2. Bears love me and hang around my bushes. Eat me and you'll end up with a purple mouth.   *Blueberry*

3. If you have a sweet tooth, I am better for you than candy. Although I live in Hawaii now, I was born in the Caribbean. I have prickly brown skin, a beautiful spiky green hat, and yellow insides.   *Pineapple*

4. I am green, high in the B vitamins, and sometimes thin people are called by my name.   *String beans*

5. Ben Franklin thought I should be the national bird, but although I do not have that title, I am still the favorite on holidays.   *Turkey*

6. I jump into eggnogs, milk shakes, yogurt, cakes, and I start my life as a black bean.

    Vanilla

7. My name sounds like I could just pop up anywhere, or I might be unruly. The Ojibway and Menominee people work really hard caring for me, so I'll be around in the future.

    Wild rice

8. Be very careful how you eat me, because I can make your mouth dry and lips pucker. Cherokees make puddings out of my yummy fruit.

    Persimmon

9. I am a grain that sounds like a girl's name, and I am very high in protein.

    Quinoa

10. I am a red and juicy fruit, rich in potassium and vitamin C that always gets mistaken for a vegetable.

    Tomato

11. I live in a bog, and although most people think I just love to hang out with turkeys, I am also a good medicine for bladder ailments.

    Cranberry

12. Several of us hang out together in a green pod.

    Peas

13. I am very nutritious, green, bumpy, and often end up as guacamole.

    Avocado

14. We are called the three sisters because when we are planted together, we always give each other exactly what we need. When we are eaten together, our proteins are as high as meat and there are lots of stories about us.

    Corn, beans, squash

15. Most kids love me and eat me ground up in a sandwich with jelly.

    Peanuts

16. Birds think I am quite the gourmet treat, but if they leave any for you, I am a nutritious snack and can even be made into bread or cookies. My plant can grow really tall!

    Sunflower seeds

Recipes

Yvonne's Cherokee or Brunswick Stew
(serves 4–8)

1 chicken or rabbit, cut up, or 8 chicken thighs
   (if using rabbit, marinate overnight in
   thyme and lemon juice)
Whole wheat flour or corn flour
3 tablespoons vegetable oil
Dutch oven or stew pot
Water
1 teaspoon thyme
1 tablespoon chili powder
1 teaspoon salt

½ teaspoon black pepper
2 bay leaves
1 onion, diced
2 large potatoes, scrubbed, cut into
   eighths, skins on
1 cup string beans, cut up
1 tomato, skinned, diced
1 8-oz. box of frozen corn
1 8-oz. box of lima beans
1 can tomato sauce

Wash and dry chicken. Dredge in flour and lightly brown in hot oil in dutch oven. Add tomato sauce and water to cover, onions, and seasonings. Bring to boil. Lower heat until simmering and cover. Cook until chicken is almost tender. Add potatoes and string beans, cover and cook for 5–8 minutes. Add tomatoes and lima beans and simmer for 3–5 minutes. Add corn last and simmer until all vegetables are tender.

Aunt Meena's Berry Cobbler
(serves 4–6)

2–4 cups strawberries, cut up (or any type of berries)
1 tablespoon cornmeal
2 tablespoons honey, concentrated apple juice, or maple syrup

Topping

1 cup cornmeal
1 teaspoon baking powder
1 teaspoon salt
1 tablespoon apple juice,
   honey, or maple syrup

½ cup milk or water
2 tablespoons melted butter
1 teaspoon lemon juice

Sauce

1 tablespoon melted butter
3 tablespoons honey, apple juice,
   or maple syrup

1 tablespoon lemon juice

Mix berries with sweetener and place in lightly oiled baking dish. Mix dry ingredients for topping. Blend liquids and add to dry ingredients, mixing quickly. Form a soft dough and drop onto berries. Mix sauce ingredients and drizzle on topping. Bake at 375 degrees for 45 minutes to an hour. Cool before serving.

Resources

<u>Students</u>

Bruchac, Joseph. *The First Strawberries: A Cherokee Story*. New York: Dial Books, 1993.
    Gives the origin of strawberries.

———. *Return of the Sun*. Freedom, CA: Crossing Press, 1990.
    There are food origin stories in this delightful book.

Bruchac, Joseph, and Michael Caduto. *Keepers of the Earth*. Golden, CO: Fulcrum, 1988.
    A wonderful science curriculum based on Native American stories.

Culleton, Beatrice. *Spirit of the White Bison*. Winnipeg, MB: Pemmican Press, 1990.
    Although this is not exactly a contemporary book, it gives a good account of cultures that were developed around the buffalo.

Henry, Edna. *Native American Cookbook*. New York: Julian Messner, 1983.
    These recipes are easy to read; adapted for the modern kitchen.

Kanena, Juanita. *Navajo Pueblo Cookery*. New York: Morgan & Morgan, 1977.
    Good cookbook, although it uses a lot of products that may need to be substituted with healthier items.

Mathers, Shirley. *Our Mother Corn*. Seattle, WA: Daybreak Star Press, 1981.
    Great curriculum: stories, games, science, and student and teacher resources.

Peters, Russell. *Clambake*. Minneapolis, MN: Lerner Publications, 1992.
    This book with contemporary photographs focuses on a young Wampanoag boy.

Regguinti, Gordon. *The Sacred Harvest: Ojibway Wild Rice Gathering*. Minneapolis, MN: Lerner Publications, 1992.
    A contemporary account of ricing. Great photographs.

<u>Teachers</u>

Buffalo Bird Woman. *Buffalo Bird Woman's Garden*. St. Paul, MN: Minnesota Historical Press, 1985.
    The title tells it all!

Carson, Dale. *Native New England Cooking*. Old Saybrook, CT: Peregrine Press, 1989.
    There are some good recipes from New England Nations in this book.

Ellis, David W., and Luke Swan. *Teachings of the Tides: Uses of Marine Invertebrates by the Nanhousat People*. Penticton, BC: Theytus Books, 1981.
    Great curriculum about peoples whose food comes from the sea.

Grinde, Donald A. *Ecocide of Native America: Environmental Destruction of Indian Lands and Peoples*. Santa Fe, NM: Clear Light Publishing, 1995.
    A definite must for teachers.

Kavasch, Barrie. *Natural Harvests: Recipes and Botanicals of the American Indian*. New York: Random House, 1979.
   This author has several books. Find one that appeals to you.

Nabhan, Gary. *The Desert Smells Like Rain*. San Francisco: North Point Press, 1982.
   Good information about desert farming peoples.

Native Foods and Nutrition: An Illustrated Reference Resource. Ottawa, ON: Canadian Health and Welfare Dept., 1985.
   This book gives very scientific information about proper nutrition.

Weatherford, Jack. *Indian Givers*. New York: Crown, 1988.
   Check out all of Weatherford's books. This one talks about the importance of all Native inventions to world survival through the ages.

Lesson  **Recreation/Sports**

Grade Level
   4–8

Materials
   Student Reading: "Sports and Recreation"; smooth strong sticks or dowels, 1½–2 feet long (small enough in circumference to grasp easily); tennis balls or bouncing balls, similar in size (one for each student); 12 dowels, ¼–½ inch in circumference (one for each student); paints; brushes (glitter, if desired)

Time
   Two class periods

Objectives
   • Students will become familiar with Eskimo-Indian Olympics, some Indian athletes, sports, and Indian sports organizations.

   • Students will participate in three Olympic events.

   • Students will make and play an Indian game similar to Jacks.

   • Students will get exercise!

Activities

Give a brief lecture based on Reading: "Sports and Recreation" or resource materials. It would be helpful if your class could view a video, newscast, or film of Eskimo-Indian Olympics. Explain that Eskimo and Aleut people live in an environment that requires toughness and stamina to survive. The various games they played over the years have helped them become strong, agile, flexible, and trained to endure all kinds of physical hardships. To appreciate the difficulty of the competitions in the World Eskimo-Indian Olympics, students will participate in just three of the several events.

• Knuckle Hopping

Object: The contestant wins who hops the farthest while keeping back straight and elbows bent.

How to Play:

1. Assume a push-up position at the starting line, but balance on knuckles and toes.
2. Hop forward, as far and as fast as possible, maintaining position.

• Kneel Jump

Object: The contestant wins who jumps farthest in specified time limit.

How to Play:

1. Contestant kneels on floor at starting line, insteps flat on the floor, soles facing upward.
2. Athlete jumps forward on knees, swinging arms to gather momentum.
3. No steps allowed.

• Stick Pull

Object: The contestant wins who can pull opponent upright or can pull the stick away from him.

How to Play:

1. Two contestants sit on floor, facing with feet pressed together, knees bent.
2. Contestants grasp a smooth stick (strong dowel) with both hands, alternating and touching.
3. On go signal, athletes pull stick, but cannot let go.
4. The best two out of three matches wins the game.
5. Change order of hands with each match.

- ## Ball and Stick (Jacks) (not part of Olympics)

This game challenges eye/hand coordination and can be used for a solo game or turned into a class competition. Sticks can be used for other purposes, for example, as Talking Sticks or Ownership Sticks. In many Nations, Ownership Sticks are placed on top of one's belongings, giving a clear message: Do not touch.

Procedure: Give each student a dowel, 12 inches in length, ¼–½ inch round, paints, glitter, and brushes. Students may decorate their sticks in any fashion. When sticks are dry, give each student a ball.

How to Play:

1. Drop stick on floor.
2. Throw ball into air.
3. Pick up stick before ball bounces on floor.
4. Catch ball after picking up stick.

Enrichment/Extensions

Community Service. Hold a Native American Games Day for younger children. Prepare and serve Native foods.

Creative Writing. Research and write reports about Indian sports figures.

Drama. Stage a sportscast and use reports as it they were being broadcast.

Physical Education. Research Delaware Football and play the game at the appropriate time between the girls and boys. Include adults, too. This is a lot of fun!

📖 Reading

Sports and Recreation

Historically, games were played for various reasons: spiritual, training for battle, developing skills for hunting and surviving, and sometimes just for fun! Indian people were known for their strength, fitness, endurance, flexibility, and agility. That reputation survives today, although Indian athletes do not get the same publicity or opportunities as other sports figures.

Some well-known American Indian athletes are Olympians Jim Thorpe, Billy Mills, Philip Osif, Buster Charles, Joe Thornton, Frank Mr. Pleasant, Jessie Resnick, Angelita Rosal, and Ellison Brown. Professional athletes include baseball players, John Meyers, Allie Reynolds; football players, John Allen, Jack Jacobs, Louis Weller; hockey player, Clarence Abel; boxers, Gordon House, Alvin Williams; and lacrosse player, Alexander Arcasa. Native people have set world records in many events, won the Boston marathon, and produced winning women's basketball teams.

The American Indian Athletic Hall of Fame, located at Haskell Indian Nations University in Kansas, was established in 1972 to honor outstanding Indian athletes. Many Nations and sports are represented by the 60 inductees.

The World Eskimo-Indian Olympics, founded in 1961, are held every July in Fairbanks, Alaska. The four days of games challenge athletic skill, concentration, endurance, strength, and agility in centuries-old sports. The Olympics also showcase Eskimo and Indian arts, dance, foods, and other aspects of indigenous culture. Even elders and babies compete in various events!

The National Indian Athletic Association promotes youth clinics for young sportsmen and women, and the Iroquois National Lacrosse Team competes internationally. Another popular Indian sporting event is the National Indian Finals Rodeo Championship held yearly in Albuquerque, New Mexico.

Running is probably the most popular Indian sport, and Native peoples have excelled in it. Wings of the West, a New Mexico Indian running club, has won two national championships sponsored by the Athletic Congress United States National Cross Country Championships.

Although Native people play a role in many sports, often they are not identified as Indians. This gives the impression that Indian athletes, like Indian people involved in all walks of life, simply do not exist.

Resources
Students

Atimoyoo, Pat. *Nehiyaw Ma Tow We Na: Games of the Plains Cree*. Saskatoon, SK: Saskatchewan Indian Cultural College, 1985.
This book gives background, play procedures, and game construction of the Plains Cree. Good illustrations and appropriate for curriculum use, too.

Board Game. Song to the Cedar Tree. Seattle, WA: Daybreak Star Press, n.d.
The object of this game is to cooperate with other players so that the tribe will have enough supplies stored in the longhouse to survive another year. Several people can play on teams.

Brescia, Bill. *A una*. Seattle, WA: Daybreak Star Press, 1982.
This handy book has recipes and games and is geared to middle elementary students.

Cowen, Agnes. *Cherokee Stick Ball*. Park Hill, OK: Cross Cultural Education Center, 1982.
Packed with historical information, this book also has a section written in Cherokee. The publisher also has biographies on some sports figures like Thorpe and Thornton.

Mills, Billy. *Wokini*. Fair Oaks, CA: Feather Publishing, 1990.
An Olympic gold medalist, Mills shares his beliefs about how to be a champion. The inspirational book includes meditations for youth, legends, and Indian philosophy.

Whitefeather, Willy. *Outdoor Survival Handbook for Kids*. Tucson, AZ: Harbinger House, 1990.
This busy book, written by a Native outdoorsman, is a fun way to learn simple and not-so-simple techniques for children (and adult children) to survive in the outdoors.

Teachers

Culin, Stewart. *Games of the North American Indians*. New York: Dover, 1975.
A cornucopia of sports of indigenous peoples, many of these games can be adapted for the classroom.

Macfarlan, A. *Handbook of American Indian Games*. New York: Dover, 1985.
These games are easily adapted for the classroom.

Nabakov, Peter. *Indian Running*. Santa Barbara, CA: Capra Press, 1981.

Oxendine, Joseph B. *American Indian Sports Heritage*. Champaign, IL: Human Kinetics Books, 1988.
Full of historical and contemporary information, there is a section of sports figures inducted into the American Indian Athletic Hall of Fame.

Smith, Gary. "Shadow of a Nation." *Sports Illustrated* (February 18, 1991): 60–74.

Wheeler, R. W. *Jim Thorpe: World's Greatest Athlete*. Norman, OK: University of Oklahoma Press, 1979.

White, Dave. *Tewaarathon: Lacrosse*. Cornwall Island, ON: North American Indian Travelling College, 1985. R.R. 3, Cornwall Island, ON, Canada K6H 5R7.
This is the most complete book of lacrosse ever written. It not only gives origins of the game, but has photographs of the manufacturing process of lacrosse equipment and historical and contemporary Native teams. It also explains rules of the game and even gives pointers. Great illustrations.

Lesson

4.8

Powwows

Grade Level
4–8

Materials
Student Readings: "Powwows," "Grand Entry," "American Flag," "Drum," "Powwow Economics," and "When a Feather Drops"; books about powwows; drawings of powwow dress; two photos of vendors; video

Time
Three class periods

Objectives
- Students learn that powwows are tribal or intertribal social events for young and old that feature beautiful outfits, drumming, singing and dancing, honoring ceremonies, feasting, special rituals, giveaways; sales of arts/crafts, and foods; that they express American Indian identity and cultural values; that they take place all over the United States and Canada throughout the year, especially in summer; and that Native people welcome non-Indian visitors.

- Students learn how to identify powwow dress of men and women.

- Students learn that the U.S. Postal Service issued American Indian Dance Stamps in 1996.

- Students learn that when an eagle feather drops in an arena, special ceremonies are required to protect and retrieve it.

- Students learn there are giveaways at powwows. An honored person and family distribute gifts of material goods to family, friends, and strangers.

- Students learn that people from other cultures also have community celebrations that express cultural values and bring people together, for example, Chinese New Year, Croatian wedding, Pakistan/Indian Mehendi party, West Africa outdooring.

- Students learn that Indian families and/or individuals rely on powwow earnings as their main source of income.

Activities

1. Duplicate the drawings of powwow dance dress (Figure 4.7, pages 90–91). Students study the eight styles of powwow dress and brief descriptions.
2. Divide the class into small groups and give each group a book about powwows. (See Resources-Students, page 96.) Working together, students identify the dress of powwow dancers.
3. Each group should look at a photograph of a dance scene. Ask each group member to contribute a line to a group essay or poem describing what is going on at the powwow. Allow at least 20 minutes. Allow each group to decide how to make its presentation: ensemble, designated spokesperson, or a line per person.
4. Create a master list of different points that each group makes regarding the powwow. If necessary, add rituals to the student list regarding a fallen eagle feather and the sacred drum. (See Readings.)
5. Find a photograph of the Grand Entry in one of the books and explain its importance. (See Resources-Students, page 96.)
6. Look at the two photographs of vendors at a powwow (Figure 4.8, page 92). Ask students if they have ever attended a powwow or an arts and crafts show. Ask students to describe why there are vendors at these events.
7. If it is possible to rent a video about powwows, show one to the class. Afterward, ask students to make observations about what they saw and add to the master list. (See Resources-Teachers, page 97.)
8. Inform students that in 1996, the U.S. Postal Service issued American Indian Dance stamps that included a fancy dancer and a traditional dancer. Have students either buy the stamp, if still available, or look it up in the most recent *Specialized Catalogue of U.S. Stamps.* (Sidney, OH: Scott Publishing), found in most libraries.
9. Ask students to bring photographs, artwork, or illustrations of a shared community celebration that combines socializing, special clothing, and special rituals. Ask the student to identify the photograph by writing a caption. (Students can take turns doing "show-and-tell" with their photos, artwork, or illustrations and/or display the visuals in the classroom. Ask students to compare powwows to their community event.)

Figure 4.7A. Women's Northern Traditional Dancer: Dress is fully beaded on shoulder or cape, fringed shawl, and fully beaded moccasins. Line work © Mary Emma Ahenakew.

Figure 4.7B. Women's Southern Traditional Dancer: Beadwork is used as an accent, fringed shawl, and accent-beaded moccasins. Line work © Mary Emma Ahenakew.

Figure 4.7C. Women's Fancy Shawl Dancer: Elaborately beaded dresses; beaded moccasins with matching leggings; brightly colored, beautifully embroidered or decorated long-fringed **shawl.** Line work © Mary Emma Ahenakew.

Figure 4.7D. Women's Jingle Dancer: Cloth dress decorated with cone-shaped metal jingles; no shawl. Line work © Mary Emma Ahenakew.

Figure 4.7E. Men's Northern Traditional Straight Dancer: Lavish circular bustle of long feathers at the dancer's waist; bone breast-plate. Line work © Mary Emma Ahenakew.

Figure 4.7F. Men's Southern Traditional Straight Dancer: Cotton or buckskin pants, a shirt, and bone breastplate that hangs to waist; porcupine headdress. Line work © Mary Emma Ahenakew.

Figure 4.7G. Men's Fancy Feather Dancer: Two large, brightly colored feather bustles (at waist and shoulders) and small bustles on arms; outfits color-coordinated and beaded. Line work © Mary Emma Ahenakew.

Figure 4.7H. Men's Grass Dancer: Outfits have long, brightly colored yarn fringe and ribbons; no bustle. Line work © Mary Emma Ahenakew.

Figure 4.8. Vendors at a powwow. Photos ©
Karen Warth.

Enrichment/Extensions

Art. Students can make a drawing, painting, or diorama of a shared community event.

Creative Writing. Students can write a poem or essay about a shared community event that they have attended. Students can further research powwow dress and make a report to the class. Students can research powwow dances and make a report to the class.

Field Trip. If possible, arrange a class trip to a powwow. See listing in Resources-Teachers for listing of *Powwow on the Red Road.*

Oral History. If a student knows someone who sells arts and crafts, ask the student to interview that person and share the interview with the class. Have the student prepare a list of questions in advance. (See Appendix A, page 209.)

📖 Reading

Powwows

Reprinted with permission of Macmillan Library Reference, USA from the *Native American Almanac,* by Arlene Hirschfelder and Martha Kreipe de Montaño. Copyright © 1993 by Arlene Hirschfelder and Martha Kreipe de Montaño.

The word "powwow" came into the English language from an eastern Algonquian language. In the Massachuset language, *pauwau* literally means "he uses divination." It refers to a shaman or medicine man, who could divine the future from information and power received while dreaming. . . . Today, "powwow" is sometimes used to refer to an important meeting, but to Native Americans it refers to a gathering of Indian people to visit, feast, sing, and dance together.

Powwows, in the Native American sense of the word, probably started in the last decades of the nineteenth century as Indian people adapted to new conditions. The majority of powwow dances were war dances, which originated with the warrior societies of the plains. When Indian people were confined to reservations, the war dances became social dances. But they did not lose their connection to warriors. People who are in the armed service today or are veterans are today's equivalent of the warriors of old, and powwows often recognize and honor them. In addition, much of the powwow clothing for men has evolved from insignia worn by warriors. The roach headdress, feathered bustles, and eagle feathers worn by men in powwows were once worn only by proven warriors. Today, they are worn by Indian men and boys as a symbol of Indian identity. Women's powwow clothing are contemporary versions of traditional clothing, usually made from buckskin or cloth.

Powwows are held outside in grassy areas or inside, often in gymnasiums, when weather dictates. The center of the powwow is the drum, which refers to the instrument and to the singers who play the drum and sing at the same time. On the northern and southern Plains, some powwow traditions differ. For example, on the southern Plains, a single drum is placed in the center of the dance arena, while in the north, one or more drums are placed at the edge. Spectators sit in bleachers or on folding chairs. Participants dance either sunwise (clockwise) or counterclockwise around the drum. In the northern tradition, men and women usually dance in opposite directions.

Powwows are not so much a performance for an audience but rather are a way of sharing, reinforcing, and expressing Indian heritage. Since many powwows are held every year, and most are open to the public, a powwow is a good way to learn about American Indian heritage. The details of the powwow vary with the location, but in general, they begin with the Grand Entry, in which all dancers, dressed in their finest regalia, enter the powwow arena dancing slowly in a parade around the drum. Inter-tribal War dances follow, interspersed with Honor dances and other special dances such as the Two-Step, Round Dance, or Crow Hop.

Contests draw dancers from far away to compete for prize money. Dancers compete in gender and in age groups. For example, there are often junior and senior as well as tiny tot divisions. Within age groups, there are categories based on styles of dancing and types of regalia worn while dancing. Dancers are judged for their dancing, their regalia, and the extent of their participation. In general, men compete in "traditional," "fancy dance," and "grass dance" categories. Popular women's dance categories are "traditional," "northern shawl," and "jingle dress."

For both men and women, the categories refer to dance styles and to the type of regalia worn while dancing. The men's traditional dance style is sedate and dignified. It is directly related to an older style where war deeds were pantomimed. The regalia of a traditional dance is based on tribal dress of the nineteenth century or earlier. The fancy dance is characterized by exuberant and strenuous high-stepping footwork, with turns and spins. Fancy dancers wear brightly colored feather bustles, elaborate beadwork, and bells. . . . Grass dancers look similar to fancy dancers, except they do not wear bustles but wear thick fringe on a yoke and their aprons. Grass dancers dance like fancy dancers but with a rhythmic rocking gait. All male dancers wear moccasins.

Women's traditional dancing is characterized by a kind of stylized gliding with a gentle knee bend and an upright posture. Buckskin dancers generally wear white buckskin dresses decorated with long fringe and intricate beadwork. Cloth dresses are of several kinds. In the Midwest, women often wear elaborate ribbon-work skirts with cloth blouses. Many women also wear cloth dresses patterned after buckskin dresses, and there are many tribal styles, such as Navajo velvet dresses and long, full-skirted Cherokee dresses. All female dancers wear moccasins and wear or carry handmade shawls with long fringe. The dance step of women's traditional dance makes the long fringe on the dresses and shawls sway to the beat of the drum.

Women who dance the northern shawl style wear cloth dresses with a beaded yoke and moccasins. Their dance steps are more like men's fancy dance steps, with high bouncing steps and twirls, which cause their shawls to spread out like wings. Northern shawl dancers move over the floor like birds circling on an updraft.

Women's jingle dresses are cloth dresses covered with many small tin cones. Their dance steps are similar to the northern shawl dancers, athletic and high stepping. When jingle dress dancers enter the arena, thousands of tin cones on their dresses add another layer of sound keeping time to the beat of the drum.

Each dancer interprets the dance individually within the canons of their particular dance category. Most dances do not have coordinated choreography; every dancer chooses steps as a way to express his or her Indian identity. As the dancers circle the drum, from communities far and near, with different customs, each one dancing a personal interpretation, all are united by the heartbeat of Mother Earth expressed through the drum.

📖 Reading

Grand Entry

The Grand Entry leads off each session of dancing at the powwow. (It has been said that this spectacular parade of dancers has been borrowed from rodeos and Wild West shows.) The flag bearers lead the way at the Grand Entry carrying the eagle staff (a staff covered with cloth and fur and hung with eagle feathers carried by a veteran and placed in the center of the dance circle or brought to the announcer's stand), the U.S. and Canadian flags, and state and tribal flags. During the Grand Entry, everyone stands and hats are removed in respect. After the flags, dignitaries file in followed by dancers arranged by category.

📖 Reading

American Flag

The American flag, a symbol of national unity, has been an inspiration for American Indians for over 100 years. Today, the American flag continues to "lead the way" at all Indian ceremonies and powwows. Indian veterans carry the American flag during the Grand Entry and tribal flag songs speak of special war deeds in defense of the American flag.

📖 Reading

Drum

The drum is more than a musical instrument. Regarded as a sacred ritual object, it is believed to be alive and represents the heartbeat of a nation, the sound of the universe. Each drum is a distinct individual with a "voice." There are many types, including the Plains large bass drum. The drum MUST be treated with respect as a sacred object. Nothing is set on a drum, nor does anyone reach across it. The term "drum" also refers to the drum group itself, which sings songs for the dancing contests.

📖 Reading

Powwow Economics

Powwows provide a marketplace for the sale of American Indian arts and foods. Many families spend their summer on the "powwow circuit," traveling from powwow to powwow participating in dance competitions and selling their handmade jewelry, clothing, blankets, and other items. For many families or individual Indians, earnings from dance competitions and other sales count as an important part of their total income.

A walk around the circle of vendors is a feast of sights, sounds, and smells. One can buy everything from fried bread to beaded baseball caps to the latest CDs of Indian music. Powwows are also a good source of resource materials for teachers because some vendors have a vast array of books and magazines about Indian people.

📖 Reading

When a Feather Drops

Tribes treat eagles with the highest respect. Eagles are said to be messengers of the Creator. Only distinguished warriors have the right to wear feathers. The notching and coloring of eagle feathers represent various brave deeds in the taking of the enemy. When an eagle feather accidentally drops to the dance floor, a dancer performs a special ceremony to pick it up. Since the feather represents the spirit of a fallen warrior, only a warrior similarly wounded is permitted to retrieve it. Once the proper rituals are performed, the warrior recounts an actual war deed or special story about his military service. Then he returns the feather to its owner. The owner usually gives a gift and the drum to the veteran in honor of the service he or she has performed.

Resources

Students

Ancona, George. *Powwow*. San Diego, CA: Harcourt Brace Jovanovich, 1993.
    Text and full-color photographs by Ancona focus on the Crow Fair, the largest powwow held in the United States.

Berstein, Diane M. *We Dance Because We Can: People of the Powwow*. Marietta, GA: Longstreet Press, 1996.
    Full-color photos show powwow dress and each photo is accompanied by words from the dancer.

Braine, Susan. *Drumbeat . . . Heartbeat: A Celebration of the Powwow*. Minneapolis, MN: Lerner Publications, 1995.
    Text and photographs by author emphasize the Northern Plains style of dancing. Giveaways are described in detail.

Crum, Robert. *Eagle Drum: On the Powwow Trail with a Young Grass Dancer*. New York: Simon and Schuster Books for Young Readers, 1994.
Full-color photographs by the author tell about the life and dress of a young dancer.

King, Sandra. *Shannon: An Ojibway Dancer*. Minneapolis, MN: Lerner Publications, 1993.
Illustrated with photographs by Catherine Whipple, this book follows a 13-year-old Ojibway girl who learns about her tribe's traditional dress from her grandmother as she gets ready to dance at a powwow.

Marra, Ben. *Powwow: Images Along the Red Road*. New York: Harry N. Abrams, 1996.
Over 100 photos illustrate the powwow event.

Parfit, Michael. "Powwow—A Gathering of the Tribes." *National Geographic* (June 1994): 89–113.
Full-color photographs by David A. Harvey give inside views of powwow life from Montana to Connecticut.

Roberts, Chris. *Pow Wow Country*. Helena, MT: American and World Geographic Publishing, 1993.
Color photos and interviews with powwow participants supply extensive information on the history, evolution, and the meaning of everything connected with powwow events.

———. "Schemitzun: The Pequot People's Feast of Green Corn and Dance." *Native Peoples: The Arts and Lifeways*. Vol. 7, no. 4 (Summer 1994): 66–70.
Full-color photographs and text by Roberts describe the 1993 powwow sponsored by the Mashantucket Pequot of Connecticut in which over a thousand dancers participated.

Steltzer, Ulli. *A Haida Potlatch*. Seattle, WA: University of Washington Press, 1984.
Photographs by the author illustrate the nature of a potlatch, which means "to give away" in the Chinook language. The distribution of gifts is done on a large and lavish scale according to a person's rank, with the audience serving as witnesses to this public event.

Teachers

Horse Capture, George P. *Powwow*. Cody, WY: Buffalo Bill Historical Center, 1989.
A catalog gives background information on every aspect of the Northern Plains powwow, including the setting, music, clothing of men and women, giveaways, and Grand Entry, as well as stunning full-color and black-and-white photos of dress, powwow scenes, and a list of "Powwows of Interest." Students could use this catalog to research dress.

Native American Co-op. *Powwow on the Red Road*. Native American Co-op, 2830 South Thrasher, Tucson, AZ 85713.
This listing of over 700 powwow events in the United States and Canada costs $25. Check/money order.

Video. "Celebration." 1979.
This video (26 minutes), filmed at the Honor the Earth Powwow held annually on the Lac Courte Oreilles Reservation in Wisconsin, shows and explains the significance of powwow dancing, feasting, giveaways, and traditional Indian team sports. Distributed by Intermedia Arts Minnesota, 435 Ontario Street, SE, Minneapolis, MN 55414.

Video. "I'd Rather be Powwowing." 1983.

This video (30 minutes) follows Al Chandler, a Gros Ventre Indian, and his son as they travel to a powwow at the Rocky Boy Reservation near Havre, Montana. The video shows scenes that capture the spirit of the powwow—socializing with friends, preparing food, assembling dance outfits, and dancing. Distributed by the Buffalo Bill Historical Center, Education Department, Box 1000, Cody, WY 82414.

Video. "Keep Your Heart Strong." 1986.

This video (58 minutes) gives an inside view of the powwow using interviews with Indian historians and elders to provide insight into the dances and traditional values powwows express. Distributed by Native American Public Telecommunications (NAPT).

Video. "Native American Men's and Women's Dance Styles." Volumes I and II, 1994.

Two-volume video covers eight styles of dancing. Men's styles include Straight Dance, Northern Traditional, Grass Dance, and Fancy Dance. Women's styles feature Southern Cloth, Buckskin Traditional, Jingle Dress, and Northern Fancy Shawl. Dancers were filmed live competing at several powwows. Volume II has some narration. Available for $19.95 from Written Heritage, PO Box 1390, Folsom, LA 70437. (800) 301-8009 or (504) 796-5433.

Video. "On the Powwow Trail." n.d.

Video follows two teenage grass dancers as they travel the powwow circuit from Oklahoma to Montana, along with a contemporary/powwow musical soundtrack. Available for $19.95 from Written Heritage, PO Box 1390, Folsom, LA 70437. (800) 301-8009 or (504) 796-5433.

Lesson

4.9

Giveaways

Grade Level
   4–8

Materials
   Student Reading: "Giveaways"; books about powwows.

Time
   One class period

Objectives
   • Students learn that through giveaways, an honored person and family distribute gifts of material goods to family, friends, and even to strangers instead of receiving them.

   • Students learn giveaways express the traditional Native belief in generosity and sharing and the belief that giving is better than receiving.

Activities

1. Find a photo of a giveaway in one of the books about the powwow and discuss the concept. Ask students to compare gift giving at a powwow and gift giving at events like birthdays, graduation parties, and weddings. (See Lesson 3.2, page 36.)
2. Each student thinks about someone they would like to honor with a giveaway. They write an essay about the kinds of gifts they would give in this person's honor.
3. Students discuss the occasions when they have given gifts to others, especially how gift giving made them feel.

Enrichment/ Extensions

Community Service. Students plan a giveaway in honor of a retiring teacher or administrator, a helpful nurse or custodian, or another deserving person.

📖 Reading

Giveaways

Giveaways are common during powwow celebrations. They are held to honor someone who has died, to commemorate joyful occasions (naming a child, or a son's or daughter's graduation from college), or to honor a soldier returning from war or retiring from service. Giveaways are given for young children embarking on a dancing career, for a loved one recovering from an illness, or for one who has passed on. Any occasion that calls for thankfulness might include a giveaway.

Instead of receiving gifts, the honored person and family give gifts to mark the occasion and to share their wealth. Those that have share with others as a point of honor. The more that people share their "wealth," the more honor or prestige they enjoy.

A family will save and work an entire year to stage a giveaway. Nothing is spared in the way of money or possessions. Gifts will be presented to family, friends, and often to strangers who have traveled far to attend the celebration. Giveaway goods include blankets, quilts, food, money, and even horses.

Resources

Students

Braine, Susan. *Drumbeat . . . Heartbeat: A Celebration of the Powwow.* Minneapolis, MN: Lerner Publications, 1995, 39–43.
Terrific description of giveaways with good full-color photos.

Horse Capture, George P. "Giveaways," in *Powwow.* Cody, WY: Buffalo Bill Historical Center, 1989, 32.
Personal account of a giveaway.

Tucker, Mark. "Contemporary Potlatches": 193–94; Charles James Nowell. "Play Potlatches": 103–4; Lorraine (Felix) Titus. "Potlatches": 189–90; Myrtle Lincoln. "They Give Away": 180, in *Native Heritage: Personal Accounts by American Indians 1790 to the Present*, Arlene Hirschfelder, ed. New York: Macmillan, 1995.

Video. "Giveaway at Ring Thunder." 15 minutes. 1982.
    Order from GPN, PO Box 80669, Lincoln, NE 68501. The video highlights the Lakota custom of strengthening ties to the community.

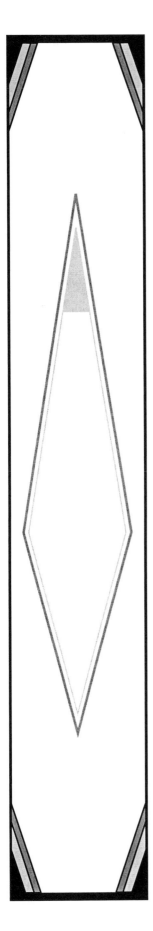

Chapter **5**

Let's Talk: Communications

Rigoberta Menchu (Quiche Maya), a recipient of the Nobel Peace Prize, said that since people always say that poor Indians can't speak and others speak for them, she learned to speak Spanish so she could speak for her people. Indian people have always been great orators and recorders of tribal histories, and today Native Americans carry on those traditions using the technology of the airwaves. They publish newspapers and operate radio and television stations. In addition, Indian reporters work for commercial presses like the *New York Daily News* and television stations like CBS. The lessons in this chapter introduce students to communications in "Indian country." If you have Native Americans in your class, they may get some of these publications and be willing to share them. However, ask them privately! Students may enjoy seeing Sherman Alexie's award-winning film, "Smoke Signals," and the parody of a reservation radio station.

Lesson

5.1

Native Press

Grade Level
7–8

Materials
Student Reading: "Native Newspapers Tell It Like It Is"; Indian newspapers; local newspapers

Time
One class period; the school year

Objectives
- Students learn that since 1828 newspapers and magazines have been published by Indian Nations, Indian individuals, and Native organizations.

- Students learn that the Indian press provides information about contemporary Native communities for Native people, while at the same time giving non-Natives a view of Native communities. The contents reflect what Native people consider to be important.

- Students learn that many U.S. newspapers do a poor job of covering Indian issues.

- Students learn to compare/contrast mainstream newspaper coverage of an Indian issue, for example, casinos with Indian newspaper coverage of the same issue.

- Students learn how to research global information sources.

Activities
1. Students read "Native Newspapers Tell It Like It Is" and discuss reasons why Indian people developed their own press.
2. Class subscribes to one of the national Indian newspapers. At least once a month, after all students have had a chance to read the paper(s), discuss five important issues in Indian country.
3. Students compare account about Indian casinos by Gel Stevenson with mainstream press. (See Lesson 7.3, page 187.)

Enrichment/Extensions
Research. Students can research the history of *Indian Country Today* (formerly called *Lakota Times*) as well as information about its founding publisher Tim Giago, Lakota, and the sale of the paper in 1998 to the Oneida Nation of New York.

📖 Reading

Native Newspapers Tell It Like It Is

From 1828 to the present, over 2,000 newspapers and magazines have been published by Indian Nations, Indian organizations, Indian individuals, Indian schools, urban Indian centers, and others. Because money for printing papers has been hard to come by, some newspapers have consisted of several mimeographed pages stapled together. While these papers did not look professional, they got the job done, providing information to people in the community. Others are full-fledged newspapers running more than 40 pages. Some of the papers ended with the first or second issue. Others folded after 30 years. But others have lasted for decades, and people around the world read them.

Today, there are several national Indian newspapers like *Indian Country Today* (weekly) and *News from Indian Country* (biweekly). (See Periodicals, page 227.) With a Native point of view, these papers cover political relations between tribes and the U.S. and state governments, gaming, legal battles, health issues, environmental issues, education, problems in Native communities, Native arts and sports, and more.

There are movie and book reviews, food recipes, photographs, poems, and opinion pieces by Native editors. Not only do Indian and non-Indian people read these papers, some senators and representatives scan them to learn what's important to Indian people.

Newspapers like *Fort Apache Scout, Cherokee One Feather*, and *Choctaw Community News* connect people within a tribe. They list tribal election dates, announce special talks at health clinics, meetings about environmental issues, festivals, and other tribal events.

Native Monthly Reader (NMR) is a newspaper especially written for all students in grades five through high school. Each month from October to May, NMR covers social studies, history and government, geography, contemporary views, language arts, science, environment, and sports from a Native point of view. Each issue always includes articles and artwork written and created by Native students.

People eager to learn about Native Americans and their communities should never depend on their local press. Nearly every American Indian community has been the subject of one-sided articles from local newspapers that feel no responsibility to Native communities and have little interest in seeking greater understanding. Many U.S. newspapers print news stories that lack cultural and/or historical information and often contain inaccuracies.

Resources

<u>Students</u>

Chu, Daniel, and Bill Shaw. "About Faces." *People* (July 22, 1991): 69–70.
    Article about Tim Giago.

Harvey, Karen D., and Lisa D. Harjo. "Tim Giago," in *Indian Country Teacher's Guide.* Golden, CO: North American Press, 1994, 81.

Johnson, Dirk. "Paper Becomes a Voice to Plains Indians." *New York Times* (September 19, 1991).
    Article about Tim Giago and *Lakota Times*.

Native Monthly Reader, PO Box 122, Crestone, CO 81131. Phone/Fax: (719) 256-4848.
    A scholastic newspaper for young adults.

<u>Teachers</u>

American Native Press Archives, University of Arkansas, Stabler Hall 502, 2801 South University Avenue, Little Rock, AR 72204-1099.
    World's largest archival collection of newspapers and periodicals by Native individuals, organizations, and tribes reflects Native publishing from 1828 to the present, with emphasis on the post–World War II period. The Archives publishes a newsletter, *American Native Press.*

Littlefield, Daniel F., Jr. "Periodicals," in *Native Americans in the Twentieth Century: An Encyclopedia.* New York: Garland, 1994, 444–45.
    History of Native American newspaper and other periodical publishing from 1828 to the present.

Littlefield, Daniel F., Jr., and James W. Parins, eds. *American Indian and Alaska Native Newspapers and Periodicals, 1925–1970.* Westport, CT: Greenwood Press, 1986.
    Also a volume 1971–1985.

Murphy, James E., and Sharon M. Murphy. *Let My People Know: American Indian Journalism, 1828–1978.* Norman, OK: University of Oklahoma Press, 1981.
    Although now a dated study, it covers the past history of the Indian press through the 1970s, limiting the study to publications "owned or managed by, intended for and speaking for Indian people."

Native American Journalists Association (NAJA).
    Established in 1984, NAJA is the largest and most significant press and organization in Native publishing. It publishes *NAJA News*, a quarterly journal.

Lesson

5.2

Native Radio Broadcasting

Grade Level
7–8

Materials
Student Readings: "Chronology of Native Radio Broadcasting" and "National Native News (NNN)"; radio; mock headset and mike

Time
One class period; the school year

Objectives
- Students learn that since the 1970s, tribal councils recognized the need to tell their stories, and so tribal radio stations began to appear.

- Students learn that National Native News (NNN), the only Indian national daily radio news program, covers important issues in Indian country.

- Students in NNN's listening areas tune in to the 10-minute program and hear firsthand Native people talking about matters that concern them. (See Appendix C for a listing of cities, call numbers, and days.)

Activities
1. Students read "Chronology of Native Radio Broadcasting" and learn that some nations have been operating their own radio stations since 1972, with some stations broadcasting in Native languages. Students discuss at least five reasons why tribes want to operate their own radio stations.
2. If "National Native News Radio Stations" (see Appendix C, page 213) is distributed to a local public radio station in the area, make arrangements for students to take turns tuning into the 10-minute program over the school year and recording the feature story. In class, set up a mock radio broadcasting center with microphone and headset. Each student can report the latest news about Indian country in mock broadcast style. Have students make up call numbers for the classroom radio station.
3. Have students monitor evening national news on television or radio to see if any station carries news about Native America. If so, have students report the story to the class.

Enrichment/Extensions
Field Trip. Students visit a local public radio broadcast studio and watch how programs are broadcast.

Research. Students can research one of the tribal radio stations or National Native News in greater depth. (See Appendix C.)

Writing. Students interested in radio broadcasting can write Youth Radio, a multicultural broadcast/journalism training program for teens dedicated to bringing youth voices to the airwaves. 1925 Martin Luther King, Jr. Way, Berkeley, CA 94704. (510) 841-5123.

📖 Reading

Chronology of Native Radio Broadcasting

Since 1972, these selected radio stations have broadcast programs in English and Native languages throughout the United States.

1972.   KTDB-FM in Ramah, New Mexico. The first Indian-owned and -operated noncommercial station in the nation. It broadcasts local, state, and national news in Navajo and English. The call letters come from Te'ochini Dinee Bi-Radio ("Radio Voice of the People"). KTDB now broadcasts from Pine Hill, New Mexico.

1975.   KRNB-FM broadcasts to Makah from Neah Bay, Washington. KEYA-AM broadcasts to Turtle Mountain Chippewa at Belcourt, North Dakota.

1976.   WOJB-FM broadcasts from Hayward, Wisconsin, to the Lac Courte Oreilles people.

1977.   KILI broadcasts from Porcupine on Oglala Sioux Pine Ridge Reservation, South Dakota. KNDN-AM broadcasts almost entirely in the Navajo language from Farmington, New Mexico.

1978.   KSHI-FM began broadcasting at Zuni Pueblo, New Mexico. KNCC-FM began broadcasting at Tsaile, Arizona, making the Navajo reservation the first reservation with two radio stations.

1982.   KNNB-FM broadcasts from Whiteriver, Arizona, to the White Mountain Apaches.

1984.   CKON-FM began broadcasting from Rooseveltown on the St. Regis Mohawk Reservation in New York.

1986.   KTNN-AM began broadcasting in Window Rock, Arizona. The radio stations air 20 percent of the programs in Navajo, Hopi, Apache, Pueblo, and Ute languages. In 1993, KTNN did the first play-by-play broadcast of an NBA game in the Navajo language during the April 24 game between the Phoenix Suns and San Antonio Spurs.

📖 Reading

National Native News (NNN)

In 1987, National Native News, beamed by satellite from Anchorage, Alaska, began broadcasting. It is the country's first and only daily radio news service covering Native American issues. From the original 30 stations using the news service (primarily in Alaska), the number has grown in 1996 to 144 public and tribal radio stations nationwide airing NNN.

National Native News is now produced in studios of the Koahnic Broadcasting Corporation, an Alaska Native organization in Anchorage, Alaska, and distributed via satellite to hundreds of radio stations. Each daily program is 10 minutes long. The first five minutes covers "hard news" about important issues affecting Native peoples. The second five-minute segment offers an in-depth feature story. Over 200 reporters throughout the nation have contributed stories that discuss everything from legislation affecting Native Americans to the ways Native people preserve identity, language, arts, and cultural lifeways.

NNN is not just for Natives. It covers pressing issues that touch Natives and non-Natives alike. These include economic development, environmental protection, health care, and urban renewal.

Resources
Students and Teachers

Haederle, Michael. "It's All Navajo, All the Time." *Chicago Tribune* (September 29, 1992).
Article concerns KNDN-AM 960 on the Navajo reservation in New Mexico.

Jones, Matthew L. "Television and Radio," in *Native America in the Twentieth Century: An Encyclopedia*, Mary Davis, ed. New York: Garland, 1994, 532–33.
General discussion.

Keith, Michael C. *Signals in the Air: Native Broadcasting in America.* New York: Praeger, 1995.
Full-length book about Native radio and television broadcasting.

Martin, Kallen. "Listen! Native Radio Can Save Languages." *Native Americas: Akwe:kon's Journal of Indigenous Issues.* Vol. 13, no. 1 (Spring 1996): 22–29.
Articles discuss how radio provides on-air language instruction along with broadcasts and programming in Native languages.

Yellowhawk, Ruth. "National Native News: The Camp Crier Comes Full Circle." *Native Peoples.* Vol. 7, no. 2 (Winter 1994).

Lesson

5.3

Native Television Reporters

Grave Level
4–8

Materials
Student Reading: "Television Reporting Native American Style"

Time
One class period

Objectives
- Students learn that several Native Americans are television reporters and that they cover news about Indians in a nonstereotypical way.

Activities
1. Students read biographies of Chino, Greene, and Kauffman and first locate the places where each was born on a map. Then locate where each now works on the map.
2. Discuss at least three reasons why it is important to have Native reporters on television.
3. Students arrange to watch Hattie Kauffman on *CBS This Morning* (broadcast week-days 7:00–9:00 A.M. EST) and compare her reporting style with other reporters.

📖 Reading

Television Reporting Native American Style

Conroy Chino, a member of Acoma Pueblo in New Mexico, has anchored Albuquerque's Channel 4 (KOB-TV) 5:30 P.M. newscast, making him one of the few Native American television news anchors in the United States.

Chino, who grew up speaking Acoma and English, has an Acoma name, *Gu We She*, that means corn silk or tassel. He was born in August when corn ripens. As a youngster, he listened to his grandfather's stories about the village and people of Acoma. These stories, he says, helped to shape his personal identity and self-esteem and gave him courage to enter an industry dominated by non-Indians.

Chino's career in television began in the early 1970s when he did general reporting. After interrupting his career to serve in a tribal office as assistant to the governor of Acoma Pueblo, he went back to television reporting in New Mexico and then covered floods, riots, and earthquakes in Los Angeles during 1991 and 1992.

As a reporter and anchor, Chino thinks he can make Native Americans more visible. "The only times the Native Americans get in the news it seems is something controversial like gaming. Or there's the powwow." Chino hopes that Indian and non-Indian viewers who see him doing a competent reporting job on television will realize that Native people are equipped to live, work, and greatly contribute to the communities in which they live and to the professions in which they have chosen to work.

Jeanie Greene, an Alaskan Inupiaq, hosts *Heartbeat Alaska*, the only Alaska television show by, for, and about Natives in Alaska. It's seen in over 250 villages in the Alaska bush, and, beamed by satellite, the program reaches northern Native people in Russia and all across Canada.

Greene, born in the logging and fishing town of Sitka in southeast Alaska, grew up listening to Eskimo stories she heard at home. She studied anthropology in college and discovered the amazing diversity of Alaska Native people. The evening news never covered any of the Native community's diversity, so she challenged the Anchorage television station to provide better coverage. Their answer was to hire Greene. She first produced and presented "Northern Lives," a five-minute Native news segment on an ABC affiliate in Anchorage. The show was so popular, she soon created and produced *Heartbeat Alaska*, an award-winning show. The Alaska Press Club gave it the 1993 Award of Excellence in the Best Public Affairs Program category.

What makes *Heartbeat Alaska* so popular with its viewers? Greene's program covers the usual hard news, but she also shows home videos by viewers. Because of the expense of getting camera crews out to remote communities of Alaska, she asked Native communities to send her home videos of community events. And they have. She has aired footage of ice floes in the Yukon River breaking up and showed a woman from the village of Savoonga reporting how hunters spared the life of a bowhead whale. To honor her fans who send her gifts, she samples on air such things as herring eggs. Says Greene, her show is "an antidote to all those negative cultural images."

Hattie Kauffman, Nez Percé, an Emmy Award–winning reporter, has been a national correspondent for *CBS This Morning* since March 1990. She heads the consumer affairs unit, providing viewers with useful information to assist them in making better consumer choices, and occasionally co-anchors the show.

Kauffman was born on the Nez Percé reservation in Idaho. Like other families, hers was poor and hungry, and her parents were gone a lot. During her childhood, television kept her company. In Seattle, where her family moved, she watched a television news reporter who she knew was Indian. That reporter stuck in Hattie Kauffman's mind.

It wasn't long before Hattie entered the world of media. She worked for the University of Minnesota radio program during her four years of college, but that's not what she wanted to do. She wanted to work in television news. Persistence and drive paid off. Before long she got a one-year apprenticeship as a reporter at KING-TV, the NBC affiliate in Seattle. It turned into a full reporter position that lasted six years, from 1981 to 1987.

In 1987, Hattie joined *Good Morning America* and left three years later to join *CBS This Morning*.

When she worked at *Good Morning America*, she took a camera crew to Lapwai, Idaho, her hometown, to cover her high school basketball team. With barely any funding for sports, the team had beaten other Idaho teams 66 games in a row. The story never would have happened if Hattie Kauffman hadn't pushed for it.

Resources

Students

Elder, Sean, and John Hannah. "Northern Star: Flamboyant TV Host Jeanie Greene's Offbeat Alaskan Show Finds a National Audience." *People* (August 22, 1994): 95–96.

Teachers

Jones, Matthew L. "Radio and Television," in *Native America in the Twentieth Century: An Encyclopedia*. New York: Garland, 1994, 532–33.

Article points out that totally controlled television stations are almost nonexistent, although some tribes are looking into it. Also notes only a few Native American professional broadcasters are in television work compared to other ethnic groups.

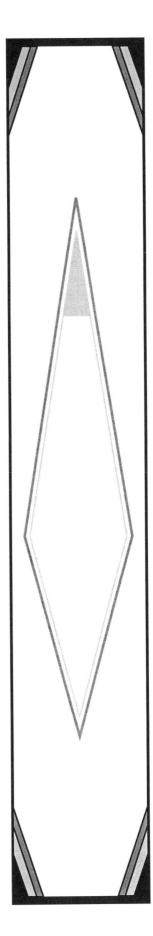

Chapter 6

Walk in Beauty: Arts

It is often said that all Indians are artists. At one time, that was probably true, because Indians made even the smallest everyday objects into works of art. However, this book is about contemporary Indians, and although many Native people still make creations of great beauty (jewelry, clothing, and rattles, to name a few), most go unrecognized. In this chapter, we present Native artists who have been recognized for their talents. Activities to motivate students to create their own art and activities are included. The doll lesson can be used with the map exercises or many other lessons in the book. The story bag activity has delighted both aspiring and reluctant writers!

Joseph Bruchac, Abenaki, took time out of his busy schedule to let us interview him. Christina Bryant, Cherokee/Shinnecock, an artist and teacher in the New York City area, contributes the Visual Arts lesson. Maestro Ray Evans Harrell, Oklahoma Cherokee, a voice and performance teacher in New York City, helped immensely with the Performing Arts section.

Lesson

6.1

Written Arts

Grade Level
4–8

Materials
Student Readings: "Joe Bruchac" and "Storyteller Bags"; pouches or bags (storyteller bags must be constructed either before or during this activity (see Contemporary-Style Native American Pouches, page 130)

Time
Four or five classroom periods; ongoing yearly reading project

Objectives
- Students will compose a story based on an event in their lives.

- Students will appreciate and become familiar with Native American writers.

- Students will begin to acquire skills for public speaking and oral interpretations.

- Students will become familiar with a Lenni Lenape storytelling technique.

- Students will practice listening to one another.

- Students will begin to develop the ability to critique writings.

Activities
First class

1. Read "Joe Bruchac" to the class. Locate Vermont and New York on a map. Ask students to compile a list of techniques, events, etc. that Joseph uses in his writing. Put their list on the board.

2. Ask them to explain the difference between oral history and written history. How did and do Native Americans use the two? Ask students for examples from other cultures, for example, the stories in the Bible were handed down for generations until they were finally written. Ask students for examples of how people recorded information other than writing it in a book: pictographs, wampum belts, hieroglyphics, etc.

3. Homework. Students will bring an example from their homes of a family story or event and how it is preserved. Births could be recorded in a family bible; souvenirs from a vacation could be kept in a scrapbook; grandfather may tell the story of how his parents came to this country, etc.

Second Class

1. Review "Joe Bruchac." Ask students to share examples they have brought from home. List different sources on the board.
2. Explain to students that they are going to use a Lenni Lenape technique for preserving stories. Locate historical and contemporary Lenape people (Delaware) on a map. Read "Storyteller Bags." Students will compose a story for their storyteller bags and share it with the class. Ask them to take a few moments to think about a personal story or event that they would like to pass down to their children and descendants.
3. Homework. Write the story for next class and bring an object to symbolize the story; examples include: photograph, souvenir, postcard, game piece, tooth, earring, etc. These are props to jog their memories.

Third Class

1. Review "Storyteller Bags." Divide the class into small groups and have them share their stories, helping each other with grammar, structure, clarity, etc. Check to see if objects match stories. Stress that this is a group project, no competition or ridicule allowed. These stories are very personal and subjective accounts that they want to stay in their families forever. Pretend that they will be shared with students' great, great, great, great grandchildren in the twenty-second century.

Fourth and Fifth Classes

1. Students have improved their written stories; now it is time to practice oral delivery in their groups. Remind them that Joseph Bruchac feels he is a good writer because he has a good memory and knows how to be a good listener. After they feel ready to share their story bags with the entire class, each student will put the object in the story bag and proceed as in "Storyteller Bags."

Enrichment/Extensions

Art. Students can design an album of all their stories and display their storyteller bags.

Career Exploration. Have students investigate all the different kinds of writing professions.

Community Service. Visit elderly people in the community and ask them to share stories. Sometimes elderly people just need someone to listen. Ask them for permission to write their stories and make a booklet. Students can perform their storyteller bags for the elderly or other children.

Creative Writing. Students can write a report of their book(s) by Native authors; make sure they include author's Nation.

Geography. Students can locate their authors on a class map of the United States.

Literature/Reading. Students can read books by Native American authors. There is a list provided in this lesson.

📖 Reading

Joe Bruchac

Joseph opened the door, stepped outside, and smiled at the morning sun, the land of the dawn, the east, the place that marks the beginning of each day. Descended from the Abenaki, Joseph imagined his ancestors greeting this same sun a few centuries before, not far from the place where he now stood. They would have given thanks for the new day as it was their custom to give thanks for all of creation. In fact, Abenaki means People of the Dawnland in the Abenaki or Wabanki language.

Joseph closed his eyes and felt the sun on his face. It felt friendly and warm. Opening his ears, he listened to the birds singing their plans for the day, the bees chatting with the clover, and the frogs scolding the flies that got away.

A whiff of marigolds that were planted around the garden almost made Joseph sneeze. He hoped the tingly scent would have the same effect on the rabbits and discourage them from eating all the lettuce. The old folks had told him to plant marigolds around his garden to keep the little critters away. Because he wanted to share with the animals, he had planted some vegetables just for them without a protective ring of marigolds. Hopefully, they would leave some vegetables for his family. Now he could smell ripe peppers, tomatoes, and cucumbers. Delicious!

Joseph ran his tongue around his teeth, enjoying the sharp taste of peppermint toothpaste. Well, it seemed as if all his senses were working this morning: sight, touch, sound, smell, and taste. The senses are important to writers and Joseph Bruchac is a writer, a gifted storyteller who is able to give readers the smell, taste, sight, touch, and sound of a story from the pages of a book.

Growing up in the small town of Greenfield Center, New York, Joseph lived with his grandparents in the very house where he now lives. It is close to the Adirondack Mountains and forests, a place to farm and fish and appreciate the natural world. His grandparents, Jesse and Marion Bowman, owned a general store, and Joseph often helped stock shelves or wait on customers. He loved to sit around the woodstove and listen to the tall tales of the farmers, lumberjacks, and elders. He began to develop the skills of listening and remembering; both would help him become a great writer.

Joseph's grandfather could barely read and write, but he taught Joseph important things like how to walk quietly in the woods, how to fish, and how to discipline without spanking. His grandmother was a law school graduate, and although she never practiced law, she taught him to read. Their house was filled with books and Joe was always reading. He especially liked stories about animals.

In elementary school, Joseph began to write and wrote some poems to his teacher. When she read one to the class, some bigger boys got jealous and beat him up after school. Joseph calls them his first hostile literary critics! Authors often have their work reviewed in newspapers and journals; sometimes the reviewers say good things and other times they say bad things about the author's story, poem, or essay.

Joseph grew up and attended college, where he met his wife, Carol. Together they moved to Africa where he taught. He said that he learned a lot from his students and feels that his time in Africa added to the richness of his life experiences, contributing to his work as a writer. Joseph's grandfather wanted Joseph, his wife, and his baby son to return to Greenfield Center, and they did.

Joseph always loved hearing stories from Native American elders and remembered them word for word. He told them to his sons and eventually he began to write them down. His first book of stories was published in 1975.

He wanted to share his gift of writing, and Joseph worked in a prison for several years, teaching inmates English and writing skills. He also taught poetry and storytelling to Native Americans, which he still does today. He once received a great honor, which he shares in the chapter titled, "Giving" from his autobiography, *Bowman's Store: A Journey to Myself.*

Each year I go to the Onondaga Indian Reservation in the center of New York State, the place where the hearth fire of the Iroquois League of Peace is kept. There I do poetry and storytelling workshops with the children of the Onondaga Nation School. And in 1980 I was given an Iroquois name.

On that particular day, I had finished class for the morning and was about to go to lunch.

Dewasentah wants to see you at her house, I was told.

I walked outside and saw Dewasentah coming toward me from her house, which is just down the road from the school. I had first met Dewasentah when I was a student at Syracuse University in 1965 and used to ride my Harley Davidson motorcycle out to the reservation. One of my dearest friends at Onondaga, she is one of the elders of their nation and the Clan Mother of the Eel Clan. She held something in her hands.

You've been coming here for such a long time, she said. And the way you use words, it has to be a gift from the Creator. So it is about time you had an Iroquois name.

She handed me what she was holding—a small lacrosse stick and an envelope with a name written on it: Gah-neh-go-he-yoh. Inside the envelope was an eagle feather.

That name, she said, Gah-neh-go-he-yoh, means The Good Mind. You know we believe that everyone has within them both a good mind and a mind that isn't good. This name will remind you that you always have to try to use your gift of words in a good way.

Joseph has lived up to his name, The Good Mind, and uses his gift of words in a good way. He has published dozens of books and cofounded Wordcraft, an organization that helps to ensure that the voices of Native writers and storytellers are heard throughout the world. Wordcraft sponsors a program where experienced Indian writers work with new writers, hold seminars and workshops for writers, and inform writers of opportunities. Joseph also helps writers by critiquing their works. He gives back his gift, as is the custom of Native Americans.

Sometimes it is difficult for Native American writers to sell their work. Publishers would often rather use non-Indian writers to write about Indian people. Joseph realized that he was fortunate to have his works published and started the North American Native Authors Catalog, which specializes in works by American Indian poets, writers, historians, storytellers, and performers. From his upstate home, Joseph and his family offer 600 different titles from novels and newspapers to children's literature. Native authors now have a place that sells their work! In 1992, the project helped put together a gathering of Native American writers held at the University of Oklahoma, called Returning the Gift. More than 200 Indian authors from across the continent attended! The gathering is held annually.

Joseph Bruchac is a busy man. Not only does he write and teach across the nation, but he travels all over the world performing storytelling, sometimes with his sister and sons in their group, the Dawnland Singers. Still he tries to be at home all summer enjoying his family, gardens, and writing.

Joseph looks up at the hill and sees his little cabin bright in the morning sun and realizes that it is time to begin work. He built the cabin away from the house so he could have a quiet, peaceful place to write. Sometimes Joseph has a deadline to complete a book and he has to work late into the night, but even if he does not have a deadline, he works from three to four hours a day just writing. Although he does not have a nine-to-five job, he has to work hard and follow a routine, probably working longer than he would if he had a regular job.

Joseph is looking forward to this afternoon, when he will speak to a group of students who want to be writers. He will tell them, "Be a really good listener. Write all the time. Don't worry about getting every word correct or in the right place. I'm a good writer, but I am a really good rewriter."

With that thought, Joseph Bruchac sets out for his work, across the same yard where Grampa and Gramma Bowman played with him as a child.

📖 Reading

Storyteller Bags

The Lenni Lenape peoples originally lived in the northeastern part of the United States, including New Jersey and New York. They were named the Delaware (see Lesson 2.1, page 18) and were forced westward by the Europeans. Today, some Lenape people still live in the Northeast, but most live in communities in Oklahoma and Canada.

Although some nations historically had a system of writing, others did not and had to remember everything. Their memories were excellent and operated almost like the computers we rely on today. Stories and oral histories were learned word for word, there was no room left for artistic interpretation! In some tribes, young people were evaluated for their ability to listen, remember, and repeat long historical accounts with every pause and sentence exactly correct. The people who excelled in these areas were educated to become orators and keepers of the knowledge and history. Because of the great oratorical and memory skills of American Indians, many ancient stories have been preserved to the present day. That is one reason why Native people do not always agree with the way that anthropologists and archaeologists interpret Native cultures from long ago. The scientists attempt to interpret the past, without even knowing the language, by looking in graves or garbage heaps. Native people, who have the gift of the oral traditions or histories, can often set the story straight!

The Lenapes, like most other Indian people, are wonderful storytellers. They traditionally do not tell stories in the summer because they believed that people should be busy tending their crops, not sitting around listening to stories and being idle. Remember that there were no supermarkets years ago, and if people did not grow enough food to last through the winter, they would starve. So if the Lenni Lenape got caught neglecting their crops, the spirits would send bugs to eat their harvests.

If the Lenape people must tell stories in the summer, they first say they are sitting on 12 skunk skins because the insects will stay away!

A technique that the Lenni Lenape people use to preserve their stories is a storyteller bag. The storyteller keeps a bag of mementos to remind him or her of the stories. When it is time for storytelling, they dump out the contents of their bags, select an object, and tell the story that goes with the object. If they tell a story of a horse, for instance, they may have some horse hair in their bags, or a story about the creation of corn could be prompted by a corn kernel. After story time is over, they put all the items back into the bag and say, "and now I tie it up."

Resources

For the best selection of books by Native authors to buy, please see the catalog section. Check the Bibliography and Resources in each chapter as well.

Students

Armstrong, Jeannette (Okanagan). *Slash*. Toronto, ON: Theytus Books, 1990.
This strong story recounts a young man's life on his reservation and his development as a political activist.

Awiakta, Marilou (Cherokee). *Abiding Appalachia: Where Mountain and Atom Meet*. Memphis, TN: St. Luke's Press, 1994.
The author grew up on the atomic frontier in Tennessee. Her poetry poses problems and solutions.

Brass, Eleanor. *I Walk in Two Worlds*. New York: Glenbow, 1987.
An activist and an author, Brass was born on the Peepeekisis Reserve in Saskatchewan and shares her family life and how she developed confidence and courage.

Bruchac, Joseph (Abenaki). *Turtle Meat*. Duluth, MN: Holy Cow! Press, 1992.
A collection of short stories, including contemporary, this book has humor, warmth and tragedy. Although Mr. Bruchac usually recounts traditional stories, his many books are appropriate at any time. Some of his works are: *A Boy Called Slow* (the true story of Sitting Bull's

childhood); *Dawn Land* (this book has everything—romance, adventure, humor, mystery); *The Faithful Hunter* (Abenaki stories); and *Thirteen Moons on Turtle's Back* (storytelling poems).

Conley, Robert (Cherokee). *The Witch of Goingsnake.* Norman, OK: University of Oklahoma Press, 1992.
   This book has short stories, all exciting, many dealing with the Indian world squeezed by white culture. Any of his books are recommended.

Hirschfelder, Arlene, and Beverly Singer (Tewa/Navajo), selectors. *Rising Voices: Writings of Young Native Americans.* New York: Charles Scribner's Sons, 1992.
   This book features poetry and prose spanning a century. Some of the topics covered are identity, family, homelands, and education. Very interesting and often compelling reading.

King, Thomas (Cherokee). *Green Grass, Running Water.* New York: Houghton Mifflin, 1993.
   A superb storyteller, King blends his contemporary Blackfeet characters with Coyote himself. Look for his other books, too.

Littlechild, George (Cree). *This Land Is My Land.* San Francisco: Children's Book Press, 1993.
   An artist, Littlechild's book is filled with art, humor, truth, and all kinds of wonderful stories.

McNickle, D'Arcy (Salish/Kootenai). *The Surrounded.* Albuquerque, NM: University of New Mexico Press, 1936.
   Any of his books are good for seventh grade and up. This one is about a man torn between his parents' separate cultures.

Monture, Joel (Mohawk). *Cloud Walker: Contemporary Native American Stories.* Golden, CO: Fulcrum Kids, 1996.
   Featuring stories of contemporary children from different tribes, this book will appeal to fourth-graders or older students on a lower reading level.

Ortiz, Simon (Acoma). *The People Shall Continue.* San Francisco: Children's Book Press, 1988.
   This is about the best account of the invasion of America for children. It offers the truth and a little bit of hope. Inviting illustrations.

Riley, Patricia, ed. (Cherokee). *Growing Up Native American: An Anthology.* New York: William Morrow, 1993.
   This anthology has excerpts from fiction and nonfiction, from the United States and Canada by Luther Standing Bear (Lakota); Ignatia Broker (Ojibway); Joseph Bruchac (Abenaki); Lame Deer (Lakota); Ella Deloria (Dakota); Michael Dorris (Modoc); Black Elk (Lakota); Louise Erdrich (Chippewa); Francis LaFlesche (Omaha); Eric L. Gansworth (Onondaga); Geary Hobson (Cherokee/Chickasaw); Linda Hogan (Chickasaw); Sara Winnemucca Hopkins (Paiute); Basil Johnston (Ojibway); Lee Maracle (Metis); John Josephs Mathew (Osage); N. Scott Momaday (Kiowa); Simon Ortiz (Acoma); Louis Owens (Choctaw/Cherokee); Vicki Sears (Cherokee); Leslie Marmon Silko (Laguna Pueblo); and Anna Lee Walters (Pawnee/Otoe).

Roman, Trish Fox, ed. (Ojibway). *Voices Under One Sky: Contemporary Native Literature.* Freedom, CA: Crossing Press, 1994.
   These stories and poems have strong cultural ties.

Walters, Anna Lee (Pawnee/Otoe). *Ghost Singer.* Albuquerque, NM: University of New Mexico Press, 1988.
> A murder mystery surrounding the theft of sacred Navajo objects. Traditional rituals must save the day.

Wheeler, Jordan (Metis). *Brothers in Arms.* Toronto, ON: Pemmican, 1989.
> These short stories tell about the lives of three Indian brothers in Canada.

Teachers

Brant, Beth, ed. (Mohawk). *A Gathering of Spirit: A Collection by North American Indian Women.* New York: Firebrand Books, 1988.
> Several of these stories can be used with students. Gives a realistic glimpse of indigenous women from their perspective.

Bruchac, Joseph, ed. (Abenaki). *Returning the Gift: Poetry and Prose from the First North American Native Writers Festival.* Tucson, AZ: University of Arizona Press, 1992.
> New writers, as well as familiar ones like Linda Hogan and Simon Ortiz, have selections in this anthology. Appropriate for the classroom.

Green, Rayna, ed. (Cherokee). *That's What She Said.* Bloomington, IN: University of Indiana Press, 1984.
> This collection of contemporary poetry and fiction by Native American women is filled with humor, sadness, tragedy, and optimism. Can be adapted for the classroom.

Hirschfelder, Arlene, ed. *Native Heritage: Personal Accounts by American Indians, 1790 to the Present.* New York: Macmillan, 1995.
> Taken from written and oral histories, autobiographies, and other sources, this anthology features 120 narratives. Some of the authors are Simon Ortiz, N. Scott Momaday, Barney Old Coyote, Bea Medicine, and Anna Lee Walters. Several accounts are suitable for the classroom.

Lerner, Andrea, ed. *Dancing on the Rim of the World.* Tucson, AZ: University of Arizona Press, 1982.
> Prose and poetry by Indians from the Northwest are featured.

A Few More Native American Authors

Alexie, Sherman (Spokane/Coeur d'Alene). *Tonto and the Lone Ranger Fistfight in Heaven.* New York: Atlantic Monthly Press, 1993.

Allen, Paula Gunn (Laguna). *As Long as the Rivers Flow: The Stories of Nine Native Americans.* New York: Scholastic Press, 1996.

Benai, Edward Benton (Ojibway). *The Mishomis Book: The Voice of the Ojibway.* St. Paul, MN: Indian Country Press, 1979.

Broker, Ignatia (Ojibway). *Night Flying Woman: An Ojibway Narrative.* St. Paul, MN: Minnesota Historical Society, 1983.

Deloria, Ella Carr (Dakota/Sioux). *Waterlily.* Lincoln, NE: University of Nebraska Press, 1988.

Dorris, Michael (Modoc). *Morning Girl.* New York: Hyperion, 1992.

Eastman, Charles Alexander (Dakota/Sioux). *Indian Boyhood.* New York: Dover, 1902 reprint.

Erdrich, Louise (Chippewa). *Grandmother's Pigeon.* New York: Hyperion, 1996.

Harjo, Joy (Creek). *She Had Some Horses.* New York: Thunder's Mouth Press, 1983.

Henson, Lance (Cheyenne). *Selected Poems 1970–1983.* Greenfield Center, NY: Greenfield Review Press, 1985.

Kegg, Maude (Ojibway). *Portag Lake: Memories of an Ojibwe Childhood.* Minneapolis, MN: University of Minnesota Press, 1991.
Includes text in Ojibway.

Mankiller, Wilma. *Mankiller: A Chief and Her People.* New York: St. Martin's Press, 1993.

Medicine Story (Wampanoag). *The Children of the Morning Light: Wampanoag Tales as Told by Manitonquat.* New York: Macmillan, 1994.

Momaday, Natachee Scott (Cherokee). *Owl in the Cedar Tree.* Flagstaff, AZ: Northland, 1965.

Mourning Dove (Colville). *Mourning Dove: A Salishan Autobiography.* Lincoln, NE: University of Nebraska Press, 1990.
(Christine Quintasket.)

Niatum, Duane (Klallam). *Ascending Red Cedar Moon.* New York: Harper & Row, 1969.

Ross, Gayle (Cherokee). *How Rabbit Tricked Otter: And Other Cherokee Stories.* New York: HarperCollins, 1996.

Sneve, Virgina Driving Hawk (Lakota). *Completing the Circle.* Lincoln, NE: University of Nebraska Press, 1995.

Tall Mountain, Mary (Koyukon). *The Light on the Tent Wall.* Los Angeles: University of California American Indian Studies Center, 1990.

Tapahonso, Luci (Navajo). *Sáanii Oahataal—The Women Are Singing: Poems and Stories.* Tucson, AZ: University of Arizona Press, 1993.

Trafzer, Clifford [aka Richard Red Hawk] (Wynadot). *Creation of a Californian Tribe: Grandfather's Maidu Indian Tales.* Newcastle, CA: Sierra Oaks, 1987.

Lesson

6.2

Visual Arts

Contemporary Native American Dolls

Grade Level

4–8

Materials

Student Reading: "Dolls"; cotton muslin 12½ inches by 8 inches (enough for each student); big eye needle; white cotton thread; polyester fill; fabric glue (Sobo/Tacky glue); doll pattern; straight pins; pencil; shears

Time

Five classroom periods

Objectives

- Students will learn that visual art has been an integral part of Native American traditions and lifeways.

- Students will learn that artistic expression shows distinct differences among the many tribes that comprise the First Nation peoples.

- Students will appreciate how the intricate care and protection of the environment was and is expressed in Native American visual art.

- Students will learn how communities and family members honor each other and pass on the history of their people through the expression of visual art.

- Students will learn that the most beautiful and expressive art was created in celebration of spiritual traditions.

- Students will construct and dress a doll (Figure 6.1) and appreciate the many different styles of dress. They will acquire skills in researching First Nation peoples.

Figure 6.1. Doll by Christina Bryant.
Photograph by John Goodwin.

Activities

1. Divide the class into groups. Assign a Native Nation from the Southwest, Northwest, Southeast, Northeast, Plains, or the West to research. Have students investigate traditional and contemporary dress of the assigned Native Nation. Have students dress their doll in either traditional or contemporary outfits. Students can make a report about the people, the state where they live, and how the people are living either on or off reservations (i.e., cities, towns, rural areas). The doll will accompany the report.

2. Duplicate the pattern for doll construction and give a copy to each student (Figure 6.2). Have students cut out the pattern around the outside of the doll line. Give each student two precut muslin pieces and the four straight pins.

3. Have students place one pin in the head of the doll, one at the feet, and one at each arm of the doll (Figure 6.3, page 124). When the doll is pinned, give out shears to cut out the fabric doll pattern. Students should cut around the outside of the doll line.

4. Place fabric-cut doll patterns together and pin at the head, feet, and arms (Figure 6.4, page 124). Give each student a sewing needle and yard length of cotton thread. Have students thread the needle.

5. Begin sewing two inches from the bottom of the doll. Students should pull the thread through the back of the doll pattern, leaving one inch of thread (Figure 6.5, page 125). Tie threads together, tying two knots. Using a simple basting stitch, sew around the pattern of the doll close to the doll edge. Keep stitches close together (Figures 6.6A and 6.6B, page 125).

6. When sewing is complete, turn the doll inside out (like a sock) and begin stuffing the doll from the bottom opening. Push stuffing into the head and neck first. Stuff hands, arms, and chest, until firm. Push stuffing into the doll with a pencil. When stuffing is complete, sew the bottom of the doll closed.

7. The doll is now ready for features and hair. Use fabric or permanent markers. Colored yarn can be glued or sewn onto the head for hair. Ready-made eyes can be glued onto the face. (Use Sobo or Tacky glue.) Use fabric scraps for clothes. A simple shirt or dress can be cut by folding a square piece of cloth about six by six inches and cutting out an upside-down "L" shape two inches long and a small slit for the head. A simple ribbon shirt for a boy can be created by adding ribbon strips across the back of the shirt, along the sleeves, and down the front of the shirt. Any color pants can be drawn or painted onto the doll itself. By increasing the length of the cloth by an additional six inches, a long dress can be made. By adding ribbons in the same manner as for the shirt, a ribbon dress can be created.

Enrichment/Extensions

Art. Students can create a picture book about their doll. Students can research and make a collage of the many types of dolls sold in stores.

Creative Writing. Students can write a history/story about their doll. Students can research the history of doll making among cultures around the world or focus on their particular culture. Students can research and write about different dolls used by boys and girls.

Field Trip. If possible, arrange a class trip to a doll factory, toy store, museum, or store that specializes in displaying and selling dolls from different cultures.

Oral History. If a student knows someone who makes or collects dolls, ask the student to interview them. (See Appendix A, page 209.) The student can also invite that person to class to present dolls to the class and lecture.

Figure 6.2. Pattern for doll construction.

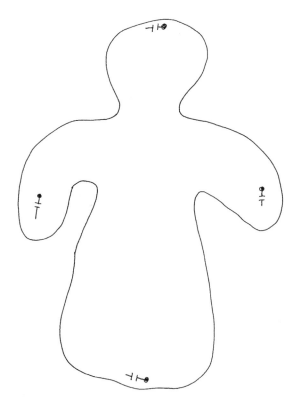

Figure 6.3. Pin placement for doll.

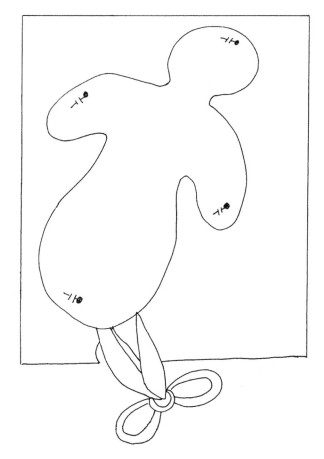

Figure 6.4. Fabric placement for doll.

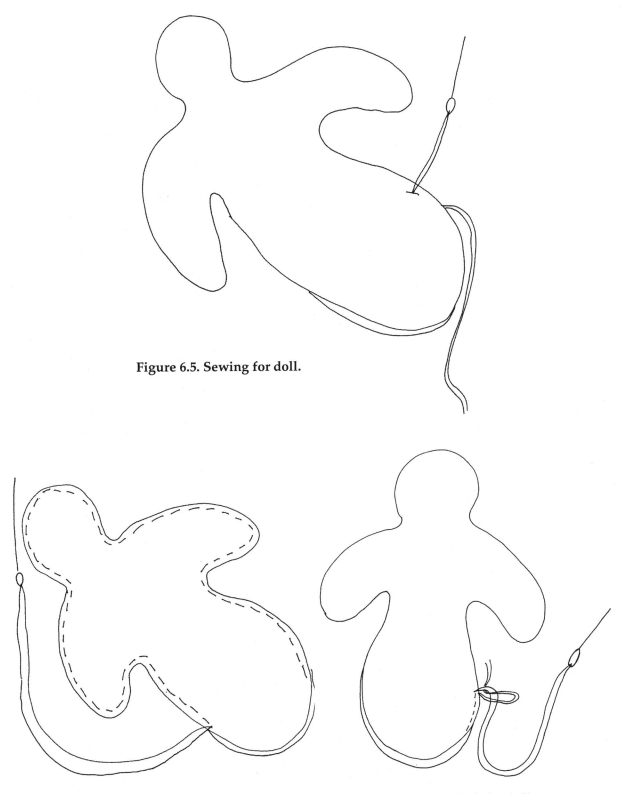

Figure 6.5. Sewing for doll.

Figure 6.6A. Basting stitch for doll.

Figure 6.6B. Basting stitch for doll.

📖 Reading

Dolls

by Christina Bryant

Visual art has always been an integral part of the traditions and lifeways of First Nation peoples of the Americas long before Europeans came to our country. We still wear our traditional dress on special occasions, at ceremonies and socials. First Nation peoples also wear traditional dress at gatherings known as powwows, which are held all year long all across America, both indoors and outside. Often the objects of visual art are created for a giveaway to celebrate a birth, wedding, honoring a warrior who served in the armed forces, a loved one who has passed, someone who has honored their people and/or family through their good deeds, or for sale/trade at the pow-wow. Students will learn that these customs are still celebrated in a contemporary expression of First Nation peoples' visual art.

Many state museums carry examples of the traditional arts and crafts work of First Nation peoples. These same museums also display contemporary arts of the people as well. The contemporary art of First Nation peoples is a unique blending of traditional expressions of the various cultures in nontraditional ways. Elders like Iris Red Elk Allrunner (Yanktonai Sioux) and Marlys M. Stiffarm (Gros Ventre), both master quilt makers, incorporate traditional ideas in modern quilt making that began before the turn of the century. Jamie Tawodi Reason (Cherokee), who has taken the art of carving cedar boxes used to hold sacred items (like gourd rattles and fans long ago), now paints them in bright colors, focusing on nature and the spiritual aspects of nature as it relates to First Nation peoples past and present. Terrance Guardipee-Last Eagle (Blackfeet) says, "I want my paintings to portray the visions and oral traditions of the Pikuni People so that the outside world may have a better understanding of traditional art through the eyes and spirit of a Pikuni member portraying traditional art." Leonda Fast Buffalo Horse (Blackfeet) has also carried this feeling into her work as a stained-glass artist. She incorporates into her art a variety of raw materials including beads, rawhide, and buckskin, along with found objects. She was able to fine-tune her craft with help from the Lodge Pole Gallery located on the Blackfeet reservation. This is an organization that provides traditional artists to teach the young the old ways used to create visual art. This gallery affords young artists of various Nations the ability to perfect their artistic skills. They are one of many such organizations both on and off the reservation that support and advance the artistic skills of young people.

The art of doll making is an ancient art among First Nation peoples across the Americas. Dolls were and are an integral part of childhood. Parents created dolls for children, who often learned the skills needed as adults when they created clothing and homes for their dolls. Some early explorers (Vitus Bering, 1741, and Captain James Cook, 1778, and missionaries to the Arctic) believed that dolls created by these people were the first dolls in North America. They reported seeing children playing with many different types. This is, of course, not true, as people of many nations created dolls reflecting their cultural tradition across North America.

Dolls of the people in the Arctic were made of clay, bone, antler, stone, ivory, cloth, and skins of various animals of the area. Dolls for girls mirrored grown women, complete with babies carried in the hood. Dolls belonging to boys were equipped with kayaks and harpoons reminding them of the hunters they would become. When visitors came, often dolls were brought out and lined up to scrutinize and greet the newcomers. Some dolls slept in the same bed as their owner, unless the children were the Ingalik of eastern Alaska. The Ingalik people feared evil spirits would enter the doll's body at night and harm the child. In some regions, girl dolls always had frowns and boy dolls always smiled.

Today, there are doll artists who create dolls as art, like Dolly Spencer from Cape Krusenstern. Her dolls are bought by collectors and have been featured in many museums like the Alaska State Museum. She learned sewing from her mother, Grace Mendenhall. Her craftswork and minute detail are unparalleled in contemporary Alaskan doll making. Her dolls are created in a traditional manner using all skin materials sewn with sinew she prepares from caribou tendons. She carves doll heads from birch, and their features often mimic well-known Alaskans.

Forest-dwelling people of the East and Mideast created their dolls from a combination of cornhusks, wood, apples, rawhide, cloth, or horse or human hair. The Iroquois people created a cornhusk doll without a face. Using horse or human hair, it was braided in Iroquois style. Some dolls were left faceless for fear a doll with human features might come alive. This was believed by many Nations, like the Kiowas, who banned dolls. However, the Delaware Nation created dolls for use in religious rites, rather than as toys.

Among the Chippewa and woodland tribes of North Dakota and Minnesota regions, the people created their dolls of buckskin with floral-style beadwork. Young girls received dolls made of cattails, pine needles, and leaves, while older girls received dolls made of slippery elm bark. After 1850, with the introduction of stroud cloth, rag dolls were stuffed with dried moss with large faces. As traditional dress changed over the years, doll dress mirrored the influence of European styles.

Among the Southeast people like the Seminoles, with the invention of the sewing machine after the 1870s, dolls mirrored the colorful patchwork clothing of the people. A little girl received her first strand of beads at the age of one. Every year more were added until she reached middle age. At this mature age a strand was removed every year until only one was left. The female dolls reflect this ancient tradition. Beaded necklaces, black bonnet hats, and patchwork dresses identify female dolls; small red hats and patchwork tunics denote the male dolls. The dolls were carved from wood or palmetto fibers and were made primarily for sale. Children, however, were left to play with bundles of rags or a stick wrapped in a piece of cloth.

Among the Cherokee of the Appalachian Mountain area, dolls were made of cloth with embroidered features. Dolls were also fashioned of cornhusk, cherry wood, and buckskin. Carved wooden dolls were created by men, but were dressed by women. Although Cherokee people didn't create dolls out of clay, in my art I incorporate the use of clay or cotton and dress the dolls in deerskin of long ago. My dolls reflect the belief of my people that there is a spirit in all living things. As the earth brings forth plants that sustain life, I create a doll that represents that plant. The mature flower ready for pollination to continue life is reflected in the face of a mature Cherokee female. I call the dolls Yvonne's Garden after a dear friend.

Plains girls practiced adult skills in fashioning and decorating clothing on their dolls. They carried their dolls in tiny beaded cradleboards, which were copies of their own cradleboards as infants. Before pony beads were introduced by traders, dolls were decorated with quillwork. By the 1840s, tiny seed beads were introduced. Translucent beads appeared in the 1870s, followed by metallic beads of the 1880s. A doll's age can often be determined by studying the size and coloring of the beaded decoration. The Lakota/Dakota people were masters of the most intricate beadwork, even beading the bottoms of their dolls' moccasins. This practice increased the doll's value.

Parents sometimes made small tipis for their daughters, who would arrange them in the same format as the larger village. The inside of the mini-tipi mirrored the inside of their families' homes. Often young male relatives would hunt small furry creatures like squirrels, mice, and moles for their fur for clothes and meat for small feasts. Like the people of the Southeast, everyday play dolls of the Plains were made of rags tied together and wrapped with a piece of cloth for hair or a shawl. While mostly girls played with dolls, boys sometimes had dolls, accompanied by horses.

Dolls were not always created for play. Sometimes an elaborately clothed doll was hung inside the tipi to remind children of their rich heritage. Rhonda Holy Bear (Lakota), a renowned Plains doll artist, began making dolls when just a young girl. She created her dolls out of whatever she could find. Her dolls are made from cloth or a combination of cloth and wood, some entirely of wood or constructed with a wire skeletal system. Holy Bear's dolls reflect the rich heritage of her people. The clothing are miniature replicas of ceremonial clothes worn depicting pre- and postreservation life. She was the first doll artist to receive a fellowship from the Southwestern Association on Indian Affairs. Holy Bear's dolls are exhibited at the Wheelwright Museum in Santa Fe, New Mexico; the Sioux Indian Museum in Rapid City, South Dakota; among other places.

For centuries the Hopi have lived on the high mesas of the Southwest. Hopi spiritual traditions are built around their desert environment. Dolls called kachinas represent the spirits that help ensure Hopi survival. A kachina is a spirit being who is impersonated by a man wearing a mask. When a man dons a kachina mask, he believes he has become one with the spirit. The men participate in ceremonial dances that guarantee the survival of the Hopi people. Hopi and Zuni people both celebrate rites concerning children at an annual festival. Masks are sometimes very frightening, scaring children into good behavior. The kachinas distribute sweets and toys like bows and arrows to boys and kachina dolls to girls.

Kachina dolls are presented to infants of both sexes as good-luck symbols. After babyhood is far behind, only girls receive the dolls. As infants, a kachina is attached to the cradleboard and is made simply. As the girl grows older, the dolls become more elaborate. They are often hung from the rafters of their homes to remind them of their heritage.

The dolls were always created by men using the dried roots of the cottonwood tree. They were covered with a thin white clay and painted using mineral and/or vegetable colors. Today, dolls are still created for children, but they are also elaborately made as contemporary doll art by master artists like Brian Honyouti of Hotevilla, Arizona and his younger brother, Ronald. They have experimented with many different varnishes, wood preservers, and oil paints to bring their dolls to life. Where before bits of cloth and feathers were attached to the doll, now craftsmen, like the Honyouti brothers, carve all the parts of the dolls out of wood.

While men only once carved kachina dolls, now women also carve them. Muriel Cainimptewa is one of the finest carvers of miniature dolls (from 3 to 4¼ inches tall). Her work, and the work of the Honyouti brothers and many other master craftspeople, are in museums and private collections around the country.

Native children of the Northwest played with simple makeshift dolls made of clay, bark, wood, and cloth. The Yurok of Oregon used a bluish mud found near streams to fashion dolls. The children carried the dolls in miniature cradle baskets. The Klamath felt doll playing was such an important part of childhood, a girl's mother or grandmother showed her how to make and play with dolls. Tlingits made simple dolls from pebbles that were pounded into shape with a hammerstone. Klikitat parents created dolls from steamed leather, dressing them in fur-trimmed parkas. The noses, eyes, and mouths were made of beads.

These are only samples of how many Native peoples across the Americas emphasized the creation of dolls as an integral part of growing up. The tradition is kept alive by far more doll artists than can be mentioned here.

Resources

Students

Note: The following two books are the best children's art books about the art of the Dakotas (Sioux) and the subject of art in general. As an art education teacher who introduces the cultures of First Nation peoples to young art students, I highly recommend their use in the classroom.

Amiotte, Arthur, ed. *Art and Indian Children of the Dakotas, Book Number One: An Introduction to Art.* Aberdeen, SD: Bureau of Indian Affairs, 1978.

———. Art and Indian Children of the Dakotas, Book Number Two: An Introduction to Art and Other Ideas. Aberdeen, SD: Bureau of Indian Affairs, 1978.

Baylor, Byrd, ed. *When Clay Sings.* New York: Charles Scribner's Sons, 1972.
Wonderful children's book that tells the story of clay use.

Facklam, Margery, and Patricia Phibbs, eds. *Corn Husk Craft.* Littlecraft Book Series. New York: Sterling, 1973.
Book of crafts ideas for contemporary and traditional use of the cornhusk.

Ingram, Jerry, ed. *They Put on Masks.* New York: Charles Scribner's Sons, 1974.
This book deals only with the creation and use of masks in Native culture.

Teachers

Alaska State Council on Arts, ed. *Eskimo Dolls Exhibit Catalog.* Anchorage, AK: Alaska State Council on Arts, 1982.
  Feature articles of master doll makers.

Hirschfelder, Arlene, ed. *Artists and Craftspeople.* New York: Facts on File, 1994.
  Several essays about well-known contemporary Native artists.

Lavitt, Wendy, ed. *The Knopf Collector's Guides to American Antiques: Dolls.* New York: Knopf, 1990.
  Complete descriptive guide to antique dolls from cultures worldwide.

Lenz, Mary Jane, ed. *The Stuff of Dreams: Native American Dolls.* New Haven, CT: Eastern Press, 1986.
  Book covers 1986 doll exhibit at the National Museum of the American Indian. A wide variety of traditional dolls are presented.

Maurer, Evan M., ed. *The Native American Heritage: A Survey of North American Indian Art.* Chicago: Art Institute of Chicago, 1977.

Contemporary-Style Native American Pouches

Grade Level
4–8

Materials
Student Reading: "Contemporary-Style Native American Pouches"; cotton muslin precut strips 16 inches long by 7 inches wide; big eye needles; white cotton thread; fabric glue (Sobo/Tacky); shears; colored yarn or leather shoestrings; fabric paint (five primary colors) or fabric markers; paste brushes; small thin brushes; paper; crayons; magic markers; (optional: seed beads, beading needles); felt strips, any color, cut 6 inches wide by 11 inches long

Time
Six class periods

Objectives
- Students will learn that all Native Americans create many varied types and styles of pouches used for carrying and/or holding various articles. Students will learn that pouches are created/designed and used by both men and women. They will learn that pouches were and are used to carry food, weapons, makeup, tools for repairing/creating clothing; personal spiritual objects; medicines and herbs for healing; as well as items for jewelry making and anything that needs to be stored for special use.

- Students will learn that the style and decoration of a pouch often identify the tribe and often the rank and/or society membership of the person carrying it.

- Students will learn that today First Nation peoples still carry/wear pouches, although their dress will be the same as any non-Native person.

- Students will learn that pouches made in the traditional styles of long ago are worn when First Nation peoples dance in their Native dress at powwows.

Activities

1. Give each student a standard letter-size sheet of white construction paper. Make magic markers, pencils, and crayons available to students. Instruct students to create a design that tells something about themselves. Explain to students how pouches were used by First Nation peoples. Remind them that all the Nations across the Americas were different, and their designs reflected their Nation and beliefs. Explain the use of designs on their pouches that say something about who they are and how they feel about the world they live in, their neighborhood, and their culture. Allow students to express themselves in their design in whatever way they wish.

2. Give each student a precut strip of muslin and a precut strip of felt of any color 6 inches wide and 11 inches long. Have students cover the felt on one side with the Sobo/Tacky glue until there is a thin white covering (Figure 6.7). Have students place the felt strip one full inch from the bottom of the muslin strip, placing it in the center. This will leave a flap of five inches at the top. Students should press the strip firmly onto the muslin.

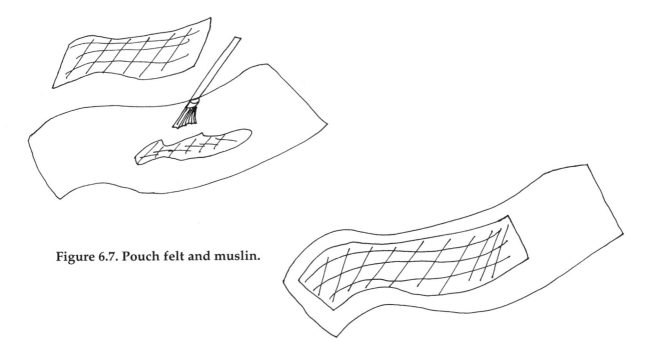

Figure 6.7. Pouch felt and muslin.

3. After the felt strip is attached, have the students fold the felt and muslin strip with the felt side out, leaving a five-inch flap of plain muslin (Figure 6.8, page 132). Give each student a big eye needle and a good long length of white cotton thread. Students will thread the needle and begin sewing the pouch at the bottom of the flap fold (Figure 6.9, page 132). Pull the thread through the pouch, leaving about one inch of thread. Have students tie the threads together making two knots. The students are now ready to stitch the pouch together using a basic basting stitch.

4. Instruct students to keep their stitches small and close together (Figure 6.10). Students will stitch the pouch around to the opposite side, staying close to the felt lining and tying a double knot when finished (Figure 6.11).

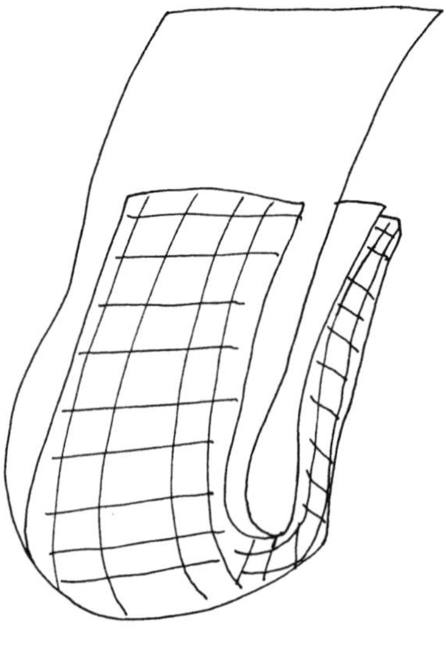

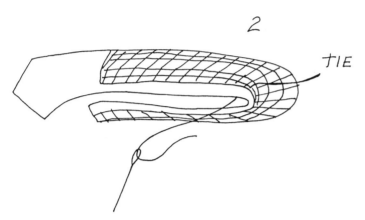

Figure 6.9. Sewing pouches.

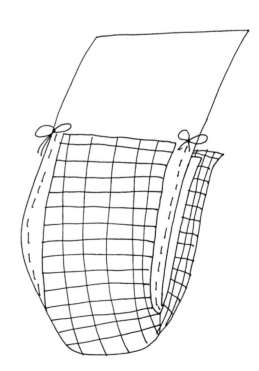

Figure 6.8. Folding pouch.

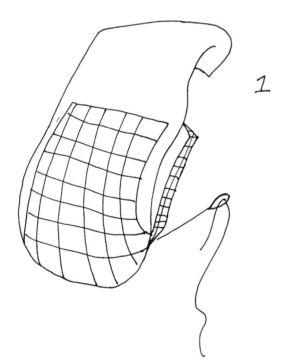

Figure 6.10. Sewing pouches.

Figure 6.11. Double knot in pouch.

5. After sewing is complete, tell students to turn their pouch inside out. Students will now apply a one-half-inch strip of paste with the paste brush all around the pouch flap. They will then fold the paste strip down, all around the flap, making a hem.

6. The pouch is now ready for the students' designs. Using the designs on the construction paper, have students copy the design onto the pouch and flap using pencils. They are ready to paint their pouch.

7. Give each student a square piece of cardboard or a plastic paint pallet (optional). If using the fabric paint, give students only two colors at a time. Each student should be given no more than a half teaspoon of paint at one time. Also, give each student one paintbrush. Let students choose their own colors and create their own mix of color (Figure 6.12). **Students' clothing should be covered.**

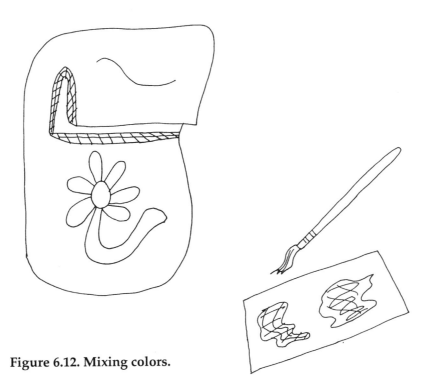

Figure 6.12. Mixing colors.

8. The small brush size will keep students from using too much paint. Caution students that less is best. Remind students that fabric paint is permanent on cloth, and they must be sure of the color they wish to use, working carefully. Students can paint the front as well as the back of their pouch. Students must paint one side, let it dry, and then paint the other side.

9. After painting the pouch, it is ready for the handle. If creating a belt pouch, use shears (teacher task) on the back of the pouch, cutting two small slits three inches apart and one inch down from the folded flap on the left side (Figure 6.13, page 134). Repeat this task on the right side. Insert one end of the leather string (or yarn) through each slit. Then tie the string together in two knots on the inside of the pouch. This will leave about a three-inch loop. Repeat.

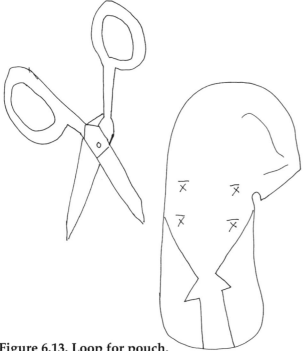

Figure 6.13. Loop for pouch.

10. If students prefer a long handle, cut one small slit on each side of the pouch at the back. Pull the string through and tie. Repeat on each side. Cut leather piece into 28-inch-long strings. If using yarn, cut three strings and braid them together before slipping through the slits and tying (Figure 6.14).

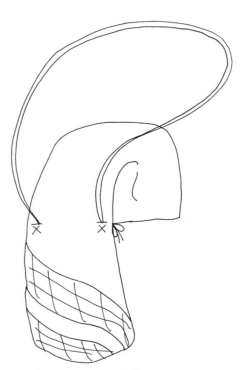

Figure 6.14. Braiding.

Enrichment/Extensions

Art. Students can draw pictures of different types of pouches, real and imagined. Students can collect pictures of different types of pouches from various cultures and create a collage.

Creative Writing. Students can write a poem or essay about the use of any type of carrying pouch by a family member.

Field Trip. If possible, arrange a class trip to a department store or small shop that sells pocketbooks or luggage. Perhaps the class can plan a trip to a museum and visit sections that display carrying pouches of different cultures, both historic and modern.

Oral History. If the student knows someone who sells or makes any kind of carrying cases, ask the student to interview that person and share the interview with the class. (See Appendix A, page 209.)

Research. Students can research the types of pouches used by different cultures around the world. Students can research and list all the different materials used to make pouches in different parts of the world.

📖 Reading

Contemporary-Style Native American Pouches

by Christina Bryant

First Nation peoples across the Americas created items using animal skins for a variety of purposes. Pouches, one of several styles of storage containers, were made out of plant fiber and tanned animal skins. Sometimes the hair/fur was scraped off, and sometimes it was left on. Sometimes the bladder of an animal like the seal or buffalo was used as a pouch. Both fur and skin pouches were created for spiritual and practical use. The style and decoration of a pouch not only identified the tribe, but also the stature of the person carrying it. Charles W. Whalen, a member of the Oglala Nation, is a hunter, taxidermist, and leather craft artist. Before beginning a leather pouch project he says, "The style of the pouch I create is dependent upon the use the owner will put it to. They must tell me what it is to be used for."

Long ago, often a particular rank or society membership was depicted by both the type of animal skin and the way the skin was prepared and decorated. Pouches were decorated using clay, mineral and vegetable mixes as paints, animal bones, claws, feathers, quills, shells, hair, and teeth. Today, fabric or acrylic paints are used, along with seed beads to decorate pouches.

The process for tanning a deer, elk, buffalo, bird, or any mammal skin varied by region. In the Southeast, the skins were soaked before scraping off hair and skin layers. Members of the Mississippi Choctaw; the Tunica Biloxi-Ofo-Avoyel-Choctaw mixed group of Marksville, Louisiana; the Biloxi-Choctaw of Bayou Lacomb and Jena, Louisiana; the Koasati of Elton, Louisiana; the Chitimacha of Charenton, Louisiana; and surrounding area; the Houma of the territory south of Houma, Louisiana; the scattered Atakapa remnants; and the Alabama (Alibamu) of Texas all still produce buckskin the old way. The Tunica and allied tribes are admired most of all the Nations in the western area of the Southeast for their buckskin products. The texture is almost velvet. Tribes came from great distances to trade for the skins of the Tunica long ago.

Tunica men carefully folded skins and then tied it with twine like a package. The package was then thrown into a nearby bayou. The end of the twine was tied to a nearby bush. The hide was allowed to soak for two to four days, depending upon the size of the animal. In the desert area, hides were laid out or staked in the sun to dry before scraping.

Tool use also varied. People in the Southeast used a scraping tool with a blunt edge, while the plains people (Lakota used an elk horn scraper called Wahintke) and woodlands people used a tool with a row of teeth. The Tunica believe the hide is made of three hides, and they must remove the two outside hides to get to the inside hide. Once all hair is removed, skins will be soaked or worked with the brains of an animal. Lakota people say that every animal has enough brains to tan itself. Skins are then hung up or stretched out to dry. The people will stretch or otherwise work the skin while it is drying. The skin will undergo another soaking before it is dried and ready to be smoked.

There are many methods for smoking, and ingredients vary by region and Nation; rotten, wet, and green wood is often used. The Oglala once used sage when smoking skins. Some woods will determine the color of the skin as it is smoked. The people were careful not to use any wood that had pitch in it. Some woods used include hemlock, aspen, poplar, Douglas fir, ponderosa pine, modrone, maple, oak, and buffalo chips.

The result of their efforts is a supple skin with a golden color ready to be cut and sewn for a variety of uses from moccasins to blankets. While many artists like Marcella Riell (Blackfeet) have their work displayed in museums; exhibited at major Indian craft shows in Chicago, New York, and Albuquerque; and featured by the National Native American Co-Operative in their worldwide exhibits and travels, others, like Charles Whalen, create pieces for everyday use, just as people did long ago.

Resources
Students

The following Shirley Glubok books are informative, easy-to-read books for young readers about the art of First Nation peoples. However, I found her descriptions very condescending. One should use these books with this in mind.

Glubok, Shirley, ed. *The Art of the Eskimo*. New York: Macmillan, 1964.

———. *The Art of the Northwest Coast Indian*. New York: Macmillan, 1975.

———. *The Art of the Plains Indian*. New York: Macmillan, 1975.

———. *The Art of the Southeastern Indian*. New York: Macmillan, 1978.

———. *The Art of the Southwest Indian*. New York: Macmillan, 1976.

———. *The Art of the Woodland Indians*. New York: Macmillan, 1976.

Hofsinde, Robert, ed. *Indian Arts*. New York: William Morrow, 1971.
This is a well-illustrated book presenting a well-rounded view of Native traditional and contemporary arts in easy-to-understand language for children.

Teachers

Coe, Ralph T. *Lost and Found Traditions: Native American Art*. New York: American Federation of Arts, 1986.
This book is organized by geographic location of tribes. It gives a clear presentation of Native arts in transition. The writer takes you along on a journey visiting various artists.

Lester, Joan A., ed. *We're Still Here: Art of Indian New England*. Boston: The Children's Museum Collection, 1987.
An informative book that presents Native people's contemporary arts and artists in the New England area.

Monthan, Guy, and Doris Monthan, eds. *Art and Indian Individualists: The Art of Seventeen Contemporary Southwestern Artists and Craftspeople*. Flagstaff, AZ: Northland, 1975.
Profiles of artists recognized as masters in their respective fields. Breathtaking pictures!

Schaefer, Arlington, ed. *The Indian Art of Tanning Buckskin*. Schaefer-Knudtsen, 1973.
    Small pamphlet describing the way a majority of tribes tanned animal skins. A how-to on tanning.

Wade, Edwin L., ed. *The Arts of the North American Indian: Native Traditions in Evolution*. New York: Hudson Hills Press, 1986.
    Wade presents the arts of Native peoples across the Americas, covering a wide variety of artistic media.

First Nation Artists

The following list of First Nation contemporary artists is categorized into seven artistic media. The list includes master artists in doll making, painting, quilting, pottery, sculpture, silversmith/jewelry, weaving, beading, basket making, leather craft, feather work, cradleboard, traditional clothing, instruments, and in many more areas. I have listed artists whose work I have had the pleasure of experiencing, who were recommended as master artists, or are friends.

In many books on Native American art, the viewer is treated to a breathtaking display, minus the name of the artists. The works are presented, it seems, as though they just appeared. The only reference to a person is usually the name of the non-Native person who acquired, donated, or is selling the work. I felt that students would better appreciate the work of the people, if they first learned about the people. With this thought in mind, I have listed only the name and Nation of the artist. Students will find the artist by researching the Nation/tribe/person. I believe this method will give the student a better understanding of the artist and traditions through which the art is given expression.

Crafts (carvers, beaders, leather and feather workers, etc.)

Robert Baker, Paiute

Amy Barber, Washoe

D. Y. Begay, Navajo

William and Mary Knight Benson, Pomo

Timothy Blue, Dakota

Birdell Bluearm, Lakota

Elizabeth Brady, Shoshone

Leah Brady, Shoshone

Clara Castillo, Paiute

Irene Cline, Paiute

Sue Coleman, Washoe

Florine Conway, Washoe

Bill Tallfeather Cueller, Cherokee

Mae Jim Curtis, Navajo

Isable Decker, Shoshone

Bernadine Delorme, Shoshone

Norman DeLorme, Washoe/Paiute

Teddy Draper Jr., Navajo

Sandy Eagle, Paiute/Washoe

Leonda Fast Buffalo Horse, Blackfeet

Adam Fortunate Eagle, Chippewa

Agnes Foster, Shoshone

Shirley Grady, Mandan/Hidatsa

James Greatwalker, Chippewa

Ray Harrell, Cherokee

Vivian High Elk, Oglala

Remonia I. Jacobsen, Iowa/
    Otoe-Missouria

Daniel James, Navajo

Isabel John, Navajo

Francis Keahna, Anishinabe

George Estes, Lower Brule Lakota

Marie Lookinghorse, Lakota
Marcie McIntire, Ojibway
Myrna Medicine Horse, Crow
Jim Nothrup Jr., Ojibway
Rosie Nuniz, Apache
Kim Ortiz, Navajo
Patty Runs After, Lakota
Melanie L. Sainz, Ho-Chunk/Dakota

Lyle Sam, Shoshone
Tootsie Dick Sam, Washoe
Jamie Tawodi Reason, Cherokee
Anne Teamer, Cherokee
Effie Tybec, Sioux
Charles W. Whalen, Oglala/
    Winnebago
Mary White, Tohono O'odham

Dolls

Annie Alowa, Siberian Yupik
Cecil Cainimptewa, Hopi
Muriel Cainmptewa, Hopi
Ronda Holybear, Lakota
Brian Honyouti, Hopi
Floyd and Amelia Kingeekuk,
    Siberian Yupik

Ina McNeil, Lakota
Deborah Ann Mullins,
    Cherokee/Catawba
Elliot Olanna, Inupiaq
Susie Paneak, Inupiaq
Dolly Spencer, Inupiaq

Painters

Norman Akers, Osage
Fred Beaver, Creek-Seminole
Joe Beeler, Cherokee
Vera Begay, Navajo
Daniel Benally, Navajo
Joanne Bird, Dakota
T. C. Cannon, Caddo-Kiowa
Al Chee, Navajo
Michael Chiago, Tohono O'odham/
    Maricopa
Hostin Claw, Navajo
Lame Deer, Northern Cheyenne
Teddy Draper Jr., Navajo
Joe Geshick, Ojibway
R. C. Gorman, Navajo
Terrance Guardipee, Blackfeet
Pretty Hawk, Yanktonais/Sioux
Jerry Ingram, Choctaw/Cherokee

David Johns, Navajo
Katsikodi, Shoshone
A. T. Lansing, Mountain Ute
Charles Lovato, Santo Domingo Pueblo
Waldo Mootzka, Hopi
Ellis Rabbit Knows Gun, Crow
Fritz Scholder, Luiseno Mission
Jackie Seiver, Northern Cheyenne
Patrick Swazo Hinds, Tesuque Pueblo
Calvin Toddy, Navajo
Irving Toddy, Navajo
Donald Vann, Cherokee
Kay Walkingstick, Cherokee
Antoine Warrior, Sac and Fox
Chief Washake, Shoshone
Laurie Whitehawk Houseman,
    Winnebago
Beatien Yazz, Navajo

Sculpture

Ed Archie Nosecap, Salish
R. G. Bowker, Sioux
Carl Cree Medicine Sr., Blackfeet
Tony Da, San Ildefonso Pueblo
Robert Haozous, Chiricahua
    Apache-Navajo
Allan Houser, Chiricahua-Apache
Douglas Hyde, Nez Percé-Chippewa-
    Assiniboine

Kovtakpaungai, Inuit
David A. Montour, Delaware/Mohawk
Leon R. Myron, Traditional Hopi
    Katsina (Tihu)
Michael Naranjo, Santa Clara Pueblo
Gerald Scoular, Coast Salish
Nanilik Temela, Inuit

Star Quilts

Mary Crow Townsend, Delaware
Florence Milligan, Osage

Marlys Stiffarm, Gros Ventre
Iris Red Elk Alrunner, Yanktonai Sioux

Pottery

Helen Cordero, Cochiti Pueblo
Tony Da, San Ildefonso Pueblo
Otellie Loloma, Hopi
Maria Martinez, San Ildefonso Pueblo

Grace Medicine Flower,
    Santa Clara Pueblo
Stella Teller, Isleta Pueblo

Silversmith/Jewelry

Leonard Gene, Navajo
Larry Golsh, Pala Mission/Cherokee
Charles Loloma, Hopi
Otellie Loloma, Hopi

Preston Monongye, Mission/Hopi
Ralph V. Thomas, Paiute
Mitchell Zephier, Lower Brule/Lakota

The artists listed can be found through their reservation/gallery/arts organization listed in the following two books and the listings of Native organizations.

Crow, John, and Martha Crow, Shannon-Jo Knows the Country, Jack Sharp, eds. *American Communication and Information Co.*, 1995. ACIC, PO Box 455, St. Cloud, MN 56302-0455. (320) 252-4190, e-mail ACIC@aol.com, fax (320) 252-6769.

National Native American Co-op, eds. *Native American Directory.* San Carlos, AZ: NNAC, 1990. PO Box 5000, San Carlos, AZ 85550-0301.

Organizations

Brule Sioux Arts and Crafts Co-op
PO Box 230
Saint Francis, SD 57572-0230
(605) 747-2019

Chahta Indian Arts & Crafts
　　Association
PO Box 371
Idabel, OK 74745

Cherokee Arts & Crafts Center
PO Box 807
Tahlequah, OK 74464

Creek Trading Post
PO Box 281
Okmulgee, OK 74447

Duck Valley Arts Council
c/o Teola Hall
PO Box 117
Owyee, NV 89832-0117
W (702) 757-3400, ext. 3015
H (702) 757-2673
F (702) 757-3663

The Eagle's Nest
Route 4, Box 100A
Norman, OK 73069
(405) 321-0611

Goombi's Indian Jewelry
1625 Homeland
Norman, OK 73069
(405) 321-9558

Indian Arts and Crafts Association
122 LaVeta Drive NE, Suite B
Albuquerque, NM 87108

Institute of Alaska Native Arts, Inc.
PO Box 70769
Fairbanks, AK 99707

Mr. Robert Blackbull
Lodgepole Gallery
PO Box 1832
Browning, MT 59417

Monkapeme
519 South Jondot
Stillwater, OK 74074
(405) 624-8378

Native American Owned and Operated
　　Arts and Crafts Business Source
　　Directory
U.S. Department of the Interior
Indian Arts & Crafts Board
Room 4004
Washington, DC 20240

Native Arts Circle
1433E Franklin, Suite 15
Minneapolis, MN 55404
W (612) 870-7173
F (612) 870-0327

Native Indian/Inuit Photographer's
　　Association
124 James Street South
Hamilton, ON, Canada L8P 224
(416) 529-7477

Navajo Arts & Crafts Association
PO Box A
Window Rock, AZ 86515
(520) 871-4090

Oklahoma Indian Artist & Craftsmen's
　　Guild
c/o Mabel Harris, President
832 North Warren
Oklahoma City, OK 73107
(405) 946-9589

Oklahoma Indian Arts & Crafts
  Cooperative
PO Box 966
Anadarko, OK 73005

Pipestone Indian Shrine Association
PO Box 727
Pipestone, MN 56164-0727
(507) 825-5463

Qualla Arts & Crafts Mutual, Inc.
PO Box 130
Cherokee, NC 28719
(704) 497-3103
Fax (704) 497-4373

Star Woman Arts & Crafts
PO Box 538
Rapid City, SD 57702-0538

Taheta Arts & Cultural Group
605 A Street
Anchorage, AK 99501
(907) 272-5829

Tiger Gallery
2110 East Shawnee Street
Muskogee, OK 74403

Tiger Family of Artists
(918) 687-7006
Wewoka Trading Post
524 South Wewoka Avenue
Wewoka, OK 74884
(405) 257-5580

Zuni Craftsmen Cooperative
  Association
PO Box 426
Zuni, NM 87327-0426
(505) 782-4425

Glossary

Contemporary Art. Continuing the visual artistic expressions of the past in a modern form.

Decoration. The act, process, technique, or art of decorating. An object or group of objects used for ornamentation and embellishment.

Giveaway. The traditional custom of an honored person distributing gifts to guests, the poor, or children, acknowledging the good deeds of a person.

Pouch. A small, flexible receptacle bag, made of leather or other relatively nonporous material.

Powwow. A word from the language of the Narraganset people, People of the Small Point. A tribe of the Algonquian Nations, who occupied southern New England. In the language, the word "powwow" was originally paw wau, meaning spiritual gathering. Today, powwows are gatherings where First Nation peoples wear their traditional clothes and celebrate their lifeways, as well as sell and/or trade craft items.

Tradition. The passing on of elements of a culture from one generation to another.

Visual Art. Having the nature of producing an image in the mind through various artistic media.

Lesson

6.3

Performing Arts

Grade Level
6–8

Materials
Student Reading: "Performing Arts"; videos; recordings (see appendices for ordering information)

Time
Five class periods, flexible

Objectives
- Students will become familiar with some Native American performers.

- Students will view at least one Native American performance.

- Students will understand that not only are American Indians involved in traditional Indian arts, but also excel in many other art forms.

Activities
Read "Performing Arts" to the class and discuss. Have the class list and discuss films they have seen that depict Native American culture, or an event that involves Indians. Most students have seen *Pocahontas* or *Dances with Wolves*. Ask students if they think that American Indians have been a part of the film: writing, directing, camera work, acting, etc. Show a segment of a film that is stereotypic and features non-Indians as Indians (*A Man Called Horse, Broken Arrow, Arrowhead, Chief Crazy Horse, Son of Cochise, Deerslayer, The Outsider,* etc.). Based on previous lessons in stereotyping, have students evaluate a film. For the next class, have students go to a video store and look for films starring Native American actors. Give them the list included in this lesson.

Second Class

Rent one of the films recommended in this lesson and view and discuss with the class. What are the differences in performances of Indians playing Indians and non-Indians playing Indians? Are Indians depicted as ordinary people or as magical, mystical, unreal people?

Third Class

View one of the suggested dance films. Research the meaning of dances. What dances are for social gatherings? Religious ceremonies? Compare Native dance with dance traditions from other cultures.

Fourth Class

Have students listen to and discuss one of the recommended recordings. How does the music make them feel? Research the musician or tribe.

Fifth Class

Adopt an artist. Have students research artists through the Internet, agents, studios, or performing companies, and write a fan letter. They can work and research it individually or as a class. Write to the artist what you have learned about the artwork, and don't forget to tell them if you enjoyed it!

📖 Reading

Performing Arts

Performance has always been an integral part of Native American culture. Spirituality, values, tribal identity, and historical events are expressed in a variety of forms from dance to theatrical presentations. In traditional societies, most celebrations, whether they are sacred or social gatherings, involve music and dance, but their purpose is not primarily for entertainment as in Euro- or Afro-American culture. Some forms of Native performance involve lighting, masks, and pantomime. The U.S. government and some religious groups have tried to suppress these events, but American Indians continue to express themselves through traditional music and dance performances.

One cultural trait of American Indians is to create beauty in all aspects of their lives. Museums are full of simple water pots or sleeping mats that were decorated beautifully centuries ago. That tradition continues today. Many traditional prayers or stories have phrases like "Walk in Beauty."

In Inupiaq and Yupik (Eskimo) celebrations in Alaska, one or more communities of all ages often gather for an evening of song and dance. Feasting and fun are a part of these events, and it is considered an honor to be invited to participate in another group's celebration. On the Northwest coast, the Native people produce elaborate performances with complicated staging, complex costuming, dramatic lighting, and masks. These events can be held in a large communal house and often involve elaborate puppets. Puppetry is used by many Indian Nations for a number of reasons from telling a story to being part of a ceremony to influence weather.

Powwows, probably the most publicized dance festivals, provide unifying social events for diverse Indian communities. (See Lesson 4.8, page 88.) Native people are also involved with different forms of dance. For example, Jack Soto, Navajo, is principal dancer for the New York City Ballet, and Maria Tallchief, Osage, was prima ballerina for the George Ballanchine Ballet Society. Some professional dance groups like the American Indian Dance Theater and the Thunderbird American Indian Dancers tour in the United States and abroad.

Most images of American Indians come directly from film and television. Indians usually have been depicted as frightening, bloodthirsty murderers, noble savages, or spiritual and childlike sages. The misleading impression that all Indian Nations are the same is inaccurate and damaging. There are hundreds of diverse Indian Nations.

To complicate matters, until recently, most Native parts were cast with non-Indians. Although there are many more American Indian actors in the business now, the quality of films has improved little. Most Indian directors rarely get to do commercial films, and non-Indian actors are often cast as Indians to guarantee box-office success. Hollywood does not like to take chances with unknown actors; however, any actor is unknown until gaining a certain amount of exposure!

A few organizations and festivals have been developed by Native artists to address the underrepresentation of Native peoples in the film industry. Some of these include the Native American Film and Video Festival in New York City, sponsored by the National Museum of the Native American; the American Indian Film Festival in San Francisco, sponsored by the American Indian Film Institute; Two Rivers Film Festival in Minneapolis; and First Americans in the Arts Foundation.

Indian actors have appeared on Broadway, in commercials and soap operas, as extras in major films, in local and regional theater, and in industrial films. Yet, directors often will not use Indian actors unless the role calls for an Indian person, as if Indians can't be mailmen or just the girl next door. As stated previously, some of the largest Indian roles in the most expensive films often go to better-known non-Indian actors.

Although most Native Americans participate in various tribal performance or dance events, there are several professional artists who earn their living by singing, acting, dancing, storytelling, composing, or playing music in all venues from experimental theater to daytime dramas. These performers combine traditional rhythms, structure, and themes with ballet, opera, folk instrumentation, jazz, or rap music. Whatever the genre, Native American performance art is memorable and enhances all aspects of the arts.

The following is a representative list of Native Americans in the arts.

Actors/Storytellers/Theater Groups

Cochise Anderson, Chickasaw
Irene Bedard, Cree
Stuart Bird, Cherokee
Joseph Bruchac, Abenaki. Storyteller
Tantoo Cardinal, Cree
George Clutesi, Nootka
Iron Eyes Cody, Cherokee
Hortensia Colorados, Nahutal
Donna Couteau, Sac/Fox
Joe Cross, Caddo
William Tallfeather Cuellar, Cherokee
Victor Daniels, Cherokee
James Apaumut Fall, Mohican
Gary Farmer, Cayuga

Hanay Geiogamah, Kiowa.
  Playwright, director
Chief Dan George, Salish
Rodney Grant, Omaha
Graham Greene, Oneida
Charlie Hill, Oneida. Comedian
Michael Horse, Apache/Zuni
Dawn Jamieson, Cayuga
Geraldine Keams, Navajo
Irma Estel LaGuerre, Tarascan/Aztec
Jane Lind, Aleut
Eddie Little Sky, Sioux
Lisa Maya, Rappahannock/Kuna
Gloria Miguel, Rappahannock/Kuna

Muriel Miguel, Rappahannock/Kuna
Elaine Miles, Umatilla
Chuck Norris, Cherokee
North American Indian Traveling College,
    Mohawk. Storytellers, mixed media
    presentations
Anthony Nukema, Karok/Hopi
Lois Red Elk, Sioux
Princess Red Wing, Winnebago
Rodd Redwing, Chickasaw
Branscombe Richmond, Apache
Marie Antoinette Rogers, Apache
Will Rogers, Cherokee
Joanelle Romero, Apache
Ned Romero, Creek
Frank Salsedo, Wintu
Will Sampson, Creek

Jay Silverheels (a.k.a. Harry Smith),
    Mohawk
Spiderwoman Theater, Kuna/
    Rappahannock.
    Feminist theater group
Medicine Story, Wampanoag. Storyteller
Nipo T. Strongheart, Yakima
Wes Studi, Cherokee
Jim Thorpe, Sac and Fox
Sheila Tousey, Menominee
Ray Tracey, Navajo
John Trudell, Santee
Katiri Walker, Potawatami
John War Eagle, Yankton Sioux
Floyd Red Crow Westerman,
    Sisseton/Wahpeton
Chief Yowlachie, Yakima

Bands

Apache Spirit. Country/Rockabilly
Kintawk, Blackfoot. Native American rock
Knifewing, Apache. Rock
Navajo Sundowners. Country/Western

Pima County, Mohave/Apache.
    Country/Western
Redbone. Rock
XIT, Navajo. Rock

Dance/Dance Groups

American Indian Dance Theater. Intertribal dances
Maria Benitz, Pueblo. Flamenco
Cape Fox Dancers, Tlingit traditional dancers
Yvonne Chouteau, Cherokee. Prima ballerina
Coastal Pomo Indian Dancers, traditional Pomo dances
Haskell Singers and Dancers, students of Haskell Indian Junior College, intertribal
Rosella Hightower, Choctaw. Prima ballerina
Belinda James, San Juan Pueblo. Modern and ballet, founded Divi Shadende
    Dance Company
Noeb Joerder, Cherokee. Broadway choreographer
Rosalie Jones, Blackfeet-Pembina-Chippewa. Modern dancer and choreographer,
    founder of Daystar Classical Dance/Drama of America

Moscelyne Larkin, Shawnee/Peoria. Classical ballerina
Kevin Locke, Standing Rock Sioux. Hoop dancer
Jim Sky Iroquois Dancers, traditional
Jack Soto, Navajo. Principal dancer, New York City Ballet
Eddie Swimmer, Cherokee. Hoop dancer
Maria Tallchief, Osage. Prima ballerina with George Balanchine's Ballet Society
Marjorie Tallchief, Osage. Premiere danseuse étoile of the Paris Opera Ballet
Thunderbird American Indian Dancers, intertribal
Juan Valensuela, Yaqui

Film and Video Makers

Maggi Banner, Hopi/Tewa
Dean Curtis Bear Claw, Crow
Gil Cardinal, Metis
George P. Horse Capture, Gros Ventre
Carol Korb, Yurok
Nettie Kuneki, Klickitat
Zacharias Kunuk, Inuit
Larry Littlebird, Santo Domingo Pueblo

Phil Lucas, Choctaw
Catherine Martin, Micmac
Victor Masayesva Jr., Hopi
Alanis Obomsawin, Abenaki
Sandra Johnson Osawa, Makah
Beverly Singer, Santa Clara Pueblo
Chris Spotted Eagle, Houma
Christine Welch, Metis

Musicians/Composers

Athabascan Old-Time Fiddlers. Alaskan group that plays fiddles, mandolins, and guitars
Louis Ballard, Quapaw/Cherokee. Composer, musician, educator. He wrote the first American Indian ballet, Koshare, which premiered in Spain.
Don Cherry, Choctaw. Jazz musician
Brent Michael Davids, Stockbridge-Munsee/Mohican. Composer
Jack Frederick Kilpatrick, Cherokee. Composer
Robert Mirabel, Taos Pueblo. Composer, double-chambered flute music
Mixashawn, Maheekanawk. Traditional flute/jazz saxophone
Russell Moore, Pima. Jazz trombonist
R. Carlos Nakai, Ute/Navajo. Composer/flautist
Doc Tate Nevaquaya, Comanche. Flautist
Jim Pepper, Kansa (Kaw). Jazz musician and composer
Don Pullen, Powhatan. Jazz musician
Anthony Joseph Rice, Mohawk. Composer
Dennis Yerry, Seneca. Composer

Singers/Singing Groups

Akwesasne Mohawk Singers

Ashland Singers, Northern Cheyenne. Traditional powwow singers

Bala-Sinem Choir, Hopi

Angela Beekman, Osage. Opera

James Bilagody, Navajo. Contemporary and traditional

Stuart Bird, Cherokee. Music theater

Chille Pop, intertribal. Contemporary musicians based on traditional music

Ned Tsosie Clark, Navajo. Traditional

Vera Colorados, Nahuatl. Music theater

Johnny Curtis, Apache. Gospel

Ray Evans Harrell, Cherokee. Opera, educator

Irma LaGuerre, Tarascan/Aztec. Opera/music theater

Lightfoot, Cherokee. Rap

Harold Littlebird, Laguna. Traditional and contemporary

Wayne Newton, Powhatan. Contemporary

A. Paul Ortega, Apache. Traditional and contemporary

Bonnie Patton, Sioux. Opera

Buddy Red Bow, Lakota. Country rock

Buffy Sainte Marie, Cree. Folk, contemporary, composer

Keith Secola, Ojibway. Contemporary

Joanne Shenandoah, Oneida. Contemporary/folk

Silver Cloud Intertribal. Powwow singers

Ulali, Intertribal. Traditional and contemporary

White Eagle, Sioux. Opera

Resources

Students

Ballard, Louis. *American Indian Music for the Classroom.* Phoenix, AZ: Canyon Records, 1973. Records, books, and how-to manual.

Weatherford, Jack. *Native Roots: How the Indians Enriched America.* New York: Crown, 1991.

Dance Videos

"Apache Mountain Spirits." 58 minutes. 1985. Silvercloud Video Production. 1321 East King Road, Tucson, AZ 85719. (602) 326-7647. $19.98.
This video weaves historical situations into the contemporary life of a teenager.

"Ceremonial," "Green Corn," and "Creek Nation Stompdance." 1994. Sold as a unit. $16. Muscogee (Creek) Nation Communications Department, PO Box 580, Okmulgee, OK 74447. (918) 756-8700.
Each video presents an important part of Muscogee (Creek) culture.

Full Circle Videos. (800) 940-8849.
    Full Circle Videos has produced the following 60-minute dance programs. Order from: Written Heritage, PO Box 1390, Folsom, LA 70437. (800) 301-8009 or (504) 796-5433. $19.95 each.

> "How to Dance Native American." 1996. How to listen to the songs and keep the beat for several social dances. Featured are Creek, Cherokee, Yuichi, and Osage.

> "Into the Circle." 1992. Explains powwow dancing and the involvement of men and women.

> "Native American Men's and Women's Dance Styles," vols. 1 and 2. 1994. Highlighted dances include Hoop Dance, Gourd Dance, Team Dancing, Rabbit Dance, and Round Dance, among others.

"Giveaway at Ring Thunder." 15 minutes. 1982. GPN. PO Box 80669, Lincoln, NE 68501. (800) 228-4530. $24.95.
    This video highlights the Lakota custom of strengthening ties to the community.

"I Know Who I Am." 28 minutes. 1979. Upstream Productions. 420 1st Avenue West, Seattle, WA 98119. $39.95.
    Dance is a part of this video, which gives a wonderful overview of Makah culture, both contemporary and historical.

KYUK Video Productions. Pouch 468, Bethel, AK 99559. (907) 543-3131. $28.
    KYUK offers the following videos:

> "Camai Dance Festival Highlights." 60 minutes. This invitational festival held at Bethel, Alaska, features Indian dancers from the United States and Canada, as well as international dancers. Six different years available: 1987, 1991, 1993, 1994, 1995, and 1996.

> "Eyes of the Spirit." 28 minutes. 1984. Public performance by the Bethel Native Dancers marks the revival of masked dancing by the Yupik Eskimo of southwest Alaska.

> "Just Dancing." 60 minutes. 1987. Intertribal dancing of several different Nations.

> "Old Dances, New Dancers. 29 minutes. 1984. Documents the first annual Young People's Eskimo Dance Awareness Festival intended to revitalize dancing by young people.

> "Yup'ik, A Dancing People." 28 minutes. 1984. Three days of dancing, gift giving, and contests by dancers and musicians from nine Yupik Eskimo villages.

"More Than Just a Week of Fun." 12 minutes. 1984. Choctaw Heritage Video. PO Box 6010, Philadelphia, MS 39350. (601) 650-1685. $25.
    An explanation of dances and activities at the annual Choctaw Fair.

"Music and Dance of the Mohawk." 25 minutes. 1983. Image Films, 300 Susquehanna Road, Rochester, NY 14618. (716) 473-8070. $28.
The spiritual significance of music and dance for the Mohawk, part of the Iroquois Confederacy.

Internet

http://virtual.atlanta.com/knifewing/index.html

http://www.fdl.cc.mn.us/natnet/refs.html

http://www.nycballet.com/DancerCasting.html

or type Buffy Saint Marie into your search program.

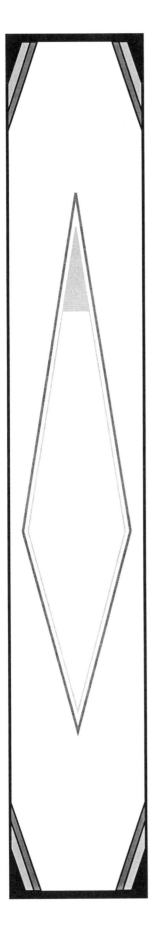

Chapter 7

Paying the Bills: Economics

Your students probably realize that the money people get from the ATM required a bank deposit at some point in time. Unfortunately, most young people cling to the old cliché, "money grows on trees," along with Nikes, CDs, Gap jeans, and Big Macs! This chapter will help students understand that Indian people have to support themselves like everyone else. Although these lessons address the tribal economy and the financial status of Indian individuals, students should be aware that Native people have the highest unemployment and poverty rates in the United States. Those Indian people who are employed work in many occupations. Native American women often complete their education after their children have grown and may have tried a number of careers in their lifetimes.

There are many opportunities to use these biographies, including Women's History Month and career awareness activities. Dr. Gelvin Stevenson, Oklahoma Cherokee, resides in New York City and is an investment counselor. He skillfully and knowledgeably contributed Lessons 2 and 3.

Lesson

7.1

Indians in Careers/Employment

Grade Level
6–8

Materials
Student Reading: "Biographical Sketches" (duplicated for each group) and biographies from other chapters, if desired; two large U.S. maps; cork or bulletin board; colored push pins; yarn; scissors

Time
Two class periods (preferably around career day or "Take Your Daughter to Work Day")

Objectives
- Students will learn that Native Americans are employed in many vocations and geographic locations.

- Students will become familiar with credentials required for some careers. Students will explore their own career possibilities and interests.

- Students will use mapping skills.

Activities
Initiate class discussion. Pose the following questions:

1. How do people choose employment?
2. Do you associate particular careers with particular ethnic groups? Give a few examples: African-American athletes, Jewish lawyers, Russian ballerinas, Korean green grocers, Greek diner operators.
3. If you associate careers with ethnic groups, why? Is this stereotyping?
4. Do you associate any particular careers with Native American people?
5. Now give examples of people whose careers differ from what they are associated with just because of their ethnicity.

Divide the class into three or four groups. Hand out different "Biographical Sketches" to each group, or use biographical information from other parts of the book. Students can select a recorder and reader. Each group will read the sketches and record the following:

1. The person's job.
2. Tribe/Nation and location of tribe/Nation.
3. Person's birthplace.
4. Location where person grew up.
5. Location of workplace.
6. Education/training required for person's employment.

After information is completed, pose the following questions:

1. Were you surprised by any of the biographies you read? If so, why?
2. Do people work in the same area where they were born? Give some examples.
3. What jobs require the most training? The least?
4. Give examples of professions that can only be done in specific areas.
5. Are you interested in any of the professions? Why?
6. Could you stay in the area where you live now and work in your chosen field? Do you want to move away from where you live now?

Mapping Activity

1. Mount maps on the bulletin board. Each group will take turns mapping information about their particular people. Choose one color push pin for birthplaces. Choose another for areas where people spent their childhood, if different. Choose another color for where people work now. Cut yarn and make a yarn line from the person's origin to where they are living now. On a second map, use one pin color to show the tribal location of each person.
2. Compare the two maps for a visual representation of where people were born, live, work, and the tribal location.

Enrichment/Extensions

Art. Draw people in biographical sketches in both their traditional outfits and their work attire. Display around maps.

Career Education. Make a list of interview questions based on information in the biographies and interview people in the community.

Drama. Have students write a skit about themselves working in their chosen careers and interacting on a community level.

Research. Look up trends in employment and employment forecasts.

Writing. Instruct students to clip a classified job advertisement from a newspaper and write an essay about it.

📖 Reading

Biographical Sketches

Dr. Zinaida Pelkey (Figure 7.1) is a Doctor of Osteopathy, living in New York City, and has ancestors who were Abenaki, Russian, French, and Irish. Born in Brooklyn, she spent her childhood in New York and Massachusetts. Medicine is Zina's third career. First, she was a nursery school teacher, and then a chef. She graduated from medical school when she was 50 years old! As an osteopathic physician, Zina looks at the whole person (mind, body, and spirit) and all things that could be affecting health. In making her diagnoses, she tries to learn why the patient's own ability to heal is not working. She pays special attention to how the structure of the body affects the way it functions. The manipulations she uses help patients heal themselves. She may also prescribe herbs, vitamins, minerals, dietary regimes, medications, and exercise, and sometimes refers patients to other health practitioners. Zina's favorite patients are children, and she likes newborn babies best! She has a private practice and also works in a hospital in the South Bronx. Part of her busy schedule involves teaching residents, doctors in training. Because Zina loves her profession, she doesn't mind working long hours, sometimes 60 or more a week. To become a Doctor of Osteopathy, she had to earn an undergraduate degree and attend medical school for four years. After she graduated, she was an intern for one year and then had to complete two years of residency in her specialty. After all that preparation, Zina had to pass three different National Board examinations before she could be a licensed doctor. She became Board certified in Osteopathic Manipulative Medicine after yet another test. To keep abreast of the latest knowledge in her field, she often attends workshops and seminars. She advises anyone interested in a medical career that if they work really hard and care about their patients, they can be successful. Zina likes to draw, hike, and walk by the ocean when she has time.

Figure 7.1. Dr. Zinaida Pelkey (L) and Yvonne Beamer (R).

Annie L. Teamer (Figure 7.2) lives in New York City where she is the volunteer coordinator for the National Museum of the American Indian. She is Blackfeet and Cherokee and was born in Tennessee and grew up there, in Michigan, and in New York. As volunteer coordinator, Annie recruits, supervises, schedules, and trains about 70 volunteers to work in the museum, which features the historical and contemporary culture and achievements of the Native peoples in the Western Hemisphere. She is also the museum's official greeter and is always on hand to welcome and direct guests and tourists. The qualifications for her job include a college background, knowledge of Native American culture, and experience working in the Native community. A volunteer coordinator has to be sensitive and at ease with people. Not only does Annie teach about the exhibits to her volunteer staff, but also prepares reports and disseminates information. Even on her days off, she has to ensure that the reception area is staffed and flyers and information are available to museum visitors. Annie loves to sew, finger weave, travel, dance, and take walking tours in her leisure time.

Figure 7.2. Annie L. Teamer.

Carmen Ketcher (Figure 7.3), Sac and Fox/Delaware, grew up and still lives in Oklahoma. She is an elementary school secretary. Her duties include recording attendance, taking care of the children's medical needs, working with parents, assisting the principal, and working with the community. Carmen is often the first person that an angry or upset parent sees in the school, and it is up to her to calm everyone and assess the situation before giving advice. Carmen acts as an intermediary between the parents and administration. To be a school secretary requires patience and tact; one must be able to complete tasks, even with constant interruptions. She works 8:00 A.M. to 4:30 P.M. 10¾ months a year; computer and good typing skills are required. Carmen is a certified professional secretary and belongs to the National Secretary Association and the BETCO Union. To become certified, she had to pass a rigid state examination and has a four-year college and business school background. She likes canoeing and playing sports with her husband and three sons. Carmen, whose Indian name is Mesh-U-Pak-With, is a member of the Bartlesville, Oklahoma Indian Women's Club.

Figure 7.3. Carmen Ketcher.

Dennis McAuliffe Jr. (Figure 7.4), Osage, was born in Pennsylvania but grew up in many different locations because his father was a career serviceman. He has lived in 48 different houses! Perhaps all of the moving around led Dennis to his career as assistant foreign editor at the *Washington Post*, the largest newspaper in Washington, D.C. The *Post* has foreign correspondents (reporters) in most places in the world. They submit articles to the paper, and it is up to Dennis to edit those stories. Once he gets a story, he makes sure that the facts are correct, the copy (text) is readable, and the story follows a logical sequence. At times, he may have to rewrite it. Finally, he selects an appropriate headline and makes the copy fit onto the page.

Dennis works the late shift, 7:00 P.M. to 3:00 A.M. Before he became an editor, he lived in other countries working as a foreign correspondent. As a high school student, Dennis worked as a sports writer, covering high school athletics. He was awarded a journalism scholarship, but interrupted his studies to serve in the army. He advises students interested in a journalism career to major in political science, history, or one of the sciences.

Journalism is becoming specialized, and it is important to enjoy reading and be very inquisitive. If someone is not a great writer, but is good at research and can put things together logically, the person can succeed in journalism. However, an editor must have good English and technical skills to make the story perfect.

To relax, Dennis plays golf, but his favorite hobby is writing books. *The Deaths of Sybil Bolton: An American History*, published by Times Books in 1994, is a mystery about his grandmother and her tragic death on Osage lands in Oklahoma. Through his research for the book, Dennis learned that 6 percent of Osage people had been murdered for their oil rights. A member of the Native American Journalists Association, he feels that the media do not cover enough Native American news. He enjoys writing articles about Native issues, and you can find Dennis McAuliffe's stories in back issues of the *Washington Post*.

Figure 7.4. Dennis McAuliffe Jr.

Audrey J. Cooper (Figure 7.5), Eastern Cherokee, was born and raised in Pennsylvania, and now lives in Ithaca, New York. Her people are from Virginia, North Carolina, and Georgia. She wears two hats, youth program director and supportive housing development coordinator. Her responsibilities include developing community programs, hiring and supervising staff, writing proposals, community relations, networking, and interacting with individuals and families who need her services. Working with the court system and other groups, Audrey ensures that at-risk and troubled adolescents follow the plan of action enacted by the court. She assists clients in goal planning, counseling, monitoring their improvement, helping them deal with crises, and ensuring they have food, shelter, and clothing. Audrey works with teen parents and victims of domestic abuse, too. She has to assess the individual and family to determine their needs.

Her agency is a not-for-profit corporation that helps the poor. Networking with other agencies to help her clients is a big part of Audrey s job. A youth program director requires a college background in social work or a related field, and years of experience in community service. Audrey is also a Certified Alcoholism Counselor and has earned certification in grantsmanship. Audrey relaxes by baking and gardening.

Figure 7.5. Audrey J. Cooper.

Carol Supernaw Bergman, Muskogee Creek, lives and works in Tulsa, Oklahoma, not far from Seminole, Oklahoma, where she was born. She is a computer systems analyst for the city of Tulsa and is in charge of applicant tracking, medical information, worker compensation, and payroll systems for city workers. She administers four major computer systems. Carol has to meet the needs of about 50 people who use the computer systems daily, and directly supervises four employees. Averaging about a 45-hour workweek, she sometimes has to work Saturday or late in the day to deal with problems. Carol helps people improve their work. A systems analyst must be good in math, science, spatial relations, and reading. Often, Carol must take special training courses to keep up with constantly changing information. Her love of reading and interest in her culture inspired Carol to open Cedar Hill Books, a company that sells quality American Indian books, primarily through mail order. Although she would much rather be selling books than working in computers, her computer expertise is very useful in the retail business. Carol's hobbies are gardening, sewing, and surfing the Net.

Frank Harris, Lumbee, has lived his entire life in Pembroke, North Carolina. He and his partner turned their love of motorcycle riding into a successful business, and Frank is now a proprietor of the Scuffletown Cycle Shop. They repair and service Harley Davidson motorcycles, sell parts, and provide customers with the latest information on Harleys. Frank works long hours—sometimes 60 hours a week. To run a successful cycle shop, he and his partner have to be expert mechanics, have good math skills, read and write well (the diagrams and manuals are very detailed and complex), and deal effectively with customers. Before Frank was able to make a profit, he and his partner had to put any money they made back into their business. Parts and tools are very expensive. They have made a lot of sacrifices; if they are ill, or must be away and cannot open the shop, they lose money. Frank needed a special resale license from the state to operate a business, and also has to file special business taxes. Although he is a master carpenter, Frank prefers running the Scuffletown Cycle Shop. Of course, his hobby is motorcycle riding, which he has been doing for 12 years. Frank stresses the importance of knowing how to ride safely. Motorcycles may look cool, but they can be very dangerous.

Beverly Wright (Figure 7.6), Wampanoag, grew up and now lives on the island of Martha's Vineyard in Massachusetts. She is chair of the Wampanoag Tribe of Gay Head/Aquinnah. Elected by popular vote, Beverly has the same responsibilities as the president of the United States, only on a smaller scale. She represents her tribe in all facets of tribal government and has to be responsive to the concerns of all tribal members. Many Indian Nations feel that a good leader has skin that is seven thumbs thick. Beverly has to have that same tough skin. No matter what difficulties or obstacles she may encounter, she has to stay strong and be able to bounce back after each adversity (at least once a day!) and still be able to smile. In Indian society a good leader lives among the people and does not set himself or herself apart. In Beverly's job, she has to be concerned with issues inside and outside the Wampanoag tribe. She has served as vice president of the United Southeastern Tribes, is a voting member of the National Congress of American Indians, National Indian Gaming Association, and United Southeastern Tribes Gaming Association, and a member of the Female Tribal Leaders Organization. Beverly enjoys traveling, reading, sewing, and gardening.

Figure 7.6. Beverly Wright.

Everett Iron Eyes, Hunkpapa, lives and works on the Standing Rock Reservation in North Dakota. He is the farm manager and irrigation coordinator for a tribally chartered farming operation on the 3.2-million-acre reservation. Not only does Everett oversee all aspects of the 2,100-acre farm that produces corn, alfalfa, soybeans, and wheat, but is also responsible for developing more farmland. That requires working with consultants who do land classification studies and investigate the cultural, environmental, and archaeological aspects of irrigating more land. Water rights are a major issue in Indian country, and Everett has struggled long and hard to ensure that Standing Rock has access to the Missouri River. Although he supervises mulching, plowing, planting, baling, and cutting, he has to know federal and state laws, treaty rights, funding sources, and congressional trends.

In the morning he may be found assisting the seasonal workers and unit managers in baling alfalfa. In the afternoon he might consult with a soil scientist. In the evening he may confer with the water rights attorney in Washington, D.C. Everett has never taught, although he holds a bachelor's degree in elementary education for natural science. However, studying natural sciences aided him in his previous position as natural resources director for Standing Rock and helps in his current position. To be a farm manager, Everett has to be able to communicate with people, including the tribal council, and be aware of new technology, like satellites to improve crop yield. Everett enjoys reading and research.

Bill Ini Igati Ugidali Cuellar (Figure 7.7), Cherokee, was born in Indian territory before Oklahoma became a state. The family moved to Texas, fleeing harassment of federal troops when he was two. He is a retired Air Force master sergeant, having served 33 years in the military. Bill began his career in the cavalry unit of the Army and transferred to the Army Air Corps. He had many jobs in the Corps, which became the Air Force in 1928, starting as airplane mechanic and finishing as an aircraft inspector. Serving in two wars, Bill was stationed in many parts of Texas, Georgia, the southwest Pacific, and Korea. He retired in 1957. To be a career serviceman requires discipline, self-sufficiency, ability to take orders, flexibility in living arrangements and locations, and self-control. In addition, one must prepare for a special or technical job in the same way as a civilian. Bill attended jet school and spent several years training in several specialties. Although he excelled in his work, he experienced ridicule and discrimination as an American Indian; he often had to struggle to ignore it. Indians were not segregated, however, as were African Americans.

After retiring, Bill moved to New Jersey to be near his wife's relatives. He has been a member of organizations like the American Indian Thunderbird Dancers. A master carver, Bill's Native American–inspired works of art are worked in bone, antler, horn, and wood. He is a singer (pop and Native American music), drummer, and plays the guitar and harmonica. Bill's many hobbies include rock, stamp, and coin collecting; horseback riding; and photography. Although he is 91, Ini Igati Ugidali dances at powwows and teaches the Cherokee language and crafts.

Figure 7.7. Rosemarie Nerl with William Tall Feather Cuellar.

Uda Nuh di Ageya Noquisi Fast Wolf (Figure 7.8), Oklahoma Cherokee, was born in Texas and moved to New Jersey when she was 10. She still resides and works in New Jersey and is a traffic engineering assistant for AT&T. Noquisi monitors telephone traffic between the United States and other countries to make sure that communications can get through. If there is a problem, she investigates to see if more or fewer circuits are needed. Often, Noquisi puts together presentation packages based on a country's needs and is adept at using computer software, including graphics and spreadsheets. She writes reports of her analysis and deals with complaints from different customers (countries). To be in traffic engineering, it is helpful to have an electrical engineering or communication background, be good in math and computers, and understand all kinds of telephone and satellite equipment. Noquisi is the eastern representative of the Intertribal Council of AT&T Employees and is a member of the Communication Workers of America. Very involved in her community, she volunteers as an emergency medical technician and teaches CPR, prehospital trauma life support and emergency medical technician courses. She is a member of the National Association of Native American EMTs. An avid equestrian, Noquisi is comfortable with both western and English riding styles.

Figure 7.8. Uda Nuh di Ageya Noquisi and nephew (on horse).

Dr. Beverly Singer (Figure 7.9), Tewa/Navajo, was born and raised in the Santa Clara Pueblo, New Mexico, but is based in New York City, where she is an independent video maker and media education consultant. A trained social worker, Beverly translates her experience and concerns with Native American wellness into film and video. She has also directed two curriculum projects that addressed cancer prevention or alcohol abuse among young Native Americans, "Native Facets" and "Join the Circle of Life." Some of Beverly's films, like "Recovery for Native America" and "Mondo's Story," are helpful to those struggling to break the cycle of addiction. Ochua Poquin, Beverly's Tewa name, feels that her art must serve the community. Recently, she worked on a video with Apache youngsters and involved them in every aspect of filmmaking: selecting the subject, writing the script, listing the shots, casting the actors, editing, choosing the music, deciding the title, and hosting the screening. The team worked very hard for 80 hours to produce a 10-minute video! A filmmaker must be creative, skilled at operating all kinds of equipment, able to make on-the-spot decisions, energetic, persistent, and able to raise money. Beverly belongs to the Native American Producers Alliance, American Studies Association, and Cancer Control Network for American Indians. Her work has earned merits like the Artist's Project Award, a National Endowment for Humanities Fellowship, and the University of New Mexico Graduate Student Award for Creative Arts. Even with Beverly's busy schedule, she earned a Ph.D. in American studies with an emphasis on popular culture and film. Beverly enjoys walking briskly through the city streets, traveling, foreign films, and horses.

Figure 7.9. Beverly Singer. Photo © George Leong.

Sybil Jones, Lumbee, is president of JR Jones Grain, Inc., a family-owned business in Pembroke, North Carolina, where she lives and grew up. A grain company buys crops from farmers and resells them to end users. Part of Sybil's job is to meet the growers; weigh and grade corn, oats, soybeans, or wheat; and determine how the grain will be used. For instance, there are several types of wheat, and while one type may be sold to a gravy manufacturer, another may be bought by a flour maker. Still another customer uses a type for animal food. Sybil must find out which customers need what grains, and how much they are willing to pay. She makes spot contracts, visits farms, looks for deals by telephone, evaluates the current grain market, and even operates like a stockbroker. During the different grain seasons, Sybil works 12 to 14 hours a day, six days a week, with no time off for holidays. The skills needed for her job include accounting, writing, speaking, computer knowledge, financial management, ability to deal with all kinds of people, and, of course, detailed knowledge of grains. JR Grain has a weigh masters license issued by the state agriculture department, and its warehouse is USDA approved. Sybil is a member of the Southeastern Grain and Feed Association and serves on the boards of the Lumbee Bank, North Carolina Indian Housing Authority, county extension service, and the Crop Promotion Association. In addition, she is a Sunday school teacher and finds time to keep in shape by running, walking, and swimming. Sybil and her husband also operate a 2,200-acre farm.

Rosemarie Nerl (Figure 7.7), Apache, is a homemaker and lives in the Bronx, New York. Her family is from New Mexico, but Rosie was born and raised in New York. Although many mothers work both outside and inside the home, Rosie laughingly refers to herself as a domestic engineer. She has six children and six grandchildren. Her duties include preparing nutritious and balanced meals, laundry, cleaning, managing the household finances, sewing, child rearing, baking, shopping, and entertaining. Because she only works at home, Rosie must keep her family on a strict budget, since they only have one income. She clips coupons, buys sale items, and finds inexpensive activities for her family's entertainment. Active as a class mother, Rosie also helps with school, Little League fund-raising, outings, and has served as a den mother. She arranges for her children's religious ceremonials and tries to live as traditionally as possible. Rosie strongly believes that there should be parenting classes and that the entire community should participate in raising children. Homemakers and parents today have to be aware of drugs and gangs and monitor their children's television programs. It is important to Rosie that her children develop good values and grow up strong and independent. She helps other mothers in the community and tries to show them how to be patient and tolerant. Her Indian name translates to Dancing Flower, and she is often the lead lady dancer at powwows. Rosie likes to lift weights, jog, and have fun with whatever she does.

Nadema Agard (Figure 7.10), Eastern Cherokee, Western Sioux (Lakota), and Powhatan, was the repatriation director for the Standing Rock Sioux Tribe in North Dakota. She researched museum inventories to find human remains and ethnographic materials belonging to the Sioux people. She arranged visits to those museums to begin the process of collecting bones of Sioux ancestors, as well as objects of cultural patrimony, famous chiefs' possessions, and religious items. It was a difficult and demanding job, and Nadema had to be very strong spiritually and emotionally to handle so much death and suffering. The bodies and objects were taken from burial sites and other places without permission of the relatives or tribe. Directing a repatriation project requires love, knowledge of Indian culture, and understanding the people's spiritual beliefs.

Nadema was born and raised in New York City and has a bachelor's and master's degree in art and education. After teaching art in New York schools for several years, she became a museum professional at the Museum of the American Indian. Nadema is also an artist and writer and enjoys photography, music, foreign films, and reading. She belonged to the American Association of Museums, Keepers of the Treasures, and ATLATL (the National Service Organization for Native American Artists). Nadema traveled extensively for her job and advised that anyone going into the repatriation specialty of museum work should do it for the benefit of the people, not personal glorification.

Figure 7.10. Nadema Agard.

Frank Schaefer (Figure 7.11) was born in Massachusetts and spent some of his childhood on the Onondaga reservation in New York State. His mother was Algonquin; his father Onondaga. A custodial supervisor, Frank oversees 18 workers in maintaining a Long Island, New York, school that has 185 classrooms, a huge pool, gigantic auditorium, oversized gym, plus several offices. He and his crew must ready the school for the next day and work from 3:00 P.M. until 11:00 P.M. They clean and repair everything in the high school that serves up to 2,800 students. To qualify for his position, Frank had to pass a civil-service examination that tested his ability to handle people and motivate without insulting subordinates. He belongs to the Industrial Workers Union. Apart from his custodial tasks, Frank lectures about Native American culture at schools and colleges. His hobbies include carving, beading, woodworking, traditional Indian dancing/drumming, and refurbishing old cars. Frank Schaefer's Indian name is Breed Nawagasa (One Who Looks After or Caretaker), and he is involved with Indian youth as an exemplary volunteer.

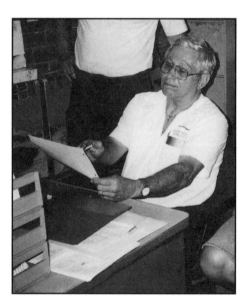

Figure 7.11. Frank Schaefer.

Jim Bruchac (Figure 7.12), Abenaki, is an outdoor educator and spent most of his life in upstate New York near the Vermont border. He is director of the Ndakinna Wilderness Project, an organization that teaches indigenous methods for tracking animals and living in the wilderness. Jim bases his instruction on Native American philosophy and folklore. People who study with Jim develop confidence and feel at ease in the woods, which helps them in other aspects of their lives. Traditional Indian music and the Abenaki language are just two of many tools he uses to help people acquire outdoor living skills. Although Jim has a bachelor's degree in American studies, he credits several sources for his vast knowledge of the natural world, including his father, elders, tracking expert John Stokes, and just being in the woods. He travels extensively, giving hands-on workshops and lectures, but still has time to perform tasks as assistant director of the Greenfield Review Press, a family business. (See Chapter 6, page 114.) An avid mountain biker, Jim loves sports, has earned a black belt in karate, and even uses martial arts techniques in his classes. He feels that two of the most important skills needed to live in the wilderness are listening and observing. Jim Bruchac's mission is to teach people to love nature, not fear it.

Figure 7.12. Jim Bruchac by wigwam he built for the Brookside Museum 1996 Native New York Festival.

Elita Dare (Figure 7.13), Oglala Sioux, is a trainer of mentally ill adults. She teaches computer skills in a model program administered by the Albany County Mental Health Association. Her tasks include individualized instruction and developing a training plan for students to help them acquire skills for independent living. All of her students have been diagnosed with mental illness.

Elita has a degree in psychology, a minor in cultural diversity, and extensive knowledge of computers. Also an herbalist, she would like to see mental illness treated with more herbal and natural remedies and fewer drugs. She cohosts a radio show that focuses on Native American issues and directs an annual Native American film festival in Albany, New York, where she cofounded the Albany Indian Center. Elita's family is from the Pine Ridge Reservation in South Dakota, but she was born in Colorado and spent much of her childhood in upstate New York. Elita Dare's Indian name translates to White Hawk Deer Woman, and she loves to attend powwows and other Indian events.

Figure 7.13. Elita Dare (L) with client Gary Chamberlain, Mohawk.

William Red Bear Smith (Figure 7.14), Cherokee, is a retired aeronautical engineer. Although he was born and raised in Oklahoma, he had to work in different places, including New York, Pennsylvania, Missouri, and California. In companies like Lockheed, where he was employed, Red Bear wrote technical orders for aircraft maintenance, concentrating on structural work, and performed tests to see how well craft would stand up in different environments. He has certificates in electronics and electrical engineering, but gained most of his knowledge from experience. Red Bear is a licensed pilot (instrument qualified) and is also a licensed aircraft and engine mechanic. He is a senior member of the Institute of Environmental Sciences and past shop steward of the Congress of Industrial Organizations. For most of his career, his work was top secret and classified. Red Bear is an active member of his tribe and community.

Figure 7.14. William Red Bear Smith.

Dr. Gelvin Stevenson (Figure 7.15), Cherokee, was born in Oklahoma and grew up in Missouri. He is an investment counselor for Indian tribes. Gelvin not only advises tribes how to invest money in stocks/bonds and other ventures, but also teaches how to monitor and evaluate investments. Tribal employees can then better protect investments from unscrupulous brokers. Gel believes that tribes can invest in ventures that help the community and local people and strengthen the local economy, including credit unions and very small businesses. He avoids business relationships with companies that pollute, discriminate, or damage Native American lands, and favors organizations that create products to solve social problems. Gel earned a doctorate degree in economics and is a member of the Social Investment Forum and a director of the First Nations Development Institute. Although Gel travels extensively through Indian country, he lives in New York City and is active in the local Native American community. Gel teaches string figures and is an avid jogger.

Figure 7.15. Dr. Gelvin Stevenson (R) with wife and son in front of his grandmother's allotment near Chelsea, Oklahoma.

Angelina C. Steves (Figure 7.16), Navajo, grew up on the Navajo reservation in Salina Springs, Arizona, near where she was born. She attended 13 different Indian schools (both boarding and day) before graduating from high school. She is a radiology technologist and ultrasound technician employed by the Ganado, Arizona hospital. Angelina performs trauma, emergency, and routine procedures on patients like barium enemas, upper gastrointestinal series, obstetrics and gynecological tests, echocardiograms and IVP tests (intravenous pyelography, an X-ray procedure that permits doctors to see the inside of the kidneys, ureters, and bladder). To become a technician, she first attended X-ray and ultrasound school and had to maintain good grades—plus do well in her clinical experience. Her courses included anatomy, physics, and physiology. Angelina earned her license by passing a very difficult, state-issued examination. She must continue taking courses and workshops to learn new equipment and procedures. Angelina belongs to both the Arizona and New York Association of American Radiologist Technologists, and her hobbies include weaving, quilting, beading, hiking, aerobics, and sheep herding.

Figure 7.16. Angelina C. Steves.

Richard Sherman, Oglala Sioux, was born and raised on the Pine Ridge Reservation in South Dakota. He is the senior wildlife biologist and coordinator of the Stewardship Program for the Oglala Sioux Parks and Recreation Authority, chartered by the Oglala Nation. Various aspects of Richard's job include managing the tribe's fisheries and wildlife resources, overseeing the Buffalo Program, and operating the Cedar Path Lodge, a concession in the Badlands National Park. He and his coworkers are responsible for 5,000 square miles! His hours can be very long, and he sometimes works seven days a week. At times he may count the animal population and chart the ratio of does to fawns; other times he is part of a search-and-rescue team that might spend hours or days finding people. Richard also helps with fund-raising for the Stewardship Program, which uses indigenous methods to ensure that the wildlife and natural resources will survive for future generations. He believes in culturally appropriate systems and learned much from his family.

Growing up so close to the land gave him the determination to put something back. Richard has an undergraduate degree in wildlife management and a graduate degree in regional planning. He spent many years away from his reservation going to school, serving in the military, and even being a seaman on the Bering Sea, but always felt the need to return because of his knowledge and love of the land. If young people were interested in a career in wildlife management, Richard would advise them to look at their land and try to enhance traditional methods to preserve and protect it. When Richard, whose Indian name is Strong Heart, is not working, he likes to camp, garden, draw, and attend art shows.

Lucia Mele, Allegheny Seneca, is an economic development specialist in San Francisco, California. She works with neighborhoods to help revitalize and promote their retail commercial corridors, while remaining true to the character of their particular community. When working with the Mission District, for instance, she helps them design businesses that keep Latino culture alive, and has herself learned to speak Spanish. Lucia meets with merchants, residents, and neighborhood groups to develop individualized plans for redevelopment and makes certain that all parties have a say. She serves on the American Indian Business Development Task Force, a subcommittee of the Human Rights Commission. Born in New York, she grew up in Princeton, New Jersey, and received an undergraduate degree in anthropology from Stanford University and a graduate degree in city planning from MIT. Lucia, whose Seneca name is Ga-NAY-gogintah, was born in Seneca Falls, New York. Her hobby is thinking up practical jokes!

Barbara Snyder (Figure 7.17) is a Southern Washoe/Northern Paiute who was born and raised in San Francisco, California. She lives in New York City, where she is a medical office manager for an orthopedic surgeon. Barbara is responsible for office administration, including supervising staff, billing, collections, scheduling appointments, booking surgeries, and hospital admissions. She learned most of her tasks on the job and completed two years of college. She needs to understand many different accents, be familiar with special medical terminology, deal with many different personalities, work with numbers, and have extensive knowledge of insurance company procedures. Barbara often works six or seven days a week. She enjoys taking her son and other neighborhood children to the park to play war games, and is very involved in Little League. Barbara's Indian name translates to Morning Dawn.

Figure 7.17. Barbara Snyder.

Jack Richardson (Figure 7.18), Stomping Elk, is from North Carolina and a member of both the Meherrin and Soponi tribes. He lives in Pennsylvania and works as a production supervisor in a manufacturing plant. His company makes pressure-sensitive label adhesive coding like medical patches. Supervising 10 workers in the adhesive mixing department keeps him busy scheduling, training, and making sure that they produce quality products. Jack learned his skills on the job and works 10 hours a day, four days a week. Understanding the regulations and specifications for the products is important in his work. In his spare time, Jack likes to work on cars, carpentry, woodworking, and plumbing. He also makes Indian drums and clothing and gives Native American cultural presentations at schools. Jack is the director of the Native American Fall Festival at the Indian Steps Museum.

Figure 7.18. Jack Richardson.

Vanesa Humer Richardson (Figure 7.19), Navajo, was born and raised in Pennsylvania, but her family is from Arizona. She is the coordinator of volunteers for a battered women and children's shelter and hires, supervises, and trains volunteers. As part of her job, Vanesa must be on 24-hour emergency room duty several times a month and ensures that standards set forth by the Pennsylvania Coalition Against Domestic Violence are implemented. She also helps monitor the Batterers Intervention Services Program. Vanesa is a trained paralegal and has a degree in business administration, but learned most of her tasks on the job and at workshops, seminars, and conferences. Her training is ongoing. She represents her agency at community events and organizations, where she often educates people about domestic violence. Vanesa serves as board member for her county conservation society and enjoys dancing, reading, hiking, biking, sewing, and is a member of a Native American drum and singing group.

Figure 7.19. Vanesa Humer Richardson.

George Strayhorn (Figure 7.20), Cayuga, is an industrial machinery mechanic, living and working in New York City. His company manufactures electrical fixtures for home and industry, and George is the only mechanic on the third shift, 12:00 A.M. to 8:30 A.M. He repairs and makes production changes for plastic compression molding machinery. To attain his present position, he worked with various machinery for a few years, was promoted to setup person, and changed molds for three years. After that, George earned a floor mechanic AA or secondary position, and finally was awarded his present job as floor mechanic A, or top grade. An industrial machine mechanic must have aptitude for mechanics, determination, discipline, and a general knowledge of hydraulics, electrical wiring, steam control, and piping. George has to learn new skills as the machines change. Currently, he is working on computer-controlled machines. He is a member of the United Auto Workers Union. Stubborn Elk (George's Indian name) was born in upstate New York, but moved to New York City as a child. He loves to fish and is an amateur photographer.

Figure 7.20. George Strayhorn.

Reginald Herb Dancer Caeser (Figure 7.21), Matinnecock and Blackfeet, lives in Queens, New York, not far from the homeland of his Nation. He is a Shiatsu master and chairperson of the Shiatsu department of the Swedish Institute, School of Massage and Allied Therapies. His responsibilities include administering the department and teaching three or four classes a semester. Reggie, a licensed massage therapist, consults with the state education department when they need help issuing licenses to other therapists. He also has a private practice where he incorporates his expertise in Swedish and Eastern healing arts including Shiatsu, Thai, and Chinese medical massage modalities, moxa, herbology, and cupping. To become a Shiatsu practitioner takes patience, discipline, and study. Reggie attended Shiatsu school for three years and then had to pass a rigid state examination to earn his license; he also studied herbal medicine and naturopathy for many years. To enhance his healing techniques, he is now studying acupuncture. He belongs to the American Massage and Therapy Association and is a certified instructor and member of the American Oriental Bodywork Therapy Association. Reggie enjoys Tai Chi and Native American dancing and singing.

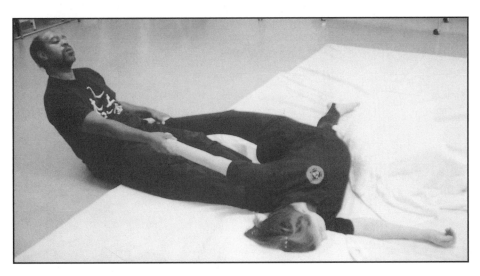

Figure 7.21. Reginald Herb Dancer Caeser.

Larry R. Chavis (Figure 7.22), Lumbee, lives in Lumberton, North Carolina, 20 miles from where he grew up. He serves as president and chief executive officer of the Lumbee Guaranty Bank, an FDIC and state-insured financial corporation. Under Larry's administration, the bank has expanded to seven branches in seven different towns, and assets are valued at over $70 million. He manages 45 employees, most of them Lumbee, who serve 18,000 customers! Lumbee Guaranty offers complete financial services, including loans and checking and saving accounts. Larry is accountable to the 1,000 shareholders, most of them Lumbee, and the all-Lumbee board of directors. He must keep abreast of legislative situations that affect banking and works with similar-sized banks to exchange information. He works about 60 hours a week and reads financial communications like the *Wall Street Journal* daily. Overseeing the bank's investments in government securities and state and municipal bonds is also part of Larry's work. Because Larry's bank is community based, he is very interested in providing low-income home financing and meeting other community needs. He has a graduate degree in business administration and a degree in bank controllership. However, he continues to take courses and seminars as needed. Larry enjoys sports with his children and is a part-time farmer.

Figure 7.22. Larry R. Chavis.

Carlos Estrella (Figure 7.23), Cherokee, was born in New Jersey and lived in Long Island, New York, before moving to Florida. He is a computer instructor, teaching corporate executives home or business applications of personal computers and software. Sometimes he travels to give classes, but usually conducts training in his company's classrooms. Carlos often has to modify the training design to fit a particular student and supplements the syllabus with his personal techniques. A computer instructor requires many hours of training and special certification. Carlos is a certified netware engineer and had to pass a lengthy and difficult examination. He is preparing for the Microsoft certified professional examination, and even after passing, he has to continuously study and learn new technology to keep his certification. In his spare time Carlos writes poetry and is skilled in Filipino stick fighting and jujitsu.

Figure 7.23. Carlos Estrella and son Kyle.

Joseph Kabance (Figure 7.24) is Prairie Band Potawatomi (Thunder Clan), from the Potawatomi reservation in Mayetta, Kansas. For most of his childhood, he lived away from his family in a South Dakota Indian boarding school and attended college in New Mexico. Presently, he is a casino poker dealer at the Foxwoods Casino located on the Mashantucket Pequot Indian reservation in Ledyard, Connecticut. To obtain his position, Joe had to attend a dealers' training school for 10 weeks and earn a Connecticut gaming license. Often working long hours, he wears a uniform and deals cards to up to eight players at a poker table. Joe deals for one and a half hours, then takes a break. There are many gambling games in the casino as well as a museum. Dealing cards is a new job experience for Joe. He attended law school and worked as an Equal Employment Opportunity coordinator for the New York State Office of Mental Health for 10 years. As an administrator for that office, he monitored agency programs and services to ensure they hired women, minorities, veterans, and the disabled. He is a member of the National Urban Indian Council and the New York State Affirmative Action Council. Also an artist, Joe's oil paintings have been featured in many exhibitions, including the Museum of the American Indian. He likes to jog, hike, play tennis, and visit art museums and shows. Joe also enjoys researching Native American issues such as images, healing, warfare, symbolism, and law.

Figure 7.24. Joseph Kabance with daughter Ohniehyah.

Dr. Paulette Fairbanks Molin, a member of the Minnesota Chippewa tribe, grew up on the White Earth Reservation in Minnesota. She now lives in Virginia where she is the director of the American Indian Educational Opportunities Program at Hampton University. She recruits, counsels, and refers Indian students, helping them get scholarships and financial aid. Paulette also teaches American Indian studies and conducts research in that field. Her academic work includes cocurating a photographic exhibition, "To Lead and Serve: American Indian Education at Hampton Institute, 1878–1923," which features the lives of early Indian students. She is responsible for procuring funds for her program and has to write proposals. That is called grantsmanship, a skill she first learned from Native American colleagues many years ago. At times Paulette travels to schools and conferences, recruiting students and networking with other educators. She usually works from 40 to 60 hours a week.

Paulette spent many years preparing for her position. She worked as a social worker in Minnesota and earned a doctorate degree in educational administration from the University of Minnesota. A recipient of the Bush Foundation Fellowship of St. Paul, she also attended Harvard University. A career in higher education requires at least a master's degree, but a doctorate is preferred. She is a member of the American Indian Engineering Society, National Indian Education Association, and serves on the board of directors of Wordcraft. (See Lesson 6.1, page 112.) In her leisure time, Paulette enjoys spending time with her family and friends and participating in community events. Most of her leisure activities are also related to her work.

Resources
Students

Avery, Susan, and L. Skinner. *Extraordinary American Indians.* Chicago: Children's Book Press, 1992.
Collection of biographies by topic.

Bataille, Gretchen, and K. Sands. *American Indian Women Telling Their Stories.* Lincoln, NE: University of Nebraska Press, 1984.
Several Indian women share their lives.

Champagne, Duane. *Native America: Portrait of the Peoples.* Detroit: Visible Ink, 1994.
There are many biographies in this book.

Grinde, Donald, and Bruce Johansen. *The Encyclopedia of Native American Biography.* New York: Henry Holt, 1995.
There are 600 biographies in this book, including every walk of life from athletes to explorers, contemporary and historical.

Klein, Barry. *Reference Encyclopedia of the American Indian.* 8th edition. West Nyack, NY: Todd Publications, 1997. 18 North Greenbush Road, West Nyack, NY 10994. (914) 358-6213.
This book has biographical sketches and a wealth of other information.

Sonneborn, Liz. *A to Z of Native American Women*. New York: Facts on File, 1998.
Profiles of over 100 women who have made contributions to both Indian and non-Indian society from the seventeenth century to the present.

United Indians of All Tribes Foundation (UIATF). *Interviews with Native American Men and Women in Various Jobs*. Seattle, WA: UIATF, 1980.
Available from Day Break Star Press.

Lesson  Indian-Owned Companies

Grade Level
4–8

Materials
Student Readings: "Indian Owned Businesses: An Overview"; "Business-Oriented Tribes"; and "A Few Indian-Owned Businesses"; art materials for a collage

Time
Two class periods

Objectives
- Students learn about the variety of Indian-owned businesses (both tribally owned and individually owned) and how they sometimes differ from non-Indian businesses.

Activities
1. Students list all the products or companies they know that contain any names of or references to Indians, e.g., Cherokee clothing, Jeep Grand Cherokee, and Winnebago (recreational vehicle). Ask students if any of these are Indian owned. If not, why do companies use Indian names? (See Chapter 1 on stereotyping.) For homework, students can bring advertisements and labels of Indian-oriented products and companies.
2. Students write to one or more of the tribes listed below and request information on businesses on their reservations that are owned by the tribe, tribal members, or Indian organizations.
3. Students discuss what "Indian-owned businesses" existed before European contact in 1492. (Teacher's hint: These related mostly to the provision of the basic economic necessities, i.e., food, shelter, clothing, transportation, healing.)
4. Students discuss what Indian-owned businesses might exist today on reservations. (Teacher's hint: The same, plus modern ones like gas stations, auto repair shops, grocery stores, video stores, etc.)
5. Students read the list of Indian-owned businesses, and then draw or construct items they can buy from Indian-owned businesses.

Enrichment/Extensions

Art. Students make a collage of products produced by Indian-owned companies. (See list of companies, page 185.)

Health. Purchase, from a store or by mail order, a food product sold by an Indian-owned company. (Most health food companies will have at least wild rice from an Indian-owned company, and maybe other products. Ask them.) Prepare the food and have students eat it together. Students discuss whether they have ever eaten these foods and how they taste.

Science. Students list businesses in their community and determine whether they are environmentally friendly. Find out whether they help the community, how many people from the community they employ, and what products or services they produce.

📖 Reading

Indian-Owned Businesses: An Overview

by Gelvin Stevenson, Ph.D.

Indians own many different types of businesses. These businesses range from huge gambling casinos and hotels to convenience stores and horse training ("bronco-busting") businesses—from small ranches to the largest irrigated farm in the United States and a helicopter manufacturer. (See list of Indian-owned businesses, page 185.) Some are owned by tribal governments, for example, the Radisson Hotel in Green Bay is owned by the Oneida tribe of Wisconsin, descendants of the people who brought hundreds of bags of corn to George Washington's hungry soldiers during their rough winter in Valley Forge, Pennsylvania. Others, including many farms and ranches, belong to families. Still others are sole proprietorships, which means individual Indians, like craftspeople, artists, and owners of small restaurants. The Jicarilla Apache own their own general store in Dulce, New Mexico. At this time, there are none that are public companies, which is to say that their shares can be bought or sold on the stock exchanges. But that could change in the near future.

Most Indian-owned businesses may not even be incorporated as businesses. They are home-based businesses that generate income for the family. Many Indians earn money producing arts and crafts like beadwork, jewelry, and clothing. (Some of these are marketed by the Zuni Silver Cooperative; others by Sky City Graphics, a gallery of Indian arts and artisans in Acoma, New Mexico.) Others earn money by catering, fixing tires, repairing cars, caring for children, gathering firewood, and performing a hundred other tasks.

Some Indian-owned businesses are located on reservations, but the great majority—some say as many as 90 percent—are located off reservations in towns and cities. First Oklahoma Bank, Native American owned, is located in Shawnee, Oklahoma. There are three Lumbee Guaranty Banks, located in different towns in North Carolina. There is an Indian-owned stock brokerage firm, First American Securities, Inc., in Minneapolis, and several Indian-owned money managers: Native American Asset Advisers in Oklahoma City and Native American Advisors outside of Atlanta.

Other Indian-owned businesses endeavor to help other Indians and non-Indians instead of just making money. The Zuni Silver Cooperative is one of these. It helps its members market their silver jewelry for prices that are fair and usually higher than they would receive from other traders or wholesalers. Some businesses owned by tribes are more interested in providing jobs for tribal members than in turning a profit (although they try not to lose money).

In Alaska, 13 Native bands were given land, resources, and/or money to establish businesses under the 1971 Alaska Native Claims Settlement Act. Some work with their resources, like lumber, minerals, oil, and hunting and fishing. One of them, Piquniq Management Corporation, provides engineering services to indigenous people all over the United States and Canada and even has an office in Central America.

Some Indian businesses operate very differently from their non-Indian counterparts. Menominee Tribal Enterprises operates a lumber and woodworking business that is known worldwide as a model of environmentally friendly, sustainable forest management. That means that only as much wood is cut down every year as grows in the forest during one year. That way the forest will always be strong and healthy. Other lumber companies, which give profits a higher priority, will cut down all the trees and then plant new ones. Even though new trees may grow back in 20 or 30 years, the forest will never be the same as it was, and the shelter and food for thousands and thousands of animals has been destroyed—and the animals will either die or move somewhere else. In 1992, Menominee Tribal Enterprises was granted the first certification in the nation for sustainable forestry. Today, it employs 260 people. They earn a living while keeping the forest strong for their children and grandchildren and other future generations.

Another tribal business in Canada has unique and creative ways of hiring. Instead of hiring a particular person, it makes an agreement with an extended family to provide a worker at a particular time and place. Then the family can decide who will show up and do the work, depending on who is needed to help the family that day. Aaxua Tannery prepares leather the traditional way, using water and other animal parts, but no toxic chemicals, like many "modern" tanneries.

Small and relatively few though they may be, Indian-owned companies are dynamic and creative, and their numbers are increasing rapidly. Keep your eyes peeled; you could be buying something from an Indian-owned business, or working for one, before you know it.

📖 Reading

Business-Oriented Tribes

Blackfeet, PO Box 850, Browning, MT 59417. (406) 338-7276.

Cherokee Nation of Oklahoma, PO Box 948, Tahlequah, OK 74465. (918) 456-0671.

Menominee Tribe, PO Box 397, Keshena, WI 54135. (715) 799-3341.

Mississippi Band of Choctaws, Route 7, Box 21, Philadelphia, MS 39350. (601) 656-5251.

Oneida Tribe of Indians of Wisconsin, PO Box 365, Oneida, WI 54155, (414) 869-2772.

White Earth Chippewa, PO Box 418, White Earth, MN 56591. (218) 983-3285.

White Mountain Apache Tribe, PO Box 700, Whiteriver, AZ 85941. (520) 338-4346.

📖 Reading

A Few Indian-Owned Businesses

Bay Bank, Packerland Drive, Oneida, WI 54155. (414) 432-0390; owned by the Oneida tribe of Wisconsin.

Blackfeet Writing Company, PO Box D, Browning, MT 59417. (406) 338-7406; produces pencils and pens.

First Oklahoma Bank, PO Box 68, Shawnee, OK 74802-0068. (405) 275-0390; owned by an individual Indian.

Gray Owl Foods, PO Box 88, Grand Rapids, MI 55744. (218) 327-2281; wild rice. Subsidiary of the Saskatchewan Indian Agriculture Program, Inc.

The Healthy Way, Cherokee, NC; retailer of health food and herbs.

Indian Country Today, PO Box 4250, Rapid City, SD 57709. (605) 341-0011; weekly newspaper covering Indian news and issues.

Native American Herbal Tea, PO Box 1266, Aberdeen, SD 57402-1266. (605) 226-2006; herbal teas.

Piquniq Management Corporation; one of 13 Native bands in Alaska given land, resources, and/or money to establish businesses under the 1971 Alaska Native Claims Settlement Act.

Radisson Inn in Green Bay and Oneida, WI; Phone: Oneida reservation; lodging and food.

Resources

<u>Students</u>

Trahant, Lenora Begay. *The Success of the Navajo Arts and Crafts Enterprise.* New York: Walker, 1996.
    This book introduces the people behind the Navajo Arts and Crafts Enterprise, a successful company for Navajo artisans to make a living at their crafts.

<u>Teachers</u>

Asian Americans, American Indians and Other Minorities (MB87-3). Bureau of the Census, Superintendent of Documents, U.S. Government Printing Office, Washington, DC 20402.

Business Alert. First Nations Development Institute, The Stores Building, 11917 Main Street, Fredericksburg, VA 22408.
    Bimonthly newsletter covers topics on culturally appropriate economic development on reservations.

Minority Business Today. U.S. Department of Commerce, 14th and Constitution, NW, Washington, DC 20230.
    This magazine covers Indian-owned and other minority businesses.

National Indian Business Association (NIBA), PO Box 40180, Albuquerque, NM 87196.

Reference Encyclopedia of the American Indian. Todd Publications, 18 North Greenbush Road, West Nyack, NY 10994. (914) 358-6213.

Tiller's Guide to Indian Country: Economic Profiles of American Indians. Albuquerque, NM: Bow Arrow, 1996.
    Order from Quality Books, Inc., 1003 West Pines Road, Oregon, IL 61061-9680.

Video. "Choctaw Story." Bob Ferguson. 1985.
    This 28-minute video highlights the achievements of the tribal administrator of Chief Phillip Martin since 1979.

Video. "Protein from the Sea." Alaskan Native Film Production (ANFP). Available from ANFP, 1515 Dexter Avenue North, Seattle, WA 98109.
    This film shows today's technically sophisticated fishing industry based on a thousand-year-old culture. It focuses on the crab and salmon processing ship, the *Al-Ind-Esk-A*, converted from a World War II naval vessel.

Lesson  7.3

Tourism and Gaming

Grade Level
4–6

Materials
Student Reading: "Tourism and Gaming in Indian Country"; materials for a collage; a map of the United States with or without reservations marked

Time
One class period

Objectives
- Students will learn about tourism on reservations and think about places they would like to visit.

- They will consider tourism and gaming from an Indian perspective and discover some of the misconceptions surrounding gaming today.

Activities
1. Students list all the things they want to see and do on a trip to an Indian reservation.
2. Students identify the reservations on a map they would most like to visit and explain in a paragraph why they chose them.
3. Students collect pictures of Indian reservations from magazines.
4. Students discuss the pros and cons of gambling, especially whether or not the amount someone gambles should be limited.
5. Students discuss the pros and cons of opening a casino from the point of view of the Indians. Pros include jobs and income for Indians and non-Indians and revenues for schools, roads, and other needs. Cons include the damage gambling can do to tribal members and others and moral objections to gaming.
6. Students discuss whether some people should not be allowed to gamble. Who? What age?
7. Students discuss the fact that people can become addicted to gambling, just like they can become addicted to alcohol, smoking, or drugs.

Enrichment/Extensions
Art. Students use the pictures of reservations to make a collage.

Creative Writing. Students write a story of a trip to a reservation. The story can be a real trip or an imaginary one.

Math. Students play games that people gamble on, like 21, bingo, or poker. Some gamblers playing 21 increase their chances of winning by counting the various cards that have been played. Have students try to figure out how that increases their odds of winning.

Students play other games. (See Lesson 4.7, page 84; research Indian games; and figure out the math involved.)

📖 Reading

Tourism and Gaming in Indian Country

by Gelvin Stevenson, Ph.D.

For hundreds of years, people have wanted to visit Indians to learn more about these first residents of North America. Early European settlers learned a great deal from Indians. They learned about foods and plants for curing illness and some ideas about how to organize societies and governments, especially democracy. Today, tourism still flourishes, and thousands of people visit reservations every year. Some go to see the beautiful scenery and some go on hunting and fishing trips with Indian guides. Other activities include attending powwows, where they can purchase authentic Indian arts and crafts, watch Indians in beautiful outfits dance traditional dances to the beat of handmade drums, and eat traditional Indian food.

Many people visit from foreign countries, particularly from Germany, Australia, Japan, and Korea. Some Japanese believe that there are many similarities between the beliefs of the Shinto religion and Native American teachings. In Germany, there are at least 60,000 people that belong to clubs devoted to Indian tribes and culture, and one German travel agent is called Lakota Tipi and Travel.

Indians are very hospitable; it is a part of their cultures. So they usually welcome visitors. However, it is important that visitors come with respect and openness. They should remember that they are visiting peoples' homes and communities. Some disrespectful visitors also try to participate in Indian religious ceremonies without being invited. That is very rude. Tourists should only visit ceremonies and gatherings that are open to the public. If they are private, tourists should attend only if invited.

A new activity that is drawing more people to reservations is gaming. In 1988, Congress granted Indian tribes the right to operate gaming enterprises by passing the Indian Gaming Regulatory Act. That law gave tribes the right to operate any gaming activity that was already being carried on in the state, but with no limit on the prizes. That meant that states allowing charities to operate bingo or "Las Vegas Nights" or any other gambling had to allow Indian tribes to operate the same games, but without any limits on the size of the prizes. But before tribes could open any gaming facilities, they had to sign an agreement or a "compact" with the government of the state where they were located.

Indian-owned casinos and bingo halls have received a great deal of publicity that has given rise to many misconceptions. Some people think that all Indian tribes operate casinos, and all are making a lot of money. In fact, some tribes, including the Navajo, who have the largest reservation in the United States, have voted not to have any gaming activities. Some traditional tribes in New York have also refused to open gaming facilities.

All in all, in 1998, 148 of the more than 550 tribes in the United States had any gaming operations; only a small number have been making large amounts of money. There has been a lot of news about the Mashantucket Pequot tribe's Foxwoods High Stakes Bingo and Casino in Connecticut. It is said to be the largest casino in the Western Hemisphere and to receive a total of $1 billion a year. (Of course, that is total receipts, not profits. Much of that is used to pay for salaries, buildings, and other expenses.) But that is the exception. Fewer than a handful of tribes are highly successful. Of those that have gaming, many have small facilities. And many reservations are located far away from urban centers. All the gaming tribes together received a total of $2.7 billion in revenues in a recent year. That's a big number, but it represented only 7 percent of the total industry in the United States. (In contrast, state governments enjoy 35 percent of all gaming revenues, earned primarily from lotteries.)

What do the successful gaming tribes do with the money? As in most matters, there is great diversity in Indian country. A few make payments to each tribal member. Most use the money to improve their economies and life and opportunities for tribal members. The Oneida tribe in Wisconsin uses its earnings for its youth and elders. It has built a beautiful school in the shape of a turtle, with modern equipment and traditional stories built into the school's tile work for its young people. The Oneida make a payment to each of their elders every year. The Ho-Chunk tribe in Nebraska is using its gaming proceeds to build hotels and invest in real estate to strengthen its reservation economy. Many tribes with gaming revenues are buying land, especially land within reservation boundaries, much of which belongs to nontribal members. Several tribes are also making contributions to local governments and charities that serve local non-Indian communities.

Indian gaming is a new phenomenon in Indian country, and it might not last very long.

Resources
Teachers

Indian Games of North America.
   (See Resources, page 87 for additional material on Indian games.)

National Indian Gaming Association, 224 Second Street, SE, Washington, DC. (202) 546-7711.
   Industry association for gaming tribes.

National Indian Gaming Commission, 1850 M Street, Washington, DC. (202) 632-7003.
   Federal agency overseeing Indian gaming.

Reference Encyclopedia of the American Indian. 7th edition, Todd Publications, 18 North Greenbush Road, West Nyack, NY 10994. (914) 358-6213.
   This edition has a section on "Casinos and Bingo Halls."

Shanks, Ralph. *The North American Indian Travel Guide.* Petaluma, CA: Castaño Books, 1991.
   This book highlights special vacation spots in Indian country. Great illustrations.

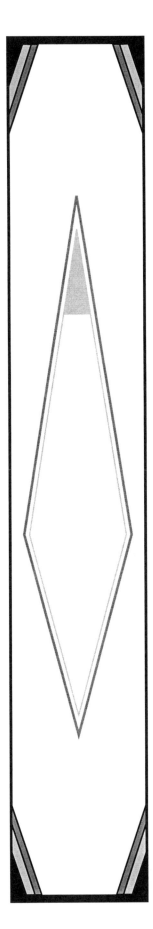

Chapter **8**

The Struggle Continues

The brilliant strategist and Shawnee leader Tecumseh said in the 1800s, "That people will continue longest in the enjoyment of peace who timely prepare to vindicate themselves and manifest the determination to protect themselves whenever they are wronged." And so the struggles continue to this day.

These lessons were developed to help students understand that Native Americans must struggle daily to protect their human rights, treaty rights, children, languages, religions, traditions, and other aspects of their cultures. They must even protect burial sites! Hopefully, these activities will be thought-provoking and may even inspire your students to support Native American rights.

The lesson on Team Names, Mascots, and Logos will be of particular interest to your students since they are probably familiar with many of the sports teams mentioned.

Lesson

8.1

Native Language Recovery

Grade Level
4–8

Materials
Student Reading: "Native Languages: Loss and Recovery"

Time
One class period

Objectives
- Students learn that many Native languages were systematically destroyed and others endangered because of U.S. government policy.

- Students learn that Native communities are trying to preserve or revive their languages.

- Students learn reasons other languages are endangered.

- Students learn how to research Indian languages in global information sources.

Activities
1. Students read "Native Languages: Loss and Recovery." First discuss the factors that endanger a language. Discuss whether other languages are spoken in students' homes. List them on the board. One by one, discuss whether any of them are endangered, and if so, why. (Age of speakers.)
2. Research the topic of Indian languages and their survival in *Readers' Guide to Periodical Literature* or InfoTrac and present an oral report based on research.

Enrichment/Extensions
Research. Students study the ways Indian languages were discouraged and/or destroyed during the Indian boarding school period (late 1870s through the mid-1930s). Give an oral report based on research.

Students research the Navajo Code Talkers whose unbreakable code based on the Navajo language played an indispensable role in World War II.

📖 Reading

Native Languages: Loss and Recovery

There never has been one language that all Indian people living in the present-day United States speak. To believe this would be the same as believing that all people in Europe speak "European" when actually they speak French, German, Spanish, Italian, and other languages. Indian languages are as different from one another as English is from Chinese. The Hopis cannot understand the Crow language any more than the Swiss can understand the Tibetan language. Experts estimate that in 1492 there were over 300 separate indigenous languages spoken by Native people in North America. Today, only about half of these languages continue to be spoken in Native communities. Why the drop?

From the beginning of European contact, efforts were made by missionaries and government officials to enforce English-only policies. In the late 1800s and early 1900s, Indian children were removed from their homes for years at a time and forced to go to boarding schools run by the U.S. government and missionary organizations. Government policy demanded that teachers instruct in English, and children were not permitted to speak their own languages and were punished when they did so. The ban was so effective that over 100 Native languages died off because people stopped speaking them.

Despite destructive policies, Native languages continue to be spoken in many Native communities. However, a significant number of them are endangered, and tribal people and communities are working to preserve languages before they slip away. They are videotaping and tape-recording elders speaking their languages. Some communities are putting their languages on CD-ROM. Tribal community colleges and public schools serving Indian communities offer bilingual programs. Some linguists are working with Indian people to produce dictionaries of unwritten Indian languages before the last speakers die. Those tribes with radio stations are using them as a tool to promote Native languages. For example, KILI in Porcupine, South Dakota, on the Pine Ridge Reservation broadcasts a four-hour morning program in Lakota.

In the late 1980s, Native Americans and non-Native educators and linguists succeeded in getting a bill through Congress to reverse the government's policy aimed at destroying Indian languages. In October 1990, President George Bush signed the Native American Language Act. The act officially recognizes the right of Native languages to exist and states it is government policy to "preserve, protect, and promote the rights and freedom of Native Americans to use, practice, and develop Native American languages."

Resources

<u>Students</u>

Aaseng, Nathan. *Navajo Code Talkers*. New York: Walker, 1992.
 History of a special group of Navajo U.S. Marines who, during World War II, developed complex code based on the Navajo language.

Barringer, Felicity. "Faded but Vibrant, Indian Languages Struggle to Keep Their Voices Alive." *New York Times* (January 8, 1991).
 Good summary of tribal efforts to preserve and revive Indian languages.

Bixler, Margaret T. *Winds of Freedom: The Story of the Navajo Code Talkers of World War II*. Darien, CT: Two Bytes Press, 1992.

Hirschfelder, Arlene, and Martha Kreipe de Montaño. "Languages" and "Code Talkers," in *Native American Almanac: A Portrait of Native America Today*. New York: Prentice-Hall, 1993.

Video. "Transitions: Destruction of a Mother Tongue." 1991. Darrell Kipp (Blackfeet) and Joe Fisher.
 This program explores the relationship among language, thought, and culture, and the impact of language disappearance in Native American communities. Distributed by Native Voices Public Television Workshop, VCB Room 224, Montana State University, Bozeman, MT 59717.

"Why Indians Must Speak Their Own Languages." Poster. North American Indian Traveling College, R.R. 3, Cornwall Island, ON, Canada K6H 5R7.

<u>Teachers</u>

Golla, Victor. "Languages," in *Native America in the Twentieth Century: An Encyclopedia*. New York: Garland, 1994, 310–12.
 Article covers language diversity, their decline and extinction, and efforts to preserve Indian languages.

Martin, Kallen. "Listen! Native Radio Can Save Languages." *Native Americas: Akwe:kon's Journal of Indigenous Issues*. Vol. 13, no.1 (Spring 1996): 22–29.
 Writer stresses the connection between Native radio and language preservation and recovery efforts.

Lesson

8.2

Burial Ground Desecration and Repatriation

Grade Level
7–8

Materials
Student Reading: "No Peace for Indian Burial Grounds"

Time
Two class periods

Objectives
- Students learn that Indian burial grounds have been desecrated, in the name of science, an example of discrimination against Indians and insensitivity to their religious beliefs.

- Students learn that Native Americans are repatriating skeletal remains and grave goods of their ancestors and reburying them.

- Students learn how to research global information sources like *Readers' Guide to Periodical Literature* and InfoTrac.

Activities
1. Students read "No Peace for Indian Burial Grounds" and discuss at least five reasons why Indian burial grounds have been destroyed.
2. Students write a "Letter to the Editor" in which they speak out against the disruption of Indian burial sites.
3. In small groups, students research in *Readers' Guide* or InfoTrac and present an oral report about the 200 graves dug up on the Slack farm in Kentucky in 1989 as well as the aftermath, or another reburial story.
4. Students discuss how they would feel if the graves of their great-grandparents were disturbed, either accidentally or deliberately.

Enrichment/Extensions
Research. Students can do a report about the repatriation work of Walter Echo Hawk.

Students can research the desecration of cemeteries of Jewish and African American peoples and community reaction.

Report on laws protecting cemeteries within the students' state. Find out if there is a state law against desecrating or robbing Indian graves. If so, what are the penalties?

Field Trip. Visit a local museum or historical society to see if any Native American human remains and/or grave goods are displayed in cases. If so, write a letter to the museum protesting the display.

📖 Reading

No Peace for Indian Burial Grounds

Thousands of years ago, Indian people laid their dead to rest above and below the ground, often surrounding them with pottery vessels, necklaces, baskets, or other sacred goods to be taken on the journey to the afterworld. Today, these ancient Indian graves—and even more recent ones—are no longer safe. Over the course of time, erosion and river flooding have accidentally exposed grave sites. Farmers plowing their fields have unearthed skeletal remains and burial goods. Urban developers have bulldozed mounds to make way for buildings. Road builders have destroyed Indian cemeteries. Land-clearing techniques and logging operations have taken their toll. But worst of all, pothunting vandals deliberately plunder Indian burial sites to steal objects buried with the dead and valued by collectors in the domestic and international markets. These grave looters scatter bones of the dead in their frenzy to find grave goods. By all accounts, Indian grave desecration and looting have reached epidemic proportions across the nation.

Nationwide, Indians and archaeologists have condemned this destruction. Archaeologists are concerned about the bulldozing and looting of burial sites because once a site is disrupted, its historical understanding is disrupted. As Winston Hurst, a Utah archaeologist explained it, "The stuff from 850 A.D. is mixed with the stuff from 850 B.C. and no one will ever be able to unscramble it."

Indians condemn the destruction of grave sites, but their protests are based on religious and moral grounds. Like cultures throughout the world, Indians have deeply ingrained attitudes about the dead. Although there is great diversity in the religious traditions of Indian Nations, Indians generally believe that when people die, their remains and any sacred objects placed with them must not be disturbed or displaced, except by natural occurrences. People who practice Judeo-Christian religions also hold these beliefs, and their views are reflected in state laws that impose criminal penalties on persons who desecrate cemeteries.

Thousands of Indian burial sites are located on federal lands managed by the Bureau of Land Management (BLM), the Forest Service, and the National Park Service. Vandals and thieves have wreaked havoc on these Indian grave sites. The BLM and Forest Service simply do not have large enough budgets or staffs to monitor millions of acres. Since the National Park Service has more law enforcement per acre than the other two agencies, it is better equipped to patrol national parks and cut down on grave desecration.

Countless Indian burial sites are also located on state and privately owned lands. These sites, too, have been looted and destroyed. One of the worst desecrations of Indian burial grounds took place in Kentucky during the fall of 1987. Ten men disturbed over 200 Indian grave sites located on 40 acres of farmland searching for ceremonial objects before the Kentucky State Police obtained a court order to halt the digging. Tens of thousands of ceremonial objects from this site and others have ended up in private or public collections, warehouses, and shops.

Indian activists want the skeletal remains of their ancestors removed from museums, universities, and warehouses and returned to their descendants for proper reburial. Eventually, Native organizations, museum curators, and archaeologists reached a compromise resulting in the passage of the Native American Grave Protection and Repatriation Act of 1990. The law applies to collections of human remains and grave goods held by federal, not state, agencies and museums receiving federal monies. The act gives tribes legal procedures to reclaim human remains and grave goods. States, too, are protecting Indian graves. Over 30 have passed burial legislation to protect unmarked Indian graves.

Resources
Students

Agard, Nadema.
   She describes her work as repatriation director for the Standing Rock Sioux Nation in North Dakota. (See her interview on page 165.)

Arden, Harvey, and Steve Wall. "Who Owns Our Past?" *National Geographic* (March 1989): 376–91.
   Article deals with plundered burials on Kentucky's Slack farm in 1987.

Barringer, Felicity. "Major Accord Likely on Indian Remains." *New York Times* (August 20, 1989): 22.
   Article deals with scientists who want to learn from the remnants of the past and the descendants who want to return them to the ground.

Brower, Montgomery, and Conan Putnam. "Walter Echo-Hawk Fights for His People's Right to Rest in Peace—Not in Museums." *People* (September 4, 1989): 44.

Buffalohead, Priscilla. "Who Owns a People's Past?," in *Modern Indian Issues . . . A Lesson Series for Secondary Teachers and Students*. Coon Rapids, MN: Anoka-Hennepin District 11, 1993, 50–52.
   Student reading deals with the digging up of Indian graves in the interest of science, and desecration of burials on the Slack farm.

Echo-Hawk, Roger C., and Walter R. Echo-Hawk. *Battlefields and Burial Grounds: The Indian Struggle to Protect Ancestral Graves in the United States*. Minneapolis, MN: Lerner Publications, 1994.
   The book examines the history of the desecration of Native American graves and describes the struggle of Native people to reclaim and rebury their dead in accord with their religious beliefs and customs. Half the book focuses on the Pawnee quest for reburial.

"Plunder of the Past." *Newsweek* (June 26, 1989): 17.
   Article deals with the plunder of the Slack farm in Kentucky and Indian grave robbing in general.

Video. "Native Americans: The People of the Great Plains," Part Two. Turner Home Entertainment, 1994.
    Arguably the most powerful and graphic five minutes ever filmed for the public. Actual footage of the repatriation (at the Smithsonian Institution) and reburial in 1993 of five skulls belonging to Cheyenne people massacred by Colonel Chivington at Sand Creek, Colorado, on November 29, 1864. Teachers should preview the video. Distributed by Turner Home Entertainment, (800) 999-0446.

<u>Teachers</u>

Preston, Douglas J. "Skeletons in Our Museums' Closets." *Harper's Magazine* (February 1989): 66–75.
    General article about Indian bones stored in museums, how they got there in the first place, why the bones are still there, and demands by Indians for their return.

Thornton, Russell. "Repatriation of Human Remains and Artifacts," in *Native America in the Twentieth Century: An Encyclopedia*, Mary B. Davis, ed. New York: Garland, 1994, 543–44.
    Reviews the long history of how Native people have been objects of study and preservation in repositories. Summarizes reasons why Natives feel repatriation and reburial must occur, and summarizes legislation enacted by U.S. federal government in the twentieth century to protect ancestral remains and sacred objects.

Time-Life Editors. "A Journey of Recovery," in *Winds of Renewal*. Alexandria, VA: Time-Life Books, 1996, 6–17.
    Photographic essay about the repatriation by the Smithsonian Institution to the Sisseton-Wahpeton Dakota of the human remains of 31 human beings belonging to that Nation.

Lesson 8.3

Sacred Objects and Repatriation

Grade Level
    7–8

Materials
    Student Reading: "Lost and Found: The Repatriation of Indian Sacred Objects"

Time
    Two class periods

Objectives
- Students learn that Native Nations have sacred objects that are used in religious ceremonies or buried with individuals.

- Students learn that sacred objects have been stolen from Indian tribes.

- Students learn that Congress passed the Native American Grave Protection and Repatriation Act of 1990.

- Students learn that Indian tribes are repatriating sacred objects.

- Students learn how to research global information sources.

Activities

1. Students first write a paragraph about an object that is sacred to their own tradition. In a second paragraph, students try to imagine their reactions if that sacred object was stolen or desecrated.

2. Students read "Lost and Found: The Repatriation of Indian Sacred Objects" and discuss the "new" meaning of repatriation.

3. Divide the class into small groups and send them to the library to research in *Readers' Guide* and InfoTrac the following sacred objects that have been repatriated: (1) the Hidatsa's Waterbuster Clan Bundle (returned by the Museum of the American Indian in 1938); (2) Zuni War Gods (over 70 returned by museums, art galleries, and private collectors all over the nation since 1978); (3) Omaha Sacred Pole (returned by Peabody Museum of Harvard University in 1989); and (4) Iroquois wampum belts (returned to Onondaga by New York State Museum in 1989 and by National Museum of the American Indian in 1996). Each group makes an oral report describing the importance to the culture of the sacred object, how the object was taken/stolen, and how it was repatriated. (See Resources, page 200.)

Enrichment/Extensions

Literature. Students can read and then present an oral book report about *Wind from an Enemy Sky* by D'arcy McNickle (Albuquerque, NM: University of New Mexico Press, 1978). The novel describes members of a tribe trying to repatriate a sacred object from a museum collector in New York City.

Research. Students research other efforts by governments to recover cultural objects in museum collections: the Greek government's effort to recover the Elgin marbles (pieces from the Parthenon that the British took in the early 1800s) from the British Museum.

📖 Reading

Lost and Found: The Repatriation of Indian Sacred Objects

Tribal ceremonies use sacred objects. Depending on the tribe, these objects may be corn ears, dolls, fans, eagle feathers, masks, pipes, rattles, drums, scrolls, or medicine bundles containing hundreds of articles, rocks, and different parts of animals and plants.

Many sacred objects, like masks, are believed to be alive. Indian spiritual leaders make and care for them according to strict tribal procedures. Certain behavior is required in their presence, during their use, and after the ceremony is over. Some sacred objects must be "fed" offerings of sacred substances like cedar or cornmeal. Other sacred objects, like the Zuni War Gods made of wood, are supposed to remain in place in sacred shrines on mesa altars until they decay and return to the earth. If sacred objects are locked up in museum cases or in private collections, they cannot breathe, nor can they receive proper care.

Over the past 100 years, several tribal sacred objects have been stolen from their original owners. In some cases, Native people who had no ownership or title to objects sold them anyway. Many sacred objects have been dug out of Native American graves. Why? There has long been a profitable market for Indian cultural objects among private collectors and museum officials. Some people believed Indians were a vanishing race, so they collected and preserved the cultural objects to do them a favor. But sometimes Indian individuals willingly turned over sacred materials to museums for safekeeping if they no longer had heirs interested in preserving the object and its traditions. The Indian people who sold these objects were often destitute and living in poverty.

For many years, many tribes have requested the return of their sacred property. Some museums cooperated. In 1938, the Hidatsa Midipadi clan petitioned the Museum of the American Indian in New York City for the return of its sacred bundle. The museum returned it reluctantly. In 1980, the Denver Art Museum returned a Zuni War God that had been stolen and later donated to the museum. In 1989, the Peabody Museum in Cambridge, Massachusetts, returned the Omaha sacred pole to its rightful owners, the tribe.

After 1990, tribes had federal law on their side to help repatriate sacred objects. In November of that year, President George Bush signed the Native American Grave Protection and Repatriation Act that gives tribes a set of legal procedures to use in reclaiming religious or ceremonial objects from museums receiving federal monies. (The law does not apply to private collectors or private museums.) Now cultural objects stolen from tribes must be returned when tribes request them. But there are museum officials in some states that are cooperating with Indian tribes and repatriating sacred objects to their rightful owners.

Resources
Students

Buffalohead, Priscilla. "Who Owns a People's Past?," in *Modern Indian Issues . . . A Lesson Series for Secondary Teachers and Students*. Coon Rapids, MN: Anoka-Hennepin District 11, 1993.

Hirschfelder, Arlene, and Paulette Molin. *The Encyclopedia of Native American Religions*. New York: Facts on File, 1992.
"Omaha Sacred Pole," "Repatriation," "Sacred Objects," "War Gods (Ahayu:da)," and "Waterbuster (Midipadi) Clan Bundle."

Suro, Roberto. "Quiet Efforts to Regain Idols May Alter Views of Indian Art." *New York Times* (August 13, 1990).
Zuni War Gods.

Video. "Return of the Sacred Pole." 1989. Produced by Michael Farrell, Nebraska Educational Television. Available from Native American Public Telecommunications (NAPT).

<u>Teachers</u>

Thornton, Russell. "Repatriation of Human Remains and Artifacts," in *Native America in the Twentieth Century: An Encyclopedia*, Mary B. Davis, ed. New York: Garland, 1994, 543–44.
Reviews the history of how Native people have been objects of study and preservation in repositories, sums up reasons why Natives feel repatriation and reburial must occur, and summarizes twentieth-century legislation enacted by the U.S. federal government to protect ancestral remains and sacred objects.

Lesson

Sacred Sites

Grade Level
7–8

Materials
Student Reading: "Sacred Sites"

Time
Two class periods

Objectives
- Students learn Native Americans worship at sacred natural sites.

- Students learn rituals must be performed at proper times and places at undisturbed sites.

- Students learn all cultures have sacred sites (natural or human-made).

- Students learn how to research global information sources.

Activities
1. Show students each of the 12 months in a sacred sites calendar. (See Resources, page 203.) Discuss the variety of sacred sites (natural versus built by humans) all over the world. Ask students how they would feel if a church, synagogue, shrine, mosque, or temple were desecrated.
2. After students read "Sacred Sites," divide the class into small groups and assign each group one of the following sacred sites: Taos Blue Lake in New Mexico; Medicine Wheel in Wyoming; Badger-Two Medicine in Montana; Devils Tower Monument in Wyoming; Mount Graham in Arizona. Ask students to research the *Readers' Guide to Periodical Literature* or InfoTrac, including information about the people who worship at the site and how each site has been endangered. (See Appendix B, page 211.) Each group presents an oral report to the class.

Enrichment/Extensions
Research. Students do a report about people in other lands that worship at sacred sites.

📖 Reading

Sacred Sites

Traditional spiritual practices of Native people are inseparably bound to land. For countless centuries, Indian people have worshipped beside lakes, streams, hot springs, caves, and mountains. Through worship, Indian people have shown respect for the Creator and other spirits, given thanks, and asked for help. The natural environment where Indian people worship becomes a kind of altar or a church in Native religions.

Some places are sacred because they are the burial places of people's ancestors or the dwelling place of spirits. Other places are sacred because religious events occurred there, or a tribe was believed to have been created at those spots. Still other places are sacred because they contain special plants, herbs, minerals, or waters with healing powers. Religious leaders travel to these sacred places to gather materials necessary for ceremonies.

Certain ceremonies are still performed at sacred sites in order to create good relationships with the spirit world. Each ceremony must be performed at the proper time for a set number of days, perhaps at the summer or winter solstice or the spring or fall equinox. No other place can be substituted for a site considered sacred. There are instructions about who may attend the ceremony and how they must behave before and after the ceremony.

No one knows exactly how many sacred sites still exist in the United States and Canada today, because many Indian people prefer not to reveal their locations. If sacred sites are discovered and disturbed, Indians fear the spirits will leave. Also, some religious ceremonies cannot take place at a sacred site that has been damaged, and many have been.

Celilo Falls in Oregon, an ancient place of worship on the Columbia River for the Umatilla, Nez Percé, Yakima, and Warm Springs Indians, was flooded by the Dalles Dam in 1957. The San Francisco Peaks in Coconino National Forest sacred to the Apaches, Hopis, Navajos, and Zunis was desecrated by the development in the 1980s of the Snow Bowl, a portion of the peaks used for downhill skiing. Today, Badger-Two Medicine in Montana, a site sacred to the Blackfeet and other tribes, is threatened by oil and gas companies that want to drill the site. Mount Graham in Arizona, a sacred site to the San Carlos Apaches and the Zunis of New Mexico, has had its summit clear-cut (cleared of trees) to make way for a telescope project.

At a 1993 hearing in Washington, D.C., tribal leaders said at least 44 sacred sites tied to Native religions in 10 states were threatened by vandals, tourism, private developers, mining, logging, road building, power lines, and hydroelectric plants. Tribal leaders said the count was underestimated because numerous Pueblo tribes do not want to disclose the location of their sites for fear they will be jeopardized.

Resources

<u>Students</u>

Calendars. *Sacred Spaces*. Golden Turtle Press, Berkeley, CA.
  Annual calendar with full-color photos of sacred natural and human-built sites from around the world, including Native America. (Look for other calendars that have similar themes.)

Charging Eagle, Tom, and Ron Zeilinger. *Black Hills: Sacred Hills*. Chamberlain, SD: Tipi Press, 1987. (c/o St. Joseph's Indian School, Chamberlain, SD 57326).
  Poetic description and photos tell about the sacredness of the hills and their desecration by gold mines.

Hirschfelder, Arlene, and Paulette Molin. *Encyclopedia of Native American Religions*. New York: Facts on File, 1992.
  Seventeen sacred sites are described.

Keegan, Marcia. *Taos Pueblo and Its Sacred Blue Lake*. Santa Fe, NM: Clear Light, 1992.
  The story and photos of the struggle of the Taos people to regain their sacred lake.

Milne, Courtney. *Sacred Places in Native North America: A Journey of the Spirit*. New York: Stewart, Tabori, and Chang, 1995.
  Over 100 photos and text examine the spiritual heritage of 50 sites.

Time-Life Editors. "The Quest to Reclaim Lost Sacred Domains," in *Winds of Renewal*. Alexandria, VA: Time-Life Books, 1996, 52–65.
  Full-color photos of six sacred sites in the United States.

<u>Teachers</u>

Gordon-McCutchan, R. C. *The Taos Indians and the Battle for Blue Lake*. Santa Fe, NM: Red Crane Books, 1991.
  Detailed story of the Taos Indians' ultimately successful fight with the U.S. government to recover their sacred Blue Lake in New Mexico.

Kelley, Klara B., and Francis Harris. *Navajo Sacred Places*. Bloomington, IN: Indiana University Press, 1994.
  Stories about sites retold.

Trope, Jack F. "Sacred Sites," in *Native America in the Twentieth Century*, Mary B. Davis, ed. New York: Garland, 1994, 564–66.
  Essay deals largely with decades-old struggle of traditional Indian people with the federal government over sacred sites.

Lesson

8.5

Team Names, Mascots, and Logos

Grade Level
7–8

Materials
Student Reading: "Chronology of Public Schools and the Mascot Issue"

Time
Two class periods

Objectives
- Students learn that Indian team names, mascots, and logos foster stereotypes and that most Indian people do not feel honored by them.

- Students learn that public schools across the nation are beginning to change their Indian-related team names, logos, and mascots.

- Students learn how to research global information sources.

Activities
1. Students survey junior and senior high schools and/or colleges in their county/city/state and categorize the names by Indian-related themes, wildlife, local industry, animals, and so on. Make a chart and report.
2. Take a survey of students and others to see if they feel the team names and logos are appropriate. Record the answers on a chart.
3. Teachers check with school coaches to see if they have a copy of their state's *Coaching Directory of High Schools*. The directory lists data about all the junior and senior high schools (including team names) within each state. Or order the 1998–1999 edition ($10.95/per state) from Clell Wade, PO Box 177, Cassville, MO 65625. The publisher also puts out a college directory ($15.95) with all the team names of colleges in the nation.
4. Students read "Chronology of Public Schools and the Mascot Issue" and discuss the reasons why school boards, faculties, and students are tossing out their Indian nicknames, logos, and mascots.

Enrichment/Extensions
Research. Students research *Readers' Guide to Periodical Literature* or InfoTrac on a high-profile college mascot issue: Chief Illiniwek at the University of Illinois (UI), the controversy between Native Americans and the UI's board of trustees that saw both of the state's senators and Illinois General Assembly taking stands. Students should write a report or make a class presentation about both sides of the issue.

📖 Reading

Chronology of Public Schools and the Mascot Issue

1987. The PTA, student council, and faculty of Southwest Secondary in Minneapolis, Minnesota, all voted to eliminate athletic team names like the Indians, Braves, or Chiefs. These names trivialize Native American heritage. Now Southwest calls its teams the Lakers.

1989. State School Superintendent Ramon Cortines ordered Lowell High School in California to phase out its mascot of an Indian warrior.

1989. The Campus Congress of students, parents, and faculty of John Jay High School in Cross River, New York, voted to abandon the mascot, Chief Katonah. Six months of debates in assemblies, classrooms, and the school newspaper led to the change.

1992. The school board of Shawano-Grisham School in Shawano, Wisconsin, voted to change the Indian nickname and mascot of Shawano High School.

1992. The Illinois State Board of Education voted to eliminate the name "Redskins" as Naperville Central's nickname. High school students opted to be known as Redhawks.

1993. Pupils at Longfellow Elementary School in Columbus, Maryland, voted to change the school mascot from an Indian to an eagle. The school's estimated 400 students came up with a new mascot.

1993. Arvada High School in Colorado changed its name from "Redskins" to "Reds." Students, alumni, and neighborhood residents voted for the change.

1993. West Junior High in Rapid City, South Dakota, changed its mascot from "Warriors" to "Wolves."

1993. Park View Middle School in Mukwonago, Wisconsin, changed its logo from a sleepy-eyed potbellied American Indian to a bulldog.

1994. Milaca High School in Milaca, Minnesota, changed its mascot from "Indians" to "Wolves."

1995. In Watertown, South Dakota, Watertown High School changed its logo from an Indian to three stars representing the body, mind, and spirit.

1995. Shawnee High School in Louisville, Kentucky, replaced its Indian mascot with a golden eagle. Students, faculty, and alumni were involved in choosing a new mascot.

1995. In Sunnyvale, California, the district's board of trustees of Fremont High School voted unanimously to retire the Indian logo and mascot. After the Indian community surrounding the school spoke with the board, it moved for the change.

1997. The Los Angeles Unified School District Board of Education, the second largest in the country, votes 6–0, with one abstention, to require three high schools and one junior high school to drop American Indian–themed names and mascots effective this school year.

1998. The Dallas, Texas public schools eliminated American Indian mascots from all of its schools.

Resources
Students

Audiotape. "The Indian in the Global Mind." Tape 5, side B, in *Spirits of the Present: The Legacy from Native America*. Smithsonian Institution and Native American Public Telecommunications (NAPT), 1992.
A 27-minute discussion includes mascots.

Giago, Tim. "Drop the Chop! Using Indians as Mascots Is a Form of Bigotry," *New York Times* (March 13, 1994): 12.
The title says it all.

Hatfield, Dolph. "Guest Essay," *Native Peoples* (Summer 1996).
Focuses on term "redskin" and Washington Redskins in particular.

Hirschfelder, Arlene, and Marthe Kreipe de Montaño. "Degrading Native American Sports Mascots," in *Native American Almanac: A Portrait of Native America Today*. New York: Prentice-Hall, 1993.
Chronology of the mascot controversy focuses on colleges that dropped their Indian mascots and nicknames.

Lidz, Franz. "Not a Very Sporting Symbol: Indians Have Ceased to Be Appropriate Team Mascots." *Sports Illustrated* (September 13, 1990): 10.
Article tells of the unsuccessful battle of Native Americans to get rid of "Chief Illiniwek," the University of Illinois mascot. Also reports about several universities that successfully dropped offensive Indian mascots.

Metz, Sharon, and Helgemo Metz. *"What Is the Point of All of This Protesting?": A Primer*. Brochure produced by HONOR, Inc., 2647 North Stowell Avenue, Milwaukee, WI 53211.
Question-and-answer format responds to the arguments people often use to defend mascots.

Video. "In Whose Honor? Indian Mascots and Nicknames in Sports." 1996.

One-hour documentary looks at the use of Indian mascots and nicknames in sports with special focus on Chief Illiniwek. Order from Jay Rosenstein, 1205 South Randolph, Champaign, IL 61820.

Teachers

Buffalohead, Priscilla. "Indian Mascots and Other Stereotypes," in *Modern Indian Issues . . . A Lesson Series for Secondary Teachers and Students.* Coon Rapids, MN: Anoka-Hennepin District 11, 1993. 11229 Hanson Boulevard, Coon Rapids, MN 55433.

Great summary of team names, logos, and mascots in sports history plus information about the battle between the owner of the Washington Redskins and Native protesters.

Considine, David M., Gail E. Haley, and Lyn Ellen Lacy. "Sports Mascots and Picture Books," in *Imagine That: Developing Critical Thinking and Critical Viewing Through Children's Literature.* Englewood, CO: Teacher Ideas Press, 1994.

Brief review of the debate in the press over sports teams with Indian names, followed by a discussion of the contents of children's books with stereotypes.

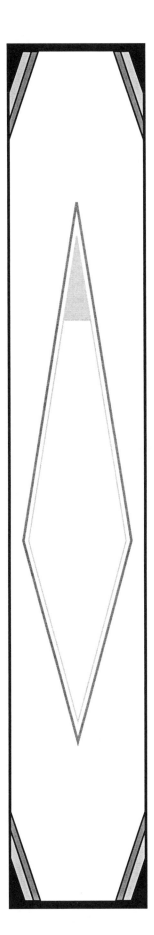

Appendix **A**

Oral History Guidelines

Make a List of Questions to Use as a Guide.

Start with general questions that cannot be answered yes or no. For example, "What are some of the things you can remember happening to you at school? NOT "Do you remember what teacher you had in first grade?" The questions should encourage the person to start talking.

You Do Not Have to Follow Your Question List Exactly.

Some things will remind your interviewee of other interesting items you might not have thought to ask about. If the speaker gets off the subject, you can bring the interview back to the topic.

You Do Not Have to Write Everything That Is Said.

It is important not to write down every word that the interviewee says, but rather to take short notes to remind yourself about what was said after the interview is over. Sit down and write what the person said as soon after the interview as possible. If you have a tape recorder you can use it during the interview and copy down what was said afterward. Be sure to ask the interviewee for permission to use a tape recorder.

A Few "Do's"

DO encourage the person to go into more depth. You can do this by asking if there is anything else about a particular thing or event that the person remembers. Ask follow-up questions. If the person says something that you think is interesting, ask more about it.

DO encourage interviewees to tell stories in their own way, rather than asking for very specific answers they may not know. Try to ask questions that are easy to answer from memory.

DO allow for pauses. The person may need some time to think. While the person is thinking, you can write down some notes or think of other questions you could ask, based on what has been said.

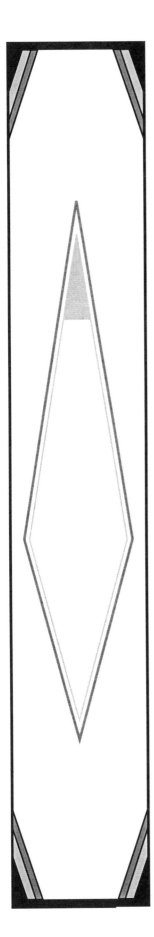

Global Information Sources

Readers' Guide to Periodical Literature. These books are issued annually and list thousands of articles in magazines. Libraries that cannot afford computer databases like InfoTrac house these books in their reference rooms or on reference shelves.

The best way to begin researching American Indian subjects in these books is to first look up "Indians of North America." Then look under topics like the following:

Antiquities (you'll find articles about repatriation of human remains under this heading)

Casinos

Foxwoods High Stakes Bingo and Casino

Industries (articles about casinos here)

Mortuary Customs (you'll find articles about reburying human remains here)

Native Grave Protection and Repatriation Act of 1990

Religion and Myth (you'll find sacred sites here)

Treatment (you'll find mascot issues here)

InfoTrac. This computer database lists thousands of articles in hundreds of periodicals. The most recent article on any given subjects appears first and the listing works itself backward until 1989. InfoTrac headings are somewhat different from the *Readers' Guide.* Look under the following topics for articles about Indian subjects.

Casino, Connecticut

Devils Tower

Foxwoods High Stakes Bingo and Casino

Mascots, Public Opinion

Mount Graham

Native Americans, Clothing

Native Americans, Dwellings

Native Americans, Games

Native Americans, Languages

Native Americans, Portrayals about, Depictions

Native Americans, Youth

Pequots

Tim Giago

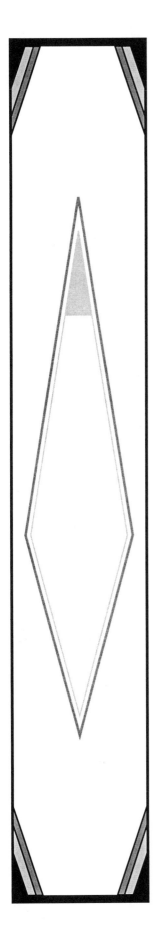

Appendix **C**

National Native News
Radio Stations

ALASKA		
Anchorage	KNBA-FM 90.3	M-F
	KRUA-AM 88.1	M-F
	KSKA-FM 91.1	M-F
Barrow	KBRW-AM 680	M-F
Bethel	KYUK-AM 640	M-F
Chevak	KCUK-FM 88.1	M-F
Dillingham	KDLG-AM 670	M-F
Fairbanks	KUAC-FM 104.7	M-F
Fort Yukon	KZPA-AM 900	M-F
Galena	KIYU-AM 910	M-F
Glenallen	KXGA-FM 90.5	M-F
Haines	KHNS-FM 102.3	M-F
Homer	KBBI-AM 890	M-F
Juneau	KTOO-FM 104.3	M-F
Kenai	KDLL-FM 91.9	M-F
Ketchikan	KRBD-FM 105.9	M-F
Kodiak	KMXT-FM 100.1	M-F
Kotzebue	KOTZ-AM 720	M-F
McCarthy	KXKN-FM 89.7	M-F
McGrath	KSKO-AM 870	M-F
Petersburg	KFSK-FM 100.9	M-F
Sand Point	KSDP-AM 840	M-F

Sitka	KCAW-FM 104.7	M-F
St. Paul Island	KUHB-FM 91.1	M-F
Talkeetna	KTNA-FM 88.9	M-F
Unalakleet	KNSA-AM 930	M-F
Unalaska	KIAL-AM 1450	M-F
Valdez	KCHU-AM 770	M-F
Wrangall	KSTK-FM 101.7	M-F
ARIZONA		
Tuba City	KTBA-AM 1050	M-F
Whiteriver	KNNB-FM 88.1	M-F
Window Rock	KTNN-AM 660	M-F
ARKANSAS		
Little Rock	KABF-FM 88.3	SAT
CALIFORNIA		
Arcata	KHSU-FM 90.5	M-THU
Hoopa	KIDE-FM 91.3	M-S
Philo	KZYX-FM 90.7	M-F
Redway	KMUD-FM 91.1	M-F
Willits	KZYZ-FM 91.5	M-F
COLORADO		
Boulder/Denver	KGNU-FM 88.5	M-THU, SUN
Ignacio	KSUT-FM 91.3	M-F
	KUTE-FM 90.1	M-F
ILLINOIS		
Urbana	WEFT-FM 90.1	M-F
KANSAS		
Kansas City/ Topeka	KANU-FM 91.5	M-F
Wichita	KMUW-FM 89.1	M-F
MAINE		
Blue Hill Falls	WERU-FM 89.9	M-F
Portland	WMPG-FM 90.9	THU

MICHIGAN		
Alpena	WCML-FM 91.7	M-F
Harbor Springs	WCMW-FM 103.9	M-F
Marquette	WNMU-FM 90.1	M-F
Mount Pleasant	WCMU-FM 89.5	M-F
Oscoda	WCMB-FM 95.7	M-F
Sault Ste. Marie	WCMZ-FM 98.3	M-F
MINNESOTA		
Austin	KMSK-FM 91.3	M-F
Duluth	KUMD-FM 103.3	M-F
Grand Rapids	KAXE-FM 91.7	M-F
Mankato	KMSU-FM 89.7	M-F
MISSOURI		
Kansas City	KKFI-FM 90.1	SAT
MONTANA		
Billings	KEMC-FM 91.7	TU-F
Bozeman	KBMC-FM 102.1	TU-F
Great Falls	KGPR-FM 89.9	M-F
Havre	KNMC-FM 90.1	TU-F
Miles City	KECC-FM 90.7	TU-F
Missoula	KUFM-FM 89.1	M-F
NEBRASKA		
Alliance	KTNE-FM 91.1	M-F
Bassett	KMNE-FM 90.3	M-F
Chadron	KCNE-FM 91.9	M-F
Hastings	KHNE-FM 89.1	M-F
Lexington	KLNE-FM 88.7	M-F
Lincoln	KUCV-FM 90.9	M-F
Merriam	KRNE-FM 91.5	M-F
Norfolk	KXNE-FM 89.3	M-F
North Platte	KPNE-FM 91.7	M-F

NEVADA		
Elko	KNCC-FM 91.5	M-F
Reno	KUNR-FM 88.7	M-F
NEW MEXICO		
Albuquerque	KUNM-FM 90.1	M-F
Dulce	KCIE-FM 90.5	M-F
Gallup	KGLP-FM 91.7	M-F
Magdalena	KABR-AM 1500	M-F
Pine Hill	KTDB-FM 89.7	M-F
Zuni	KSHI-FM 90.9	M-F
NEW YORK		
Southampton	WPBX-FM 88.3	M-F
NORTH CAROLINA		
Fayetteville	WFSS-FM 91.9	TUE
NORTH DAKOTA		
Belcourt	KEYA-FM 88.5	M-THU
Bismarck	KCND-FM 90.5	TU-F
Dickinson	KDPR-FM 89.9	TU-F
Fargo	KDSU-FM 91.9	TU-F
Grand Forks	KUND-FM 89.3	TU-F
Jamestown	KPRJ-FM 91.5	TU-F
Minot	KMPR-FM 88.9	TU-F
New Town	KMHA-FM 91.3	M-F
Williston	KPPR-FM 89. 5	TU-F
OHIO		
Columbus	WCBE-FM 90.5	MWTF
OKLAHOMA		
Edmond/ Oklahoma City	KGOU-FM 106.3	M-F
Oklahoma City	KROU-FM 105.7	M-F
Stillwater	KOSU-FM 91.7	M-F

OREGON		
Bend	KOAB-FM 91.3	M-F
Corvallis	KOAC-AM 550	M-F
Pendleton	KRBM-FM 90.9	M-F
Portland	KBOO-FM 90.7	MON
SOUTH DAKOTA		
Aberdeen	KDSD-FM 90.9	M-F
Brookings	KESD-FM 88.3	M-F
Faith	KPSD-FM 97.1	M-F
Lowry	KQSD-FM 91.9	M-F
Martin	KZSD-FM 102.5	M-F
Pierre	KTSD-FM 91.1	M-F
Porcupine	KILI-FM 90.1	M-F
Rapid City	KBHE-FM 89.3	M-F
Sioux Falls	KCSD-FM 90.9	M-F
St. Francis	KINI-FM 96.1	M-F
Vermillion	KUSD-FM 89.7	M-F
UTAH		
Salt Lake City	KRCL-FM 90.9	SUN
WISCONSIN		
Hayward	WOJB-FM 88.9	M-F
Rhinelander	WXPR-FM 91.7	M-F
WYOMING		
Aston	KUWA-FM 91.3	M-F
Gillette	KUWG-FM 90.1	M-F
Jackson	KUWJ-FM 90.3	M-F
Laramie	KUWR-FM 91.9	M-F
Newcastle	KUWN-FM 90.5	M-F

Contact Koahnic Broadcast Corporation for information about new listings, call numbers, and broadcast times. Natural Native News: (907) 258-8895. Native America Calling: (907) 258-8896.

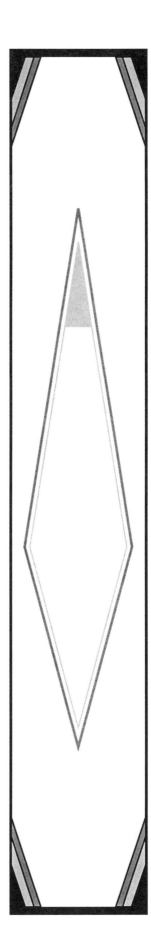

Appendix D

Web Sites

After cruising around the Web, we found these sites emerged as the most informative about Indian issues. Included here is the name of each site, the address, and a brief description of the site's contents. These addresses are only starting points. Much more material is out there, and though digging around takes a little time, it will pay off.

Reminder: The Web is an ever-changing universe, and unfortunately, many sites disappear. We apologize in advance if any of these sites no longer exist.

Census Data for American Indians
  http://www.census.gov/

Under "A" find American Indian [choose "Businesses" or "Population"] or Alaska Native [Businesses or Population]

Home Pages of Native Artists and Authors
  http://www.hanksville.org/

An index provides links to the home pages of Native artists and authors as well as Native American resources on the Internet, including culture, language, history, health, education, and indigenous knowledge.

Indian Country Today (newspaper)
  http://Indiancountry.com/

The weekly national newspaper, *Indian Country Today*, covering national news and events and distributed in all 50 states and in 12 foreign countries, can be accessed online.

Native American Home Pages

> http://info.pitt.edu/~/mitten/indians.html

This megasite, maintained by Lisa Mitten, a Mohawk urban Indian who is a librarian at the University of Pittsburgh, provides access to the home pages of individual Native Americans and Nations and to other sites that provide solid information about Native people. Topics include Native organizations and urban Indian centers, tribal colleges, Native studies programs, the mascot issue, powwows and festivals, sources for Indian music, businesses, and general Indian-oriented home pages.

Native American Resource Center

> http://www.wco.com/~berryhp/broadcast.html

Produced by radio producer Peggy Berryhill, this site is a "gateway" to Native American public broadcasting and media organizations along with community radio information.

Native American Public Telecommunications

> http://www.Nativetelecom.org

This site is the national distribution system for AIROS (American Indian Radio on Satellite), Native programming to tribal communities and to general audiences through Native American and other public radio stations as well as the Internet. "Native American Calling," the nation's first live talk-radio show geared toward a Native American audience, is also available at this site. This one-hour electronic talking circle can be heard Monday through Friday, 1:00–2:00 P.M. ET on local public radio stations and on the World Wide Web. Some stations opt to air the program on tape delay. Call a particular station for broadcast time. Before listening on the computer, it is necessary to click onto the RealTime Audio web site and download its program at no charge. The site is www.realaudio.com.

This site also has music programs like "Native Sounds–Native Voices" featuring traditional and contemporary Native American music.

Native Americas

> http://nativeamericas.aip.cornell.edu/   or
> http://www.news.Cornell.edu/general/July97/NatAm.Online

Native Americas is the quarterly publication of Akwe:kon Press of the American Indian Program at Cornell University. The journal features articles that cover important issues of concern to indigenous peoples throughout the Western Hemisphere. Visit the site and find subscription information, Native happenings, and information on Akwe:kon Press.

NativeNet

> http://www.fdl.cc.mn.us/natnet/

The NativeNet page provides an excellent connection to a group of NativeNet mailing lists as well as list archives. Also lists references to selected Web resources relating to indigenous peoples. Good for ongoing and past topics.

NativeWeb

http://www.nativeweb.org/

NativeWeb exists to utilize the Internet to educate the public about indigenous cultures and issues and to promote communications between indigenous peoples and organizations supporting their goals and efforts. The content of NativeWeb is predominantly about the Americas, from the Arctic to Tierra del Fuego. Lists Native-owned enterprises, deals with issues of cultural property, genealogy, and lots more.

Repatriation Issues

http://www.uiowa.edu/~anthro/reburial/repat.html

Deals with the Native American Grave Protection and Repatriation Act of 1990, case studies, state laws, articles, organizations, and bibliographies.

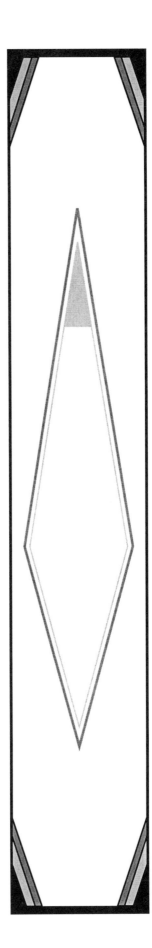

Resources

American Indian Curriculum Units or Sources

Abenaki Self-Help Association, Inc. PO Box 276, Swanton, VT 05488.

Allen, Paula Gunn. *Studies in American Indian Literature: Critical Essays and Course Designs*. New York: Modern Language Association of America, 1983.

American Friends Service Committee. *The Wabanakis of Maine and the Maritimes: A Resource Book About Penobscot, Passamaquoddy, Maliseet, Micmac and Abenaki Indians*.
Available in North American Native Authors Catalog. (See Catalogs of Native American Books, page 226.)

American Indian Curricula Development Program. United Tribes Technical College, 3315 University Drive, Bismarck, ND 58501.

American Indian Education Unit, California Department of Education. *The American Indian: Yesterday, Today and Tomorrow: A Handbook for Educators*. Sacramento, CA: California Department of Education, 1991.

American Indian Institute. University of Oklahoma, 555 Constitution Avenue, Norman, OK 73037.

Anishinabe Reading Materials. Duluth Indian Education Advisory Committee, Independent School District, 709 Lake Avenue and Second Street, Duluth, MN 55802.

Anoka-Hennepin Indian Education Program. *Inside the Culture.* 1988.
(See Catalogs of Native American Books, page 226.)

Ballard, Louis. *American Indian Music for the Classroom.*
(Available through Canyon Records. See Audiovisual Resources, page 225.)

Bigelow, Bill, Barbara Miner, and Bob Paterson. *Rethinking Columbus: Teaching About the 500th Anniversary of Columbus's Arrival in America.* Milwaukee, WI: Rethinking Schools, 1991.

Blackfeet Heritage Program. School District #9, Browning, MT 59417.

Caduto, Michael J., and Joseph Bruchac. *Keepers of the Earth: Native American Stories and Environmental Activities for Children.* Golden, CO: Fulcrum, 1988.
(Also *Keepers of the Animals, Keepers of the Night,* and *Keepers of Life*—all wonderful science curricula.)

Chinle Unified School District #24. Curriculum Center, PO Box 587, Chinle, AZ 86503.

Choctaw Heritage Press. Mississippi Band of Choctaw Indians, Route 7, Box 21, Philadelphia, MS 39350.

Cornelius, Carol. *The Six Nations Series: Student's Guide and Teacher Guide.* American Indian Program. Cornell University, 300 Caldwell Hall, Ithaca, NY 14853.

Cross-Cultural Education Center. PO Box 66, Park Hill, OK 74451.

Daybreak Star Press. PO Box 99100, Seattle, WA 98100.

Ecumenical Program on Central America and the Caribbean. 1470 Irving Street, NW, Washington, DC 20010.

ERIC/CRESS. PO Box 1348, Charleston, WV 25325.
They will do a free computer search by subject. Example: curriculum materials about North Carolina Indians. (800) 624-9120.

Harvey, Karen D., and Lisa D. Harjo. *Indian Country: A History of Native People in America* (readings and lesson plans) and *Indian Country Teacher's Guide.* Golden, CO: North American Press, 1994.

Harvey, Karen, Lisa Harjo, and Jane Jackson. *Teaching About Native Americans.* Bulletin No. 84. National Council for the Social Studies, 1990.

Kraft, Herbert, and John Kraft. *The Indians of Lenapehoking.* South Orange, NJ: Seton Hall University Museum, 1985.

Miller, Susan. *Fresh Tracks: Pathways to the Past.* 1988. Susan Miller, PO Box 752, Brooklyn, NY 11231.
This unit has a 300-page teacher's guide complete with videos about precontact and contemporary New York area Native peoples, the Lenni Lenape.

Minneapolis Public Schools. Planning, Development and Evaluation Department, 807 Northeast Broadway, Minneapolis, MN 55413.

Minnesota Chippewa Tribe. PO Box 217, Cass Lake, MN 56633.

Minnesota Historical Society. 1500 Mississippi Street, St. Paul, MN 55101.

Native American Materials Development Center. 407 Rio Grande Boulevard NW, Albuquerque, NM 87104.

Network of Educators' Committees on Central America. PO Box 43509, Washington, DC 20010.

OHOYO Resource Center. c/o M. Cherry, 4712 Florist, Wichita Falls, TX 76302.

Robinson, Barbara. *Native American Sourcebook: A Teacher's Resource on New England Native Peoples.* Concord, MA: Concord Museum, 1988.

Saskatchewan Indian Cultural College. Curriculum Department, PO Box 3085, Saskatoon, SK, Canada S7K 3S9.

Science: An Indian Perspective. Indian Education Division of Elementary and Secondary Education, Department of Education and Cultural Affairs, State of South Dakota Education Department, 1975.

Social Studies Education. Bureau for Program Development, Division for Instructional Services, 125 South Webster Street, PO Box 7841, Madison, WI 53702.

Tohono O'odham Education Department. PO Box 837, Sells, AZ 85634.

Verrall, Catherine, and Lenore Keeshig-Tobias. *All My Relations: Sharing Native Values Through the Arts.* Canadian Alliance in Solidarity with Native Peoples, PO Box 574, Station P, Toronto, ON, Canada M5S 2T1.

Zuk, W. M., and D. L. Bergland. *Art First Nations: Tradition and Innovation.* Elementary Program Teacher's Guide, Champlain, NY: Art Image Publications, 1992.

Audiovisual Resources

(Films, Videos, Posters, Photographs, Recordings)

The American Audio Prose Library. PO Box 842, Columbia, MO 65205.

American Museum of Natural History. Division of Photography, Central Park West and 79th Street, New York, NY 10024.

ATLATL. PO Box 34090, Phoenix, AZ 85067-4090.

Big Moon Traders (great maps). 676 Desoto Street, Salt Lake City, UT 84103.

Canyon Records. 4143 North 16th Street, Phoenix, AZ 85016.

Featherstone Productions, Inc. PO Box 487, Brookings, SD 57006.

Folkway Records. Birch Tree Group, Ltd. 180 Alexander Street, Princeton, NJ 18540.

Four Worlds Development Project. University of Lethbridge, 4401 University Drive, Lethbridge, AB, Canada T1K 3M4.

Indian House. PO Box 472, Taos, NM 87571.

Indian Records. Box 47, Fay, OK 73646.

Library of Congress. Music Division, Recorded Sound Section, Washington, DC 20540.

National Anthropological Archives, Smithsonian Institution, Washington, DC 20560.

Native American Public Telecommunications. PO Box 83111, Lincoln, NE 68501-3111.

Native Americans on Film and Video. 2 volumes. National Museum of the American Indian, George Gustav Heye Center, Public Information Department, One Bowling Green, New York, NY 10004.

North American Indian Travelling College, R.R. 3, Cornwall Island, ON, Canada K6H 5R7.

Office of Folklife Programs. 955 L Enfant Plaza, Suite 2600, Smithsonian Institution, Washington, DC 20560.

Rounder Records. PO Box 154, North Cambridge, MA 02140.

Shenandoah Film Productions. 538 G Street, Arcata, CA 95521.

SOAR (Sound of America Records). PO Box 8606, Albuquerque, NM 87198.

Catalogs of Native American Books

American Indian Books. American Indian Science and Engineering Society, 4730 Walnut Street, Suite 212, Boulder, CO 80301.

Curriculum Materials. Akwe:kon. 300 Caldwell Hall, Cornell University, Ithaca, NY 14853.

Curriculum Materials. Anoka-Hennepin Independent School District 11, 11299 Hanson Boulevard NW, Coon Rapids, MN 55433.

Cherokee Publications, Inc. PO Box 256, Cherokee, NC 28719.

Children's Book Press. 1461 9th Avenue, San Francisco, CA 94122.

Council for Indian Education. 1240 Burlington Avenue, Billings, MT 59102-4224.

Highsmith Multicultural Bookstore. W5527 Highway 106, PO Box 800, Fort Atkinson, WI 53538-0800.

North American Native Authors Catalog. Greenfield Review Press, PO Box 308, 2 Middle Grove Road, Greenfield Center, NY 12833.

Oyate. 2702 Mathews Street, Berkeley, CA 94702.

Pemmican Publications. 412 McGregor Street, Winnipeg, MB, Canada R2W 4X5.

Saskatchewan Indian Cultural College. Curriculum Department, PO Box 3085, Saskatoon, SK, Canada S7K 3S9.

Sierra Oaks Publishing Company. PO Box 255354, Sacramento, CA 95865-5354.

Sinte Gleska College Bookstore. Rosebud Sioux Reservation, PO Box 156, Mission, SD 57555.

University of Arizona Press. 1230 North Park Avenue, Tucson, AZ 85719.

University of Nebraska Press. PO Box 880484, 312 North 14th Street, Lincoln, NE 68588-0484.

University of New Mexico Press. Albuquerque, NM 87131-1591.

University of Oklahoma Press. 1005 Asp Avenue, Norman, OK 73019-0445.

Periodicals

(Magazines, Journals, Newspapers)

Aboriginal Voices: A Native North American Magazine. Suite 201, 116 Spadina Avenue, Toronto, ON, Canada M5V 2K6.

American Indian Art Magazine. Circulation Department, 7314 East Osburn Drive, Scottsdale, AZ 85251.

American Indian Culture and Research Journal. American Indian Studies Center, University of California at Los Angeles, 3220 Campbell Hall, Los Angeles, CA 90024.

American Indian Quarterly. University of Nebraska Press, PO Box 880484, Lincoln, NE 98588-0484.

The Circle. Minneapolis American Indian Center, 1530 East Franklin Avenue, Minneapolis, MN 55404 (Newspaper).

Honor Digest. 6435 Wiesner Road, Omro, WI 54963.

Indian Country Today. Box 4250, Rapid City, SD 57709 (Newspaper).

NARF Legal Review. 1506 Broadway, Boulder, CO 80302.

Native Americas: Akwe:kon's Journal of Indigenous Issues. American Indian Program, 300 Caldwell Hall, Ithaca, NY 14853.

Native Monthly Reader. PO Box 122, Crestone, CO 81131 (Newspaper for young adults).

Native Peoples. Media Concepts Group, PO Box 18449, Aneheim, CA 92817-9913.

News from Indian Country. 7831 N. Grindstone Ave., Hayward, WI 54843 (Newspaper).

News from Native California. PO Box 9145, Berkeley, CA 94709.

Tribal College Journal. PO Box 720, Mancos, CO 81328.

Winds of Change. AISES Publishing, Inc. American Indian Science and Engineering Society, 4730 Walnut Street, Suite 212, Boulder, CO 80301.

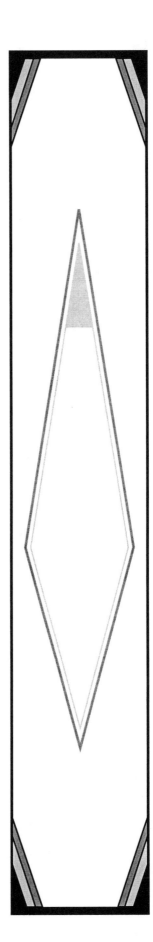

Bibliography

Books for Students and Teachers*

*Indicates selections for teachers.

Amiotte, Arthur. *Art and Indian Children of the Dakotas*. Washington, DC: Government Printing Office, 1985.

Ancona, George. *Earth Daughter: Alicia of Acoma Pueblo*. New York: Simon & Schuster, 1994.

Armstrong, Jeanette. *Slash*. Penticton, BC: Theytus Books, 1988.

Ashabranner, Brent. *Morning Star, Black Sun: The Northern Cheyenne Indians and America's Energy Crisis*. New York: Dodd, Mead, 1982.

*Aveni, Anthony. *Native American Astronomy*. Austin, TX: University of Texas Press, 1979.

Awiakta, Marilou. *Rising Fawn and the Fire Mystery*. New York: Ibis Press, 1983.

Begay, Shirley M., and Horace Spencer. *Hooghan Baahane : A Book About the Hogan*. Rough Rock, AZ: Rough Rock Press, 1982.

Begay, Shonto. *Navajo: Visions and Voices Across the Mesa*. New York: Scholastic, 1994.

Benton-Banai, Edward. *Generation to Generation: A Short Story*. Hayward, WI: Indian Country Communications, 1991. Route 2, Box 2900-A, Hayward, WI 54843.

230 Bibliography

*Berger, Thomas. *Village Journey: The Report of the Alaska Native Review Commission.* New York: Hill and Wang, 1985.

Bowen, Du Wayne. *One More Story: Contemporary Seneca Tales of the Supernatural.* New York: Bowman Books, 1991.

Browne, Vee. *Maria Tallchief: Prima Ballerina.* New York: Simon & Schuster, 1995.

Bruchac, Joseph. *The Faithful Hunter and Other Abenaki Stories.* New York: Bowman Books, 1988.

———. *Return of the Sun.* New York: Crossing Press, 1990.

Champagne, Duane. *Native America: Portrait of the Peoples.* Detroit: Visible Ink, 1994.

*Closs, Michael. *Native American Mathematics.* Austin, TX: University of Texas Press, 1990.

Conley, Robert. *The Witch of Goingsnake and Other Stories.* Norman, OK: University of Oklahoma Press, 1988.

*Deloria, Vine. *American Indian Policy in the Twentieth Century.* Norman, OK: University of Oklahoma Press, 1985.

*Dooling, D. M., and Paul Jordan-Smith. *I Become a Part of It: Sacred Dimensions in Native American Life.* New York: Parabola Books, 1988.

Ekoomiak, Normee. *Arctic Memories.* New York: Henry Holt, 1988.

George, Jean Craighead. *Arctic Son.* New York: Hyperion, 1997.

*Green, Rayna. *Women in American Indian Society.* New York: Chelsea House, 1992.

Griffin-Pierce, Trudy. *The Encyclopedia of Native America.* New York: Penguin, 1995.

Harlan, Judith. *American Indians Today.* New York: Franklin Watts, 1987.

Hill, Norbert, ed. *Words of Power: Voices from Indian America.* Golden, CO: Fulcrum, 1994.

Hirschfelder, Arlene. *Happily May I Walk: American Indians and Alaska Natives Today.* New York: Charles Scribner's Sons, 1986.

Hoig, Stan. *People of the Sacred Arrow: The Southern Cheyenne Today.* New York: Cobblehill Books, 1992.

Hoyt-Goldsmith, Diane. *Apache Rodeo.* New York: Holiday House, 1995.

———. *Lacrosse: The National Game of the Iroquois.* New York: Holiday House, 1998.

Johnston, Basil. *How the Birds Got Their Colors.* Toronto, ON: Kids Can Press, 1978. 585 Bloor Street West, Toronto, ON, Canada M6G 1K5.

*Josephy, Alvin. *Now That the Buffalo's Gone.* Norman, OK: University of Oklahoma Press, 1988.

Katz, Jane. *Messengers of the Wind: Native American Women Tell Their Stories.* New York: Ballantine, 1994.

Klein, Barry. *Reference Encyclopedia of the American Indian*, 8th edition. West Nyack, NY: Todd Publications, 1997. 18 North Greenbush Road, West Nyack, NY 10994.

Krull, Kathleen. *One Nation, Many Tribes: How Kids Live in Milwaukee's Indian Community*. New York: Lodestar Books, 1994.

Lesley, Craig, ed. *Talking Leaves: Contemporary Native American Short Stories*. New York: Dell, 1991.

Lourie, Peter. *Everglades: Buffalo Tiger and the River of Grass*. Honesdale, PA: Boyds Mill Press, 1994.

*Lyons, Oren. *Exiled in the Land of the Free*. Santa Fe, NM: Clearlight, 1992.

Martinson, David. *Angwamas Minosewag Anishinabeq/Time of the Indian*. Cass Lake, MN: Chippewa Tribe of Minnesota, 1979. Box 217, Cass Lake, MN 56633.

McLuhun, T. C. *Touch the Earth*. New York: Promontory, 1987.

Monture, Joel. *Cloudwalker: Contemporary Native American Stories*. Golden, CO: Fulcrum Kids, 1996.

Moore, Reavis. *Native Artists of North America*. Santa Fe, NM: John Muir, 1993.

*Nabokov, Peter, ed. *Native American Testimony: A Chronicle of Indian White Relations from Prophecy to Present*. New York: Penguin Books, 1991.

Ortiz, Simon. *The People Shall Continue*. Emeryville, CA: Children's Book Press, 1977.

Page, Suzanne. *A Celebration of Being*. Flagstaff, AZ: Northland Press, 1989.

Peters, Russell. *The Wampanoags of Mashpee*. n.p.: Nimrod Press, 1989. (Available from North American Native Authors Catalog, Greenfield Review Press).

Prucha, Francis. *Atlas of American Indian Affairs*. Lincoln, NE: University of Nebraska Press, 1991.

Riley, Patricia. *Growing Up Native American: An Anthology*. New York: William Morrow, 1993.

Rockpoint Community School. *Between Sacred Mountains: Navajo Stories and Lessons from the Land*. Tucson, AZ: University of Arizona Press, 1984.

Sneve, Virginia Driving Hawk. *High Elk's Treasure*. New York: Holiday House, 1995.

Stark, Raymond. *Guide to Indian Herbs*. Blaine, WA: Hancock House, 1989.

Strete, Craig. *When Grandfather Journeys into Winter*. New York: Greenwillow Press, 1979.

Swamp, Jake. *Giving Thanks: A Native American Good Morning Message*. New York: Lee and Low Books, 1995.

Swentzell, Rina. *Children of Clay: A Family of Potters*. Minneapolis, MN: Lerner Publications, 1992.

Tall Bull, Henry, and Tom Weist. *Northern Cheyenne Fire Fighters.* Billings, MT: Council for Indian Education, n.d.

Thomson, Peggy. *Katie Henio, Navajo Sheepherder.* New York: Cobblehill, 1995.

Trafzer, Clifford. *American Indian Identity.* Sacramento, CA: Sierra Oaks Publishing, 1989.

Ugvwiyuhi. *Journey to Sunrise.* Claremore, OK: EGI Press, 1977. PO Box 1397, Claremore, OK 74017.

Williams, Neva. *Patrick DesJarlait: Conversations with a Native American Artist.* Minneapolis, MN: Lerner Publications, 1995.

Wilson, Gilbert. *Waheenee: An Indian Girl's Story.* Lincoln, NE: University of Nebraska Press, 1981.

Wood, Nancy. *The Serpent's Tongue: Prose, Poetry, and Art of the New Mexico Pueblos.* New York: Dutton, 1997.

Wood, Ted, with Wanbli Numpa Afraid of Hawk. *A Boy Becomes a Man at Wounded Knee.* New York: Walker, 1992.

Contemporary Art Books

Archuleta, Margaret, and Rennard Strickland. *Shared Visions: Native American Paintings and Sculptors of the Twentieth Century.* Phoenix, AZ: Heard Museum, 1991.

Broder, Patricia Janis. *American Indian Painting and Sculpture.* New York: Abbeville Press, 1981.

Coe, Ralph. *Lost and Found Traditions: Native American Art 1965–1985.* Seattle, WA: University of Washington Press, 1986.

Hill, Rick. *Creativity Is Our Tradition: Three Decades of Art At the Institute of American Indian Arts.* Santa Fe, NM: Institute of American Indian and Alaska Native Culture and Arts Development, 1992.

Jacka, Jerry, and Lois Jacka. *Beyond Tradition: Contemporary Indian Art and Its Evolution.* Flagstaff, AZ: Northland, 1988.

McMaster, Gerald, and Lee-Ann Martin. *Indigena: Contemporary Native Perspectives.* Vancouver, BC: Douglas & McIntyre, 1987.

Monthan, Guy, and Doris Monthan. *Art and Indian Individualists.* Flagstaff, AZ: Northland, 1975.

Tanner, Clara Lee. *Southwest Indian Painting: A Changing Art.* Tucson, AZ: University of Arizona Press, 1973.

Wade, Edwin L., and Rennard Strickland. *Magic Images: Contemporary Native American Art.* Tulsa, OK: Philbrook Art Center, and Norman, OK: University of Oklahoma Press, 1981.

Photography Books

(The following books contain photographs of Native peoples involved in many different activities: ceremonial, work, recreation, etc.)

Brill, Charles. *Red Lake Nation: Portraits of Ojibway Life.* Minneapolis, MN: University of Minnesota Press, 1992.

Conners, Dennis, ed. *Onondaga: Portrait of a Native People.* Syracuse, NY: Syracuse University Press, 1993.

Doll, Don. *Vision Quest: Men, Women and Sacred Sites of the Sioux Nation.* New York: Crown, 1994.

Farber, Joseph. *Native Americans 500 Years After.* New York: Crowell, 1976.

Gilpin, Laura. *Enduring Navajo.* Austin, TX: University of Texas Press, 1994.

Grimes, Joel. *Navajo: Portrait of a Nation.* Englewood, CO: Westcliffe Publishers, 1992.

Haegert, Dorothy. *Children of the First People.* Vancouver, BC: Tillacum Library, 1983.

Hubbard, Jim, selector. *Shooting Back for the Reservation: A Photographic View of Life by Native American Youth.* New York: New Press, 1994.

Keegan, Marcia. *Pueblo People: Place, Space and Balance.* Santa Fe, NM: Clear Light, 1995.

McAuley, Skeet. *Sign Language: Contemporary Southwest Native America.* New York: Aperture Foundation, 1990.

Morgan, Lael. "Alaska's Native People." *Alaska Geographic.* Vol. 6, no. 3. Anchorage, AK: Alaska Geographic Society, 1979.

Neel, David. *Our Chiefs and Elders: Words and Photographs of Native Leaders.* Vancouver, BC: UBC Press, 1992.

New Eyes: Visions of Young Lakota Photographers/Wicista Teca: Lakota Wici Towapi. Rapid City, SD: Dahl Fine Arts Center, 1993.

Page, Jake. *Navajo.* New York: Harry N. Abrams, 1992.

Running, John. *Honor Dance: Native American Photographs.* Reno, NV: University of Nevada Press, 1985.

Smith, Paul Chaat, Theresa Harlan, Jolene Rickard, et al. *Strong Hearts: Native American Visions and Voices.* New York: Aperture Foundation, 1995.

Stowell, Cynthia. *Faces of a Reservation: A Portrait of the Warm Springs Indian Reservation.* Portland, OR: Oregon Historical Society, 1987.

Time-Life Editors. *Winds of Renewal.* Alexandria VA: Time-Life Books, 1996.

Trimble, Stephen. *The People: Indians of the American Southwest.* Santa Fe, NM: School of American Research, 1994.

Trimble, Stephen, ed. *Our Voices, Our Land.* Flagstaff, AZ: Northland, 1986.

Viola, Herman. *After Columbus: The Smithsonian Chronicle of the North American Indians.* Washington, DC: Smithsonian Books, 1990. (Last chapter).

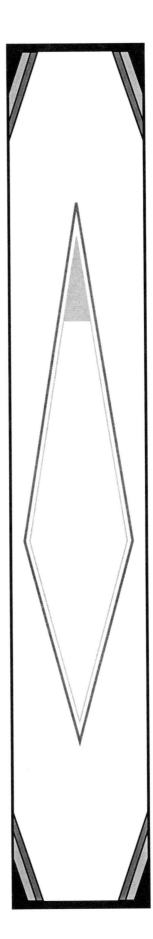

Glossary

Assimilation Policy. In the Indian context, this policy meant that the federal government, missionaries, teachers, and "reformers" all wanted to integrate Indians into Anglo-American society.

Bureau of Indian Affairs. A subdivision of the Department of the Interior. This agency has the major responsibility for implementing the trust relationship between Indian Nations and Congress. The central office is in Washington, D.C., and there are 12 regional offices.

Clan. A group in American Indian society that traces its descent from a common ancestor. Membership in a clan establishes membership in a tribe. Descent and consequently clan membership can be traced through the mother or the father's line.

Corrugated Cardboard. A piece of material with alternate furrows and ridges.

Elder. The Nation Indian Council on Aging defines an elder as anyone over 55 years of age.

Giveaway. The traditional custom of an honored person distributing gifts to guests, the poor, or children, acknowledging the good deeds of a person.

Periodical. A magazine or other publication that is issued at regular intervals.

Pouch. A small flexible receptacle made of leather or other relatively nonporous material.

Repatriation. This term generally applies to human beings when they are returned to their own country. In the context of Indian affairs, the term refers to the process of returning, by museums, collectors, and others, human remains and/or sacred objects to their rightful owners—Indian people.

Reservation. A piece of land that belongs to one or more groups of American Indians. There are hundreds of federal and state Indian reservations. Reservations are not public property like parks, and they are not part of the states surrounding them. Reservations have definite boundary lines just like states. These lines separate reservations from the states in which they are located.

Sacred. Persons or objects connected with religion.

Sovereignty. The right to rule or govern oneself. Tribes have the right to govern themselves, but Congress has the power to limit or even abolish tribal powers—and it has.

Termination. This is the process by which Congress has abolished a tribe's government and ended the tribe's special relationship with the federal government. Between 1954 and 1964, Congress terminated many tribes, and federal programs were no longer available to them.

Time Line. A visual design to show a chronology of events.

Tradition. A way of life. Tradition is made up of things a group of people do the same way over and over again, from generation to generation. Native traditions are practiced in songs, dances, ceremonies, prayers, food, and art. Native traditions have endured for thousands of years.

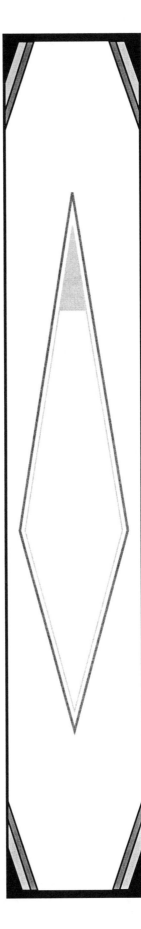

Index

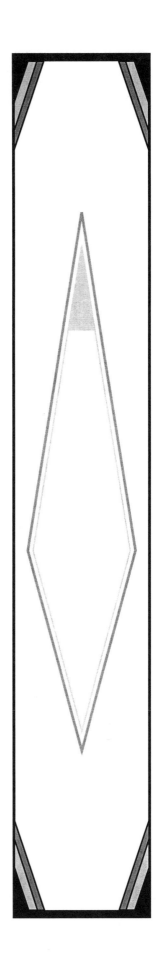

About the Authors

Arlene Hirschfelder is the author of award-winning non-fiction books, as well as curricula and bibliographies concerning Native Americans. Hirschfelder, who also teaches about Native histories, cultures, and literature, worked for the Association on American Indian Affairs for over 20 years.

Yvonne Beamer Wakim, Cherokee and Arab, has worked in Indian education and community services for over 25 years. She is also a writer and multicultural consultant. Presently she works with Nitchen, Inc., a holistic program for American Indian families.

from **Teacher Ideas Press**

Diversity Resources

FOUR GREAT RIVERS TO CROSS: Cheyenne History, Culture, and Traditions
Patrick M. Mendoza, Ann Strange Owl-Raben, and Nico Strange Owl

The culture and history of the Cheyenne come alive through stories told through the voices of Old Nam Shim (which means grandfather) and a little girl named Shadow. Discussion questions, extension activities, vocabulary lists, and a glossary of Cheyenne terms are provided. A valuable resource for multicultural units. **Grades 3–8.**
x, 131p. 8½x11 paper ISBN 1-56308-471-6

EXPLORING DIVERSITY: Literature Themes and Activities for Grades 4–8
Jean E. Brown and Elaine C. Stephens

Take the riches of multicultural literature beyond the printed page and into the classroom. With a variety of themes, discussion questions, and activities that challenge misconceptions and stereotypes, this book gives students the opportunity to develop an understanding of and an appreciation for their own and other cultures. **Grades 4–8.**
x, 210p. 8½x11 paper ISBN 1-56308-322-1

TEACHING U.S. HISTORY THROUGH CHILDREN'S LITERATURE:
Post World War II
Wanda J. Miller

This new book contains more great resources to help you combine recommended children's literature with actual events in U.S. History, from World War II to the present. Similar to Miller's earlier book, *U.S. History Through Children's Literature: From the Colonial Period to World War II.* **Grades 4–8.**
xiii, 229p. 8½x11 paper ISBN 1-56308-581-X

MULTICULTURAL FOLKTALES: Readers Theatre for Elementary Students
Suzanne I. Barchers

Introduce your students to other countries and cultures through the traditional folk and fairy tales in these engaging readers theatre scripts. Representing more than 30 countries and regions, the 40 reproducible scripts are accompanied by presentation suggestions and recommendations for props and delivery. **Grades 1–5.**
xxi, 188p. 8½x11 paper ISBN 1-56308-760-X

COOKING UP WORLD HISTORY: Multicultural Recipes and Resources
Suzanne I. Barchers and Patricia C. Marden

Take students on a culinary trip around the world and introduce them to other cultures through the recipes, research, readings, and related media offered in this tasty resource. More than 20 countries and regions frequently studied in elementary and middle schools are represented. **Grades K–6.**
xv, 237p. 8½x11 paper ISBN 1-56308-116-4

 Teacher Ideas Press
Dept. B046 • P.O. Box 6633 • Englewood, CO 80155-6633
800-237-6124 • Fax: 303-220-8843 • www.lu.com/tip

Gricha caché

Claire Ubac
Annick Bougerolle

Père Castor
Flammarion

Que fait la famille Ours
quand le ciel est bleu, bleu,
bleu comme aujourd'hui ?
Un pique-nique dans la forêt.

La famille Renard
et la famille Corbeau ont eu
exactement la même idée.
Aussi, tout le monde
se retrouve pour déjeuner.

Après le dessert, les parents
s'apprêtent à faire la sieste.

Gricha l'ourson, Nina
la renarde et Boris le corbeau
partent jouer à cache-cache.
– N'allez pas trop loin,
dit Mère Ourse en bâillant.

Appuyée
contre un grand chêne,
Nina compte la première :
– 1, 2, 3... et 5 !

Cette maligne découvre
les autres tout de suite.
– Peuh, bien sûr, ce n'était pas
difficile, fait Boris. Mais moi,
je sais compter jusqu'à dix.

Au milieu du jeu,
Gricha s'écrie :
– J'en ai marre, on me trouve
toujours en premier !
– Fais attention,
lui souffle Boris. Nina triche ;
elle regarde où tu vas.

Cette fois, Gricha
s'éloigne tout en surveillant
Nina et court jusqu'à
un buisson. Mmm, non,
c'est encore trop facile.
S'il grimpait plutôt
dans ce petit chêne ?

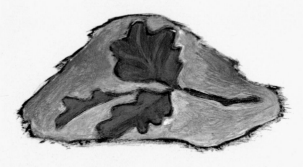

Mais Gricha aperçoit
un arbre creux qui ferait
une bien meilleure cachette.

Vite, il descend
de sa branche,
s'approche et saute de joie :
le trou de l'arbre est juste
à sa taille. Ici, Nina
ne le découvrira jamais.
Au loin, la voix
de son amie retentit : 
– Gricha, je t'ai vu !

Gricha pouffe de rire
au fond de son arbre. C'est
une ruse de Nina, bien sûr,
mais il ne sortira pas.

Gricha s'enfonce
profondément dans son trou
comme dans un nid
tout doux. Si doux
qu'il s'endort pour de vrai.

Quand Gricha
se réveille,
il ne sait plus
où il se trouve.
Il se croit dans son lit,
ne reconnaît pas sa chambre.
Puis il distingue le ciel
par le trou de l'arbre, là-haut,
et il se souvient.

Gricha veut se lever,
mais rien à faire : le nid
le retient et l'emprisonne.
Il essaie et essaie encore,
mais n'arrive même pas
à se retourner.

Gricha a très chaud
et un peu mal au cœur.
Et s'il restait coincé là
pour toujours ? Il essaie
de crier… mais son appel
est étouffé par l'écorce.

Personne ne le trouvera
jamais dans cet arbre !

Gricha sent une grosse boule
qui monte vers sa gorge et
va bientôt exploser en larmes.

Alors une petite voix
au fond de lui murmure :
– Allons, gros bébé,
tu ne vas pas pleurer ?
Réfléchis plutôt au moyen
de sortir de là !

Gricha écoute la petite voix
qui le réconforte.

Il se calme, regarde
autour de lui et aperçoit
une branche morte.

Gricha sort péniblement
son mouchoir de sa poche
et l'attache
au bout de la branche.
Puis il lève son bras
bien au-dessus de sa tête.
Comme ça, le mouchoir
dépassera du trou de l'arbre
et les autres le verront
peut-être s'agiter.

Gricha remue son bras
très vite, puis bien moins vite…
Il se fatigue de plus en plus.
Et surtout, personne ne vient.

Cette fois, les yeux
de Gricha se brouillent.
Des larmes se mettent
à couler. Les autres
l'ont cherché, c'est sûr,
pendant qu'il dormait,
et maintenant, ils doivent
être tous partis.

Il imagine Père Ours
et Mère Ourse rentrant,
les épaules basses, à la maison.
Son petit lit restera vide
pendant que lui, Gricha,
passera la nuit ici.

Bientôt il fera
complètement noir.
Gricha entendra
des bruits
qu'il ne connaît pas
et Père Ours
ne sera pas là
pour les lui expliquer.
La chouette hululera
tout près de lui,
et Mère Ourse ne sera pas là
pour le prendre dans ses bras.
Et le loup ? Le loup le flairera
et viendra le manger !

Les poils de Gricha
se hérissent de frayeur…
Il se bouche les oreilles,
se cache les yeux. Il entend
déjà la bête s'approcher.
Elle griffe le bois : crââ, crââ…

– Croâ ! Croâ !

Il est là, je l'ai trouvé !

La silhouette noire
de Boris se découpe
au-dessus de Gricha.

Père Ours tire son fils
et le dégage du trou.
– Eh bien toi,
tu nous en as fait, une peur,
dit-il en le serrant
dans ses bras.

– Je croyais que vous étiez
partis ! sanglote Gricha.

Mère Ourse se penche
sur son petit et lui murmure :
– Crois-tu qu'un papa ours
et une maman ourse
repartiraient à la maison,
sans leur ourson ? Voyons,
ils le cherchent partout
jusqu'à ce qu'ils l'aient trouvé.
N'oublie jamais ça,
mon Gricha !

Autres titres de la collection :

Une rentrée sans maîtresse
Lorsque le jour de la rentrée,
la maîtresse manque à l'appel,
il faut bien s'organiser

La poule, le coq et le cochon
La veille de Noël, deux pauvres fermiers
se résignent à manger leurs animaux…
mais la poule, curieuse, a tout entendu !

Hubert et les haricots verts
Hubert déteste les haricots verts
et refuse de les manger. Le Grand
Mamamouchi est obligé d'intervenir…

C'est mon nid !
Un matin de printemps, Loly la lutine
trouve un œuf tombé de son nid.
Elle l'installe chez elle. L'œuf éclôt…

Chacun chez soi
Léa et Léo déménagent.
Ils sont contents d'avoir maintenant
chacun leur chambre. Mais le soir…